LEADING
MULTICULTURAL
TEAMS

We appreciated very much all that you have written in this book. It is a very comprehensive guidebook that covers all the essential areas. This book is very helpful in understanding the complexity of a multicultural team, the challenge to leading such a team, and how an organization can restructure, support, and help those involved, whether they are leaders, members, or mentors/coaches. The book has given many good examples—it is very well written and presented, and very "meaty."

– Chiew Yoke and Phaik See Lee, Asia-Pacific Regional Directors, WEC International

The chapter on conflict is much the best presentation I've seen of cross-cultural ways of dealing with conflict. Greatly needed material!

– Ministry Trainer with the Church Missionary Society, Middle East

I think this is the best book I have read on the subject, because it is up to date, with lots of references to the most recent research and abreast with all the latest theory. The bibliography is a gold mine. At the same time it is very practical. There are lots of tips and insights for team leaders. It is also realistic about the pain and difficulty of establishing multicultural teams that are really synergistic.

– Julyan Lidstone, Area Leader, Operation Mobilization, Western and Central Asia

LEADING
MULTICULTURAL
TEAMS

EVELYN & RICHARD HIBBERT

WILLIAM CAREY
LIBRARY

Leading Multicultural Teams
Copyright © 2014 by Evelyn and Richard Hibbert

Unless otherwise indicated, all Scripture quotations are taken from the Holy Bible, New Living Translation, copyright © 1996, 2004, 2007, 2013 by Tyndale House Foundation. Used by permission of Tyndale House Publishers, Inc., Carol Stream, Illinois 60188. All rights reserved.

Scripture quotations marked "NIV" are taken from THE HOLY BIBLE, NEW INTERNATIONAL VERSION®, NIV® Copyright © 1973, 1978, 1984, 2011 by Biblica, Inc.® Used by permission. All rights reserved worldwide.

Published by William Carey Library
1605 E. Elizabeth St.
Pasadena, CA 91104 | www.missionbooks.org

Aidan Lewis, editor
Brad Koenig, copyeditor
Hugh Pindur, graphic design

William Carey Library is a ministry of the
U.S. Center for World Mission
Pasadena, CA | www.uscwm.org

Printed in the United States of America
18 17 16 15 14   5 4 3 2 1 BP 300

Library of Congress Cataloging-in-Publication Data

Hibbert, Evelyn.
  Leading multicultural teams / Evelyn Hibbert, Richard HIbbert.
      pages cm
  Includes bibliographical references.
  ISBN 978-0-87808-541-5
  1. Christian leadership. 2. Multiculturalism--Religious aspects--Christianity. 3. Teams in the workplace. 4. Interpersonal relations--Religious aspects--Christianity. 5. Leadership--Religious aspects--Christianity. 6. Leadership. I. Title.
  BV652.1.H535 2014
  253--dc23
                              2014000627

CONTENTS

PREFACE

We began our quest to be part of a synergistic multicultural team over twenty-five years ago. Since that time we have been part of many groups that called themselves teams, but only two that achieved synergy—one multicultural and one monocultural. We have visited, coached, and advised teams, and taught about teams in many different countries and contexts across the globe. Highly effective teams, monocultural or multicultural, are the exception rather than the rule in all the contexts we have seen. High-performing multicultural teams are very rare, but they do not have to be.

There is a wonder and joy in being part of a team that achieves synergy. You want to get up every morning and be with your colleagues. There is a confidence that you can overcome obstacles together. There is anticipation about what you will be able to achieve together. There is security in feeling that your teammates are 100 percent there for you and will always back you up in front of others. There is joy in seeing each team member grow and develop, and a genuine, ever-continuing delight in discovering the different strengths each member brings to the team. Being part of a team that becomes what a team is meant to be is an awesome privilege. Too few teams reach this state of synergy, but it is within reach of most teams. Achieving synergy in multicultural teams requires disciplined commitment to building relationships, especially during team formation, and dogged perseverance through the major storms that arise.

This book is designed to help leaders and organizations help their teams become highly effective. We have developed the ideas in this book through reflecting on our experiences and through studying what others have written in many fields of human knowledge. These fields include intercultural studies, cultural anthropology, missiology, business, management, organizational studies, peace and conflict studies, Whiteness and indigenous studies, multiculturalism, education, and social justice. Sometimes Christians can think that they do not need to learn from secular fields of study. But many people have spent many years researching and thinking about human interaction in many different contexts and have gained insights that can help us understand the interpersonal and intercultural dynamics that occur in the hotbed of a multicultural team. Multicultural team leaders as well as their team members need to be continual learners, and we have much to learn from the research in these areas.

If you are not a Christian or you work in a secular organization, we believe that the principles described in this book about how to facilitate reflective teamwork, healthy community, and good relationships apply to all teams. You may not find the biblical and theological discussions about multicultural community so relevant, but the emphasis on relationships and equity in human organizational structures is essential for all teams, as are the insights concerning intercultural differences. We interviewed team members, leaders, and supervisors from Christian mission agencies and secular organizations as part of the research behind this book. Our interviewees stressed character qualities such as humility and patience; these were as much a concern for non-Christian team supervisors, leaders, and members as for Christian.

This book begins by describing what a healthy team looks like and extends this to multicultural teams by considering how cultural differences affect multicultural teams and what healthy multicultural community looks like. It then explores the implications of understanding these insights for leaders of multicultural teams, including the things the leader needs to do to establish the team, build a healthy team community, balance personalities and roles on the team, and manage conflict. The characteristics and competencies of good multicultural team leaders are then described, and ways leaders can develop these are explored. The book concludes with recommendations for organizations about how to select and train multicultural team leaders and how to develop and strengthen multicultural teams.

We recommend the adventure of being part of a multicultural team to everyone who wants to experience the wonder of synergy that can develop when people of very diverse backgrounds learn to appreciate each other and work together. However, be prepared for a bumpy ride! And only set out on the journey if you are convinced the destination is worth arriving at, as it will take a great deal of commitment and perseverance to get there. Multicultural teams are wonderful, but they are also hard work.

ACKNOWLEDGMENTS

We could not have written this book without the help of several groups of people. First we would like to thank our teammates who worked with us in the Middle East, Bulgaria, England, and Australia. You gave us the privilege of experiencing what it is like to achieve more together than we could ever have done on our own. This book is the product of your struggling together with us to discover how to work together in multicultural teams.

Thank you too to all the people we interviewed about their experiences of working in other multicultural teams. You have given us hope that multicultural teams can work and be a deeply enriching experience. Your experiences and insights have formed a vital part of this book. Thank you especially for being willing to share the difficulties and pain you experienced in the process.

A dedicated band of busy people who have many years of experience in working in and leading multicultural teams carved time out from their busy lives to review the first draft of this book. Your comments and suggestions have made the final product much better than it would otherwise have been. Thank you so much! One of this group of reviewers reminded us that working in a multicultural team is a transformative experience. Even when it is difficult, we can be confident that God's Spirit is at work in us to mold us into the image of Jesus.

Finally we want to thank everyone who has believed in us and encouraged us over the years. Without your encouragement we would not have attempted this task. Thank you especially to Elizabeth Hentschel, who conducted some of the interviews as she visited different teams around the globe.

CHAPTER 1

THE CHALLENGE OF LEADING MULTICULTURAL TEAMS

Leading a multicultural team is a great adventure. But it is also a complex task that involves huge challenges. Over the past twenty years, as our roles have shifted from being mission team leaders to consultants and trainers of missionary teams, we have met many leaders of multicultural teams who are struggling with those challenges. One leader told us, "I've been on . . . several multicultural teams and in at least two of them, if the question was asked, 'Are multicultural teams worth the effort?' I'd give an unequivocal no as the answer." Another leader admitted, "At a certain point in our team leadership I began to doubt the real value of multicultural teams. It seemed like so much hard work with little payoff in terms of ministry effectiveness."

These two leaders are not unique in questioning whether the effort involved in multicultural teams is worth it. Despite these questions and doubts, organizations including mission agencies and churches are continuing to recruit and build multicultural teams either intentionally or out of necessity. Are multicultural teams really worth the effort? Yes! We need the creative answers to complex problems that multicultural teams are able to generate. We need the close commitment to each other that effective multicultural teams offer in order to be able to cope with the demands of ministry in our rapidly changing world. And we need practical, biblical models of intercultural harmony in a world ruptured by interethnic tensions.

Multicultural ministry teams commonly face challenges in the areas of communication, making decisions, and managing conflict. In our interviews with church planting teams in one large international mission agency, team members reported that their leaders were especially weak in clarifying expectations and team members' roles and in confronting problems. They and their team leaders strongly felt the need for more support and training in these areas. Chapter 10 will address the question of how organizations can more proactively support their leaders and teams.

Research into multicultural teams suggests that multicultural teams have the potential to become exceptionally effective but also to experience serious conflict. In our own research into multicultural church planting teams, we discovered some seriously damaged relationships and many team members who felt their leader's style of leading was hindering their team's effectiveness.[1] Lorraine Dierck, a missionary to Thailand who studied multicultural mission teams there, found that two out of twelve teams in her research disintegrated due to intercultural conflict.[2]

The failure of a ministry team can be a devastating experience. Although chronic conflict does not always lead to the team disbanding, it inevitably results in damage to relationships. Christian workers who are unprepared for conflict in team relationships expect unity and harmony to be relatively straightforward. This is rarely the case. Conflict and misunderstanding are normal between people in all contexts, but in intercultural interaction they are greatly amplified. Team leaders need to be skilled at managing intercultural conflict on their teams, and chapter 7 discusses this issue.

A major cause of conflict in multicultural teams is the differences between the cultural values of team members. Paul Hiebert defined culture as "the partially integrated system of ideas, feelings, and values encoded in learned patterns of behavior, signs, products, rituals, beliefs, and worldviews shared by a community of people."[3] Culture affects all dimensions of human

---

1   Richard Hibbert, "Enhancing WEC Church Planting Teams: A Study of the Factors Influencing Their Effectiveness" (DMin diss., Columbia International University, 2002), 167, 169.

2   Lorraine Dierck, "Teams That Work: Leadership, Power, and Decision-making in Multicultural Teams in Thailand" (DMiss diss., Biola University, 2007), 9.

3   Paul Hiebert, *The Gospel in Human Contexts: Anthropological Explorations for Contemporary Missions* (Grand Rapids: Baker Academic, 2009), 18.

experience. It is inculcated into us from birth and profoundly affects the way we interact with other people.

One of the most powerful functions of culture is that it defines for the members of each cultural group what is right and acceptable and how things should be done. Because our culture is so fundamental to who we are, it is hard for us to understand and accept that what seems obvious to us is only our own culture's perspective. This attitude is called ethnocentrism. One of the consequences of ethnocentrism is that we judge people who behave or think differently to us as wrong. When things seem "wrong" we feel bad. We want to fix those things up so that we do not feel bad anymore. We feel a need for the world to be "right" and cannot just leave things in what we feel is a "wrong" state.

An example of a cultural value that varies across cultures is orientation to time. When we were working in the Middle East, we had an American coworker who invited us for the evening meal. For most Australians it is usually acceptable and even considerate to be up to half an hour late for such an engagement. When we arrived half an hour late, he was furious at what he considered to be our sinful lack of punctuality. In contrast, it was normal for the host people of the country to arrive one or even two hours late for an appointment, and not to wait patiently for them was considered extremely inconsiderate. If your team consists of people from many different cultures with very different views on the reasonable limits of punctuality, major conflict is highly likely.

Outward behaviors are linked to deeply held cultural values. In the example above, our American coworker believed that time is valuable and should not be wasted, whereas the members of the host culture held that people are of primary importance and that time is limitless, relatively unimportant, and not controllable. In both cases, cultural values strongly affected behavior and emotions.

When people from other cultures act in ways that we see as inappropriate, we tend to make negative judgments about them. It is not uncommon for Christians from one culture working with Christians from another culture to judge them as not even Christians because they see them as behaving in ways that are unacceptable in their own culture. In a multicultural ministry team, this can have devastating effects.

Differences in cultural values also mean that good leadership is perceived differently by people from different cultures. Leaders will naturally use the model of leadership that is familiar to them, even though this may be inappropriate or even offensive to members of the team from other cultures, who expect their leaders to lead in ways that are familiar to them. Two dimensions of culture described by Geert Hofstede that particularly affect people's views of leadership are power distance and collectivism.[4]

High power distance inclines people to be more accepting of a leader's decisions, whereas people from low-power-distance cultures tend to expect more direct involvement in decision making. If differences in power distance are not understood and managed well, they can have negative consequences for multicultural teams. Western cultures are generally low-power-distance cultures, and this is reflected in their strong emphasis on democratic leadership. The majority of the world's cultures are more comfortable with high power distance. In high-power-distance cultures, followers accept and expect that their leaders will have more power than they do. Leaders are given higher status but are also expected to be aware of individuals' needs. High-power-distance cultures ascribe status according to age and social seniority and expect their leaders to direct rather than discuss.

Differences in power distance can cause tensions in multicultural teams. Australians, for example, are relatively low in power distance, whereas Chinese and people from most of Asia are much higher in this cultural dimension. Peter,[5] an Australian in his early forties, became the senior pastor of a multicultural church with a large Chinese membership. During his first weeks in the church, he worked hard to have democratic meetings with the ministry team, where he said little and tried to get all the staff to contribute to discussions in order to reach a consensus on the church's direction. The Chinese co-pastor seemed to withdraw more and more, and soon there were significant tensions within the leadership team. The Chinese co-pastor expected his leader to be much more directive in his leadership. In a ministry team in Eastern Europe, another Australian was appointed as the leader of

---

4   Geert Hofstede, Gert Jan Hofstede, and Michael Minkov, *Cultures and Organizations: Software of the Mind* (New York: McGraw-Hill, 2010).

5   Although all the examples given in this book are from real life, names and some other details have been changed to preserve anonymity.

a team that included local believers and Asian missionaries, who were all older than him and from high-power-distance cultures. Within days it was clear that there were major tensions in the team. Discussions were ineffective and tension increased. In each of these cases, the leader was considered to be too young by his high-power-distance team members, and his nondirective approach reinforced his lack of credibility. In both cases, the teams failed. The effect of these and other cultural dimensions on multicultural team leadership is discussed in more detail in chapter 2.

Many Christians misunderstand the concept of Christian unity to mean never having any disagreements and everyone having the same values. They can therefore find it difficult to discuss their reservations about multicultural teams and think that Christian unity means that it is unacceptable to not always be in total agreement with their teammates.

We will not always be able to work harmoniously with other Christians who have different cultural values. Some people may not be able to make the compromises necessary to becoming part of an effective multicultural team. An Australian missionary couple was recently assigned to work in a team with Koreans for their prefield orientation. They found that they were unable to cope with the differences in communication style and cultural values between them and their Korean teammates. As a result, they decided not to join the mission agency and said that the effort of working in multicultural teams was one of the main reasons for their decision. This was not a failure but an insightful recognition of their personal limitations. Multicultural teams require compromises on the part of everyone in them. If it is not possible for team members to make those compromises, it is totally acceptable for them to work in another context.

THE VISION: A HEALTHY MULTICULTURAL TEAM

Healthy multicultural teams are beacons of hope in a world that is struggling with intercultural conflicts, racial prejudice, and socioeconomic inequity. With increasing migration and highly diverse international cities, multicultural teams are becoming more and more common. But many workplaces and teams are still dominated by one culture, and people from minority cultures are often forced to compromise at least some of their values and practices in order to survive and make a living. Christian multicultural teams should be different.

As the world becomes more and more complex, we need the capacity to creatively solve problems, a capacity that multicultural teams are able to provide. An effective team works in such a way that the whole team is built up and becomes fruitful in a way that would have been impossible if each individual had acted independently. This dynamic is called synergy. Synergy comes from team members working interdependently. Team members need each other in order to achieve the team's purpose. Many ministry situations are extremely demanding spiritually, emotionally, psychologically, and sometimes physically. The support of team members is invaluable. Synergy and interdependence are illustrated in Ephesians 4:1–16 and 1 Corinthians 12:12–31, in which members of the body of Christ use their gifts for the benefit of the church, and the whole church grows to become more like God wants it to be as each member does the work God has given them to do. Difference creates a kaleidoscope of human experience that enriches everyone on a multicultural team and those who benefit from its work.

The Bible presents a picture of people from all cultures being equal but different. The story of the Tower of Babel (Gen 11:1–9), the description of the coming of the Holy Spirit at Pentecost (Acts 2:5–11), Paul's teaching that Christians from different backgrounds are "all children of God through faith in Christ Jesus" (Gal 3:26), and the descriptions of the crowd from every tribe, people, nation, and language worshiping in heaven (Rev 5:6–14; 7:9–12) all emphasize this reality. Christian unity and harmony are often misunderstood as meaning uniformity. However, around the throne of the Lamb, there is a celebration of the diversity of those who have been saved to worship God for eternity. The challenge for Christians working in multicultural teams is to learn practically how equality in diversity can produce creative synergy.

WHAT IS A TEAM?

A good team is one you want to work in. Relationships are healthy, each person feels safe and valued, there is a sense of common identity, and members are learning and growing. Together with these relational indicators of health, the team is making progress towards its goals and there is an excitement, joy, and expectation of success generated by purposeful, corporate, creative activity. This is the kind of team that this book aims to help leaders and organizations develop. It can be defined as a small number of people with complementary skills who are committed to a single purpose, each other, and a common working approach and values for which they hold themselves mutually accountable.[6]

A team, then, is a group of people who are committed to a common vision and to one another, who hold each other accountable to the accomplishment of that vision, and who work interdependently and according to commonly agreed values to accomplish their vision.

Not every group that is called a team is a team. The word "team" is often used indiscriminately to refer to any group of people who work together, but many of these groups do not have the qualities outlined in the above definition. This can cause confusion and frustration for new team members who have conflicting expectations of what a team is.

John and Mary were young professionals who joined a large, international missionary organization that advertised its commitment to working in multicultural teams. They had worked in interdisciplinary teams in their secular professions prior to becoming missionaries. They were passionate about the goals of the organization and looked forward to working together with highly committed teammates from other nations to plant churches in an unreached area. The organization continued to use and promote team language, but in the context where John and Mary were assigned, individuals were dispersed throughout the country and pursued their own goals with little accountability. When John and Mary questioned the lack of focus, cohesion, and accountability, it was explained that this team was like a track-and-field team, in which each member had their own individual ministry that functioned independently of the others, in contrast to a basketball team, in which all members work interdependently towards the same goals. When John and Mary attempted to establish a basketball-style team, they came into conflict with the rest of the group, who felt threatened by the focused

---

6   This definition has been developed from the one provided in Jon Katzenbach and Douglas Smith, *The Wisdom of Teams: Creating the High-performance Organization* (New York: HarperCollins, 1999), 45.

accountability these kinds of teams require. John and Mary eventually resigned in frustration and disillusionment.

When individuals work in parallel towards individual or organizational goals, this is called a working group. In their book *The Wisdom of Teams*, Jon Katzenbach and Douglas Smith define a working group as one in which

> [t]he members interact primarily to share information, best practices or perspectives and to make decisions to help individuals perform within his or her area of responsibility. Beyond that, there is no realistic or truly desired "small group" common purpose, incremental performance goals, or joint work-products that call for either a team approach or mutual accountability.[7]

There is nothing wrong with working groups. In many situations a working group may be the best option for working together. Teams, however, are characterized by synergy and interdependence. Their task requires them to work together in an interdependent way.

This book is for those who want to work in, support, or facilitate basketball-style teams, where everyone interdependently strives to get the ball through the same hoop. There is no individual glory or agenda in a basketball team. Team members think in terms of "we" rather than "I." The team achieves or fails together.

KEY INGREDIENTS AND STAGES OF TEAM DEVELOPMENT

The most important feature of a team is that it forms for a specific purpose. A team revolves around that purpose and should disband once that purpose has been achieved. If the group decides to adopt a new focus, it effectively becomes a new team, as the dynamic of the team is inseparable from its specific vision and goals. The synergy of a team comes from working together towards a common purpose. Efficacy, the most potent predictor of a team's

---

7   Ibid.

success, is closely related to its purpose. Team efficacy is the degree to which team members believe their team is able to achieve its purpose.

An effective team has three main ingredients: clear goals, balanced roles, and healthy relationships ("souls"). These ingredients are outlined in the table below.

GOALS	Shared commitment to a clear vision, goals, and mutually agreed-on strategies
ROLES	Balanced roles and skills, with an understanding and appreciation of each other's roles and skills
SOULS	Healthy in terms of caring, communication, conflict resolution, and accountability High levels of trust, support, and participation Interdependence

Table 1: Ingredients of an effective team

Teams have distinct stages that they pass through, and may return to, before they reach optimal effectiveness. These are commonly referred to as "forming," "storming," "norming," and "performing."[8] These stages of team development are described in the following table:

---

8   Bruce Tuckman, "Developmental Sequence in Small Groups," *Psychological Bulletin* 63 (1965): 384–99.

STAGE	CHARACTERISTICS
Forming	**THE HONEYMOON STAGE** Expectations are unclear. Members test the water. As they explore the boundaries of acceptable group behavior, they tend to avoid conflict and carefully watch each other's behaviors. There is politeness, formality, and a sense of awkwardness. Members feel anticipation and optimism but have only a tentative attachment to the team. Little is achieved on the team's task.
Storming	**CONFLICT** Differences among team members become more obvious, and the team wrestles with negotiating these differences. There is conflict and polarization around interpersonal issues and a questioning of commitment. There is impatience at lack of progress on the task, and some members may resort to trying to work alone rather than with the team. Arguments, competitiveness, and factions may develop.
Norming	**ACCEPTANCE** Members begin to accept the team, its core values, their own roles, and the other members. They develop norms for working together, resolving conflict, and making decisions. Standards and procedures are agreed on, core values are established, and members' roles are defined. Competition gives way to cooperation. There is more friendliness and openness than in the "storming" stage.
Performing	**SYNERGISTIC, EFFECTIVE WORK** Most of the issues about how to work together have been resolved. Roles are more flexible and functional, and group energy is channeled into the task. Members are tolerant of each other's strengths and weaknesses and are satisfied with progress. Work is done effectively.

Table 2: Stages of team development
(adapted from Tuckman 1965)

Knowing which stage of development a team is at can help us understand the dynamics in the team. For example, a lack of conflict in a team's forming stage is a natural result of team members' uncertainty about each other and the lack of deep interaction among them. Teams in the storming stage can be encouraged that the discomfort they are experiencing is normal and will eventually reduce to a more manageable level. The team leader's role should also be modified according to the stage the team is in, with the earlier team stages requiring more direction and intervention.[9]

It takes multicultural teams much longer than monocultural teams to get through the storming stage and reach the norming stage. Diversity has a detrimental effect on team functioning in the early stages of forming and norming. The initial period of turmoil at the start of a new multicultural team is much greater than in a monocultural team. Multicultural teams consistently need more time to solve problems and make decisions than homogeneous groups. There are greater initial difficulties in problem solving and greater potential for conflict in negotiating tasks and processes. Team members commonly misinterpret what their teammates are saying, and this slows the team's progress. Negotiating these misunderstandings and differences between team members and working to understand one another takes time. Differences must be faced and worked through, and teams that try to avoid this process will find they encounter much bigger problems in the future and run the risk of failing.[10]

Perfect agreement and harmony is unrealistic even in monocultural teams. In organizations that place a high value on having multicultural teams, team members can tend to avoid conflict and make unnecessary compromises for fear that team unity will be undermined and that their team will not live up to their organization's expectations. It is not possible or helpful to avoid the storming stage in multicultural team building.

There are few resources that are specifically designed to help multicultural teams tackle culture-related issues that arise in the storming stage. The vast majority of books about teamwork are written with the assumption that all readers and team members come from the same culture and that they will respond in the same way as people from the culture of the

9   One tool for assessing the stage a team is currently in can be found in Donald Clark, "Teamwork Survey," Big Dog and Little Dog's Performance Juxtaposition, August 22, 2010, http://www.nwlink.com/~donclark/leader/teamsuv.html.

10   Christopher Earley and Elaine Mosakowski, "Creating Hybrid Team Cultures: An Empirical Test of Transnational Team Functioning," *Academy of Management Journal* 43 (2000): 26–49.

writer (who is generally North American or European). Yet it is crucial that the cultural background of team members is appreciated, because culture affects every dimension of people's experience of and interaction with the world. Team members' cultures affect their concept of what a team is, their understanding of team effectiveness, and how they view goals.[11] There is widespread agreement that increasing the number of cultures on a team leads to an increase in the team's diversity and complexity. As a result, the potential for conflict and personal dissatisfaction also increases as the number of cultures rises.

Cultural differences are not always acknowledged, even in international Christian organizations. Sometimes this can be due to a fear of stereotyping people from minority cultures, but the most common reason is an unconscious assumption by people from more dominant cultures that their way is the "right" one. To develop healthy multicultural teams, cultural differences must be recognized and valued.

TOWARDS A THEORY OF MULTICULTURAL TEAM LEADERSHIP

Multicultural teams are more complex and difficult to establish than monocultural teams, primarily because of the value differences between cultures. The easily visible differences between cultures, such as differences in greetings and language script, are relatively simple to describe, understand, and manage. Values, on the other hand, are less visible, more difficult to articulate, and associated with strong emotions. Members of multicultural teams are often not aware of their deeply held values until their teammates from other cultures contravene those values. Even then, a team member whose value has been challenged is often unable to explain what has happened but feels confused, angry, or depressed. When people come from very different cultural backgrounds, some value differences are irreconcilable unless team members are willing to make major adjustments.

---

11   Cristina Gibson and Mary Zellmer-Bruhn, "Metaphors and Meaning: An Intercultural Analysis of the Concept of Teamwork," *Administrative Science Quarterly* 46, no. 2 (2001): 274–303.

Cultural values are deeply embedded in people through their family
and schooling. They ensure that everyone within each culture knows exactly
what is expected of them. These values are mostly implicit in the culture,
which means that people assume that their ways of doing things are "normal" and "right" rather than simply one cultural expression of how people
can interact. In this book we will use the term "team values" to describe the
values according to which the people in the community of a team agree to
interact with each other. In a monocultural team the team values are largely
implicit and shared by all team members because they are the same as their
commonly shared cultural values. In a multicultural team the team values
need to be negotiated, explicitly articulated, and agreed on.

Team leaders are human beings who have finite personal resources of
time and energy. When team members all come from the same culture, the
cultural values for relationships, communication, decision making, and managing conflict are well understood by everyone. When there is dysfunction
in the team, team members' shared understanding of these cultural values
means that they are able to take initiative to help resolve the dysfunction in
ways that are understood by the whole team. This allows the leader to focus
his or her time and energy on the vision, goals, and strategy of the team.

The diagram on the next page (fig. 1) illustrates the process of team
formation in a monocultural team. The team leader and members all come
from the same cultural background and do not have to compromise any
cultural values in order to work together. Their shared cultural values of
interaction enable them to fit well together into a working unit. The process
of team formation is relatively straightforward as team members are able
to help the leader with the team-building process by applying the shared
cultural values.

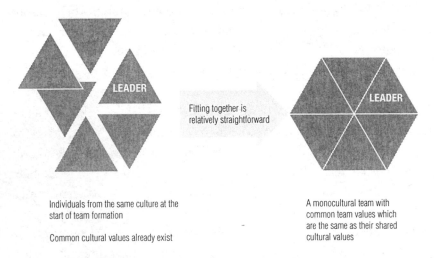

Fitting together is
relatively straightforward

Individuals from the same culture at the
start of team formation

Common cultural values already exist

A monocultural team with
common team values which
are the same as their shared
cultural values

Figure 1: Monocultural team formation

When there are two cultures on a team (that is, the team is bicultural), the leader has two options. The first of these is for the leader to impose the dominant culture's values on the team. This happens especially in countries or organizations where one culture has traditionally dominated, such as a European manager in a European company operating in an Asian country. The other option is majority rule. This means that the cultural values of the majority are imposed, usually by default rather than informed choice, by the team members who are in the majority. If the leader is not from the majority culture (for example, an American leading a largely Korean team in an African country), he or she needs to learn, understand, and operate according to the cultural values of the majority culture in order for the team to become effective. In this book, we will refer to this approach to leadership as the cross-cultural approach.

If the team members from both cultures in a bicultural team are unable to agree on common team values, competition and a feeling of "us versus them" can develop between them. Leaders in this situation have to take the initiative to learn the ways of the culture that is unfamiliar and help each group to adapt to the ways of the other. In the real world of finite time and energy, this means that the cross-cultural leader has to invest significantly more time in managing the interpersonal dimension of teamwork than the monocultural team leader.

The diagram below (fig. 2) illustrates the process of team formation in a bicultural team where the team members all come from one cultural background and the team leader comes from another. Team members in this situation do not have to compromise any cultural values in order to work together. The leader has to learn the cultural values of the team members' culture and be willing to make major adaptations to his or her own values and leadership style in order to fit well with the rest of the team. The ease of team formation is dependent on the cross-cultural leader's ability to adapt.

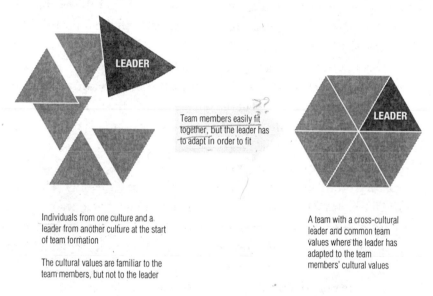

Team members easily fit together, but the leader has to adapt in order to fit

Individuals from one culture and a leader from another culture at the start of team formation

The cultural values are familiar to the team members, but not to the leader

A team with a cross-cultural leader and common team values where the leader has adapted to the team members' cultural values

Figure 2: Team formation when the leader is from one culture and all the members are from another culture

In a multicultural team, in which members come from more than two cultures, there are no cultural values that are shared by the whole team. As team members generally lack awareness of most of their cultural values because they are implicitly and deeply held, they need to be helped to understand their own values by learning to reflect on their emotional reactions when these values have been inadvertently transgressed, confronted, or disrespected by their teammates. Such reflection needs to be intentionally facilitated by the leader or a team coach, as it rarely happens without outside help. Without training or experience that raises awareness of potential areas of value conflict, the leader is unable to anticipate and prepare the team for conflict and can only react to it after problems arise. This reactive approach to problems usually results in prolonged and often agonizing conflict, especially during the early stages of team life.

Even when the leader is experienced, multicultural team formation takes longer than in monocultural teams. The extra time and conflict that is both intrinsic to and unavoidable in multicultural team formation arises from the difficulty of establishing commonly agreed team values that govern how team members interact and work together. These new team values will be specific and unique to each multicultural team and can only be established through a complex negotiation process. This means that the finite time and energy of the multicultural team leader, especially during the early stages of team life, will be almost completely utilized in the interpersonal processes of building good team relationships and a strong team community. The team leader will have minimal time or energy left to focus on the tasks and goals of the team. The leader of a multicultural team must invest much more time in building the team than either the monocultural or cross-cultural team leader.

The diagram on the next page (fig. 3) illustrates the process of team formation in a multicultural team. The team leader and members all come from different cultural backgrounds and do not have any shared team values. The process of learning about each other and adapting sufficiently so that the individuals begin to fit well together into a working unit is complex and highly demanding for all team members, and especially for the leader. The lack of shared team values, the lack of awareness of deeply held cultural values, and the difficulty of communicating and building relationships with people from unfamiliar cultures means that team members find it difficult to help the leader with the team-building process. In fact, team formation in a multicultural team is so difficult that it is rare for an inexperienced leader to be able to do it well without help from outside the team.

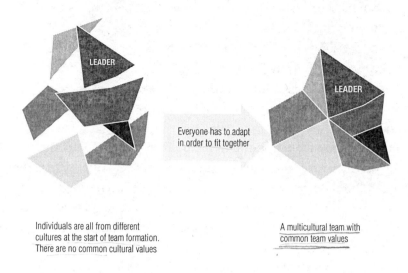

Individuals are all from different
cultures at the start of team formation.
There are no common cultural values

Everyone has to adapt
in order to fit together

A multicultural team with
common team values

Figure 3: Multicultural team formation

The rule in multicultural teams, especially where members come from
different cultures, is that everyone will have to accept compromise. The leader's
role is to facilitate the processes of mutual negotiation and compromise at
the same time as building a strong and healthy team community that is able
to manage its conflicts well.

CHARACTERISTICS OF GOOD MULTICULTURAL TEAM LEADERS

A good multicultural team leader enables all members of the team to become
fully participating members of the team. Hofstede describes multicultural
leadership in the following way:

> Learning to become an effective leader is like learning to
> play music: Besides talent, it demands persistence and
> the opportunity to practice. Effective monocultural lead-
> ers have learned to play one instrument; they often have
> proven themselves by a strong drive and quick and firm
> opinions. Leading in a multicultural and diverse environ-

ment is like playing several instruments. It partly calls for different attitudes and skills: restraint in passing judgment and the ability to recognize that familiar tunes may have to be played differently. The very qualities that make someone an effective monocultural leader may make her or him less qualified for a multicultural environment.[12]

Cultural difference cannot be ignored, as it affects all dimensions of human existence. Successful multicultural team leaders recognize and understand cultural difference. They are aware of and accept the deeply held cultural values of team members, which may even be in opposition to the leaders' own cultural values. Since transgression of cultural values generally evokes an emotional reaction, multicultural team leaders need to be able to recognize intercultural variations in emotional expression and be able to tactfully help team members reflect on their emotional responses and the cultural values that underlie them. As cultural value differences may be difficult, and in some cases impossible, to reconcile, the multicultural team leader has to be a skilled negotiator and mediator who can facilitate a process that enables all team members to agree on a unique set of team values that will form the foundation for a healthy team community.

---

12   Geert Hofstede, foreword to *Leadership in a Diverse and Multicultural Environment: Developing Awareness, Knowledge, and Skills*, ed. Mary L. Connerley and Paul Pedersen (Thousand Oaks, CA: SAGE, 2005), ix.

CHAPTER 2

HOW CULTURAL DIFFERENCES AFFECT TEAMS

All human beings are cultural beings. From the time we are born, we are acculturated with the values, beliefs, and practices of our parents, families, and societies. Language and culture are also inextricably intertwined, as the way language is constructed and developed reflects the values of culture. When we grow up in a monocultural context, we are usually unaware that there are other ways of doing things and perceiving the world. This lack of awareness tends to make us assume that our way of doing things is the best way.

Assuming that our way is the best or only way of doing things works well as long as we do not encounter people from other cultures; it keeps society cohesive and guards its values. When we are confronted with a culture that is very different than our own, however, assuming our culture's way is best often means that we judge the other culture's ways as wrong or dangerous. This is a completely normal human reaction but is very unhelpful when people from different cultures attempt to live and work together. All human beings are ethnocentric to some extent, meaning that all of us assume our own culture's ways of thinking and acting are the correct way. This chapter explores some of the deep differences in thinking and behavior between cultures and the impact these can have in multicultural teams.

Culture involves more than differences in ways of greeting, eating, and other easy-to-see behaviors. Geert Hofstede describes culture as being a "software of the mind," meaning patterns of thinking, feeling, and acting that are like mental computer programs that determine what we do.[13] Different cultural groups have different mental programs—different patterns of thinking, feeling, and acting. Each of us views and interacts with the world according to the social environment we grew up in, and this programming is "hardwired" into our language. Regardless of our background and cross-cultural training or experience, we tend to relate to others using our own cultural style.

Our culturally learned mental programming leads us to behave differently to people from other cultural backgrounds in ways that are easy to see, such as different ways of greeting other people or of washing dishes. Books on cross-cultural interaction often focus on these easy-to-see differences between people from different cultures, especially actions that can easily cause offense. This is a good starting point that aids us in the first stages of getting to know people, but it is inadequate for working closely with people from other cultures. These superficial cultural elements are easy to see and to communicate to others, and relatively easy to forgive when transgressed. But cultures also include assumptions about the world that are often difficult to identify and articulate. It is these deeply held values and assumptions that pattern the way people think about life.

Most people are unaware of their mental programming, and this is especially true of the deeper and more implicit levels of culture—cultural values and worldview assumptions. These are what people use to think with rather than what they think about. Just as humans develop and adapt to the changing circumstances they encounter, cultures are also constantly changing. Each human culture embodies what a society considers most important for their collective identity and well-being. Having a sense of collective identity is deeply important to every society, and preservation of this sense of "us" is so strongly defended that any perception of threat such as a contradiction of our values by others—as so often occurs in intercultural interactions—can result in a strong, negative emotional response.

While it is possible to learn a lot about other cultures by reading about them or hearing about them secondhand, it is only when we interact face-to-face with people from another culture that we experience the strong, deep emotions that arise from having our cultural values and worldview chal-

---

13   Hofstede, Hofstede, and Minkov, *Cultures and Organizations*, 4–5.

lenged. It is this challenge to what is most precious to us, and the emotional response arising from that challenge, that makes working in a multicultural team difficult. Even people who have learned a lot about other cultures before joining a multicultural team still experience these strong emotions.

It can be difficult for Christians from countries in which one large ethnic group dominates to work well in multicultural teams. One of the main reasons for this is that we tend to assume that there is a biblical culture that is supracultural, and that this biblical culture is reflected in our church or Christian group. While there are certainly supracultural biblical values, such as the command to love our neighbors as ourselves (Lev 19:18; Matt 22:39) and to forgive one another (Eph 4:32; Col 3:13), these values of love and forgiveness are expressed in different ways in different cultures. Christians from different cultures express biblical values in ways that are shaped by their own cultures. Assuming that our Christian culture is the most godly way to do things is part of our ethnocentric tendency to assume our way is right. Sadly, this assumption can lead us to judge Christians from other cultural backgrounds who express biblical values in ways that are different from our ways as being sinful, and may even cause us to think they are not Christians.

Most books on teamwork and leadership written in English reflect English/Dutch/German-speaking background (EDG) cultural values.[14] These values include individualism, efficiency, task orientation, an emphasis on written team agreements, and relatively little emphasis on relationships except as an instrumental factor in achieving tasks. Amanda Sinclair suggests that American "values of individualism and universalism . . . have

---

14   We have struggled to find a term that best describes the dominant cultural cluster that incorporates the individualistic, low-context values (described later in this chapter) expressed by people from British, German, and Dutch heritage, including their descendants in the USA, Canada, New Zealand, and Australia. This cultural cluster is particularly significant because of the large numbers of missionaries sent out from these countries over the last two centuries. Other terms that are sometimes used include Western, Global North, northern European, Minority World, Anglo-Saxon background, or White Australian/American. Each of these terms is problematic, either because it is too broad (e.g., Western) or because people have difficulty accepting it (White Australian). The terms are also problematic because they make it difficult to account for mixed identities such as Chinese American or Fijian Australian or Australian Lebanese. We have decided to adopt the acronym EDG (for English/Dutch/German-speaking background) to indicate English/German/Dutch-speaking, low-context, individualist cultural background as a general but not exclusive group, which readers can choose to identify with or attribute to others as appropriate.

percolated into the work on leadership." She describes the consequences of this as being "individual-centric explanations for success, and . . . universal rules for leadership that can be distilled and applied regardless of context."[15]

This EDG instrumental orientation to leadership has also permeated much of the literature on cross-cultural leadership. EDG leadership values are particularly focused on what the leader has to do to get followers to achieve tasks. In the same way, most books on cross-cultural leadership focus on helping leaders understand cross-cultural differences so that they can adjust their leadership style in order to cause those they are leading to achieve what the organization wants. In this approach, which we have called the cross-cultural approach to leadership, explained in chapter 1, the burden is on the leader to adapt to each culture represented on the team. Leaders using this approach become like instruments or tools in order to manipulate culture to make the team fulfill its task. They try to adapt their leadership style to the culture of each team member to make it fit better with each member's expectations of leadership, and they do their best not to offend them. In effect, leaders who adopt the cross-cultural approach have to become cultural chameleons. Adaptation is a serial, one-way process that is highly demanding on the leader.

A cross-cultural approach to leadership assumes that if leaders learn enough about each of their team members' cultures, they should be able to sufficiently replicate each culture's leadership style towards each member in such a way as to guarantee followership. A leader who uses this approach has an overwhelmingly complex and demanding task, as they have to make multiple adjustments to suit each member. The burden is on the team leader to make adaptations in their leadership style to cancel out the effects of cultural difference, so that the team functions like a monocultural team. In this approach to leadership, culture is treated as something that can be manipulated. It assumes that when the leader is able to make the necessary adjustments to the cultural norms of their team members, the team will be harmonious and effective. Team members are regarded as passive elements in the process.

---

15   Amanda Sinclair, *Leadership for the Disillusioned: Moving beyond Myths and Heroes to Leading That Liberates* (Crows Nest, Australia: Allen & Unwin, 2007), 23.

The cross-cultural approach to leadership is a good starting point for leading a multicultural team, but it is inadequate on its own. It helps as a starting point because it emphasizes the need for the leader, as well as all team members, to be aware of and sensitive to each member's cultural background. But it becomes untenable when a leader has to deal simultaneously with team members from very different cultures who have opposing expectations of leaders. When team members' cultural expectations of leadership are irreconcilable, the cross-cultural approach to leading a multicultural team is a recipe for leadership failure and burnout. In the next section we explore dimensions of cultural difference that help to make it clear why there can be irreconcilable differences in expectations of team members from different cultures.

UNDERSTANDING CULTURE AND CULTURAL DIFFERENCES

A culture is the way in which a group of people orders their lives and determines what is or is not appropriate behavior. Cultures are constantly changing in response to the world around them. Some people resist cultural definitions, predominantly due to fears of stereotyping or that they are being put into boxes. Nevertheless, whenever groups of people from different cultures get together—in a university classroom, for example—they invariably talk about the differences between cultures such as language, greetings, food, or childcare. Cultural difference is a fact of life.

Culture has a stabilizing influence in that it forms a large part of any group's sense of identity. Since we all acquire our culture through socialization that starts very early in life, culture is a deep and usually subconscious influence on our values and behaviors and the development of our concept of who we are. One of the main ways that members of each ethnic group define their group's distinct identity is to find cultural features that make their group distinct and to emphasize these as boundary markers around their group. Key cultural features are used to define the boundary of the ethnic group and, in this way, exclude other people from the group.[16] Theologian

---

16   Fredrik Barth, introduction to *Ethnic Groups and Boundaries: The Social*

Miroslav Volf explains that we exclude others because we see difference as dangerous and feel the need to remove those differences in order "to ward off the perceived threat of chaotic waters rushing in."[17]

One way people exclude culturally different others is by stereotyping them. Often these stereotypes are negative. Paul Hiebert traced an extreme example of stereotyping in the ways many Europeans defined the people they came across in their travels in Africa and Latin America in the eighteenth and nineteenth centuries. European explorers initially saw the new people they encountered on their travels as savages whom they could use as slaves. Later the dominant perception shifted to seeing them as primitives needing enlightenment and civilization or as children needing education. It was not until the twentieth century that the majority of Europeans began to see people from other cultures as fully human.[18] Such dehumanizing stereotyping is not restricted to the past and to Europeans; it is a widespread human response to ethnic and cultural difference. Most people have negative expectations about communicating with people from other cultures, have negative stereotypes of them, and are convinced that their own group's way of seeing things is the correct one.[19]

In order to understand what happens and what often goes wrong when people from different cultures try to work together, it is helpful at the outset to have a model for understanding culture. Hiebert proposed a very helpful three-level model of culture. At the surface level are the people's behaviors that are easily observable and the first thing that an outsider sees. Underlying these are the people's beliefs and values that provide a scaffold for interpreting the world. At the deepest level are the largely implicit assumptions that

---

Organization of Culture Difference, ed. Fredrik Barth (Long Grove, IL: Waveland, 1969), 9–38.

17   Miroslav Volf, *Exclusion and Embrace: A Theological Exploration of Identity, Otherness, and Reconciliation* (Nashville: Abingdon, 1996), 78.

18   Paul Hiebert, "Western Images of Others and Otherness," in *This Side of Heaven: Race, Ethnicity, and Christian Faith*, ed. Robert Priest and Alvaro Nieves (Oxford: Oxford University Press, 2007), 97–110.

19   William Gudykunst, *Bridging Differences: Effective Intergroup Communication* (London: SAGE, 2004), 115–31.

underlie both beliefs and behaviors and provide the rationale for why the people believe and behave as they do.[20]

In practice, culture is complex and dynamic. Behaviors and assumptions are not independent of each other. Assumptions affect behaviors, but, at the same time, as people interact with the physical world, they may have to change the way they do things, such as moving from subsistence farming to technology-driven approaches to farming, and this affects the assumptions they have about the world.

People continually seek to understand and explain their world. To do this they create meaning frameworks that help them to interpret the things they experience. Jack Mezirow proposes that when we encounter something that is alien to our framework, we try to work out how to attach or incorporate it into our personal framework. If we are unable to incorporate it, we tend to reject it.[21]

Meaning frameworks form a bridge between people's deep, implicitly held assumptions and the things they do that are at the surface of their culture and easy to observe. Meaning frameworks incorporate beliefs, values, and feelings. Beliefs are statements that summarize assumptions and are considered widely accepted facts by the people of any culture. Beliefs are constructed with words. It is more difficult to describe the essence of values and feelings, because they are not based on words. But to try and understand them we still have to use words. Values define what is good, right, and beautiful and how things should be. They enable people to make judgments about what is acceptable and what is not. Feelings are people's positive or negative emotional responses to what they encounter.

EDG cultures are highly biased towards beliefs. People from EDG cultures tend to confuse values with beliefs and virtually ignore emotion. They are quick to judge other people negatively when they consider that they have not used the right words to express what EDG people consider to be of value. Most other cultures put much less emphasis on words, and interpret and evaluate what they encounter using feelings, intuition, experience, and the

---

20   Paul Hiebert, *Transforming Worldviews: An Anthropological Understanding of How People Change* (Grand Rapids: Baker Academic, 2008), 32–33.

21   Jack Mezirow, "How Critical Reflection Triggers Transformative Learning," in *Fostering Critical Reflection in Adulthood*, ed. Jack Mezirow (San Francisco: Jossey-Bass, 1991), 1–20.

accumulated wisdom of tradition. There are massive mismatches between the meaning frameworks of different cultures. As each culture's meaning framework provides the scaffolding for how experience is interpreted and responded to, team members from different cultures see and experience the same things but interpret and react to them in completely different ways. Helping multicultural team members to understand, articulate, and negotiate a compatible common meaning framework is one of the challenges in team formation.

A simple example of how we use our meaning framework occurs when we are given something to eat that is forbidden in our own culture. Although our culturally different friend is eating the same food, we refuse to even consider eating it because our meaning framework does not allow it. It is not only things that are alien to our framework that we reject; we also decide not to engage with things when we consider they are the same as our previous experience. This often happens in short-term mission teams when people interpret what they are seeing as being the same as in their own culture and assume that they understand what is happening when in fact there are crucial differences. Members of a short-term team from a relatively affluent country, for example, may have been given a meal by their much less affluent host people to welcome them and interpret it as equivalent to a welcome meal in their own culture. They can easily fail to appreciate the sacrificial hospitality of their hosts, and because they cannot see its sacrificial nature, they cannot be challenged by it or learn from it.

Mezirow suggests that there is an optimal level of discomfort that makes people experiencing the discomfort aware of inadequacies or holes in their own meaning frameworks such that they want to fix the inadequacies. The multicultural team leader has to help each team member appreciate the incompleteness of his or her own meaning framework, and help them learn from each other so that they can together build a corporate meaning framework that is compatible with each team member's personal framework and which then binds them together.

The diagram on the next page (fig. 4) is a model of culture developed from Hiebert's and Mezirow's ideas. Behaviors are depicted at the surface level of culture, and assumptions at the deepest level. The meaning framework binds the two layers together using beliefs, values, and feelings. These three layers are dynamic and constantly interacting with and affecting each other.

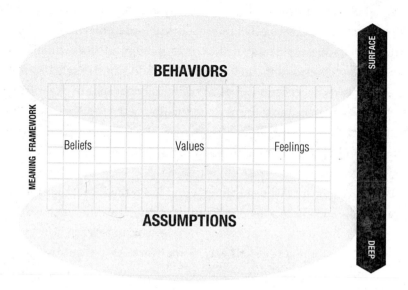

*Figure 4: Model for understanding culture
(adapted from Hiebert,* Transforming Worldviews, *32–33;
and Mezirow, "Critical Reflection")*

When people interact with a new culture for the first time, the superficial differences such as the climate, the new food, the new modes of transport, the presence or absence of people on the streets, and the way people shop are what first impress them. They also start to observe differences in the behavior of the people such as the ways they greet people, talk, and eat. Although these differences will be a challenge for new visitors, they will usually be able to adjust to them. This stage of cross-cultural encounter is often referred to as the "honeymoon" phase. At this point visitors are engaging primarily with differences in behavior. These expressions of culture can be seen and touched in some way and encountered with minimal language. Many cross-cultural workers develop personal strategies for managing these kinds of differences but fail to progress to a deeper engagement with the belief system of the host culture.

If visitors stay longer, begin to learn the language, and delve beneath the surface of the culture, they soon discover barriers of difference that are more difficult to adjust to. They will begin to interact with the beliefs and values of the people that are learned from an early age, repeated frequently, and often not examined. These beliefs and values provide a meaning framework by which the local people evaluate new information. Visitors will often find these beliefs and values difficult to understand and will struggle to communicate their own beliefs and values meaningfully because of the mismatch between their own meaning framework and that of the local people. We will refer to this mismatch as cultural dissonance. The struggle to communicate or understand the local people clearly can result in severe frustration and is a major aspect of culture stress or culture shock.[22]

With time, visitors who stay longer and learn the local language begin to see how differences in behavior are underpinned by differences in beliefs and values. While it is usually easy for the new worker to learn how to adjust to greeting people in a different way, it may be very difficult for them to adjust to the meanings of these greetings, as, for example, when greetings embed different approaches to social hierarchy. An Indian with a preference for hierarchy may find it nearly impossible to refer to an egalitarian Dutch coworker, who is older and more senior, using a first name, and the Dutch person may find it very hard to show appropriate respect to the older and more senior Indian coworker. Being required to do so can seem like an attack on personal integrity as it forces people to act in ways that go against all they have ever done and believe in. The same would apply to an egalitarian Australian being required to accept and follow a Korean leader's instructions without any opportunity to discuss the instructions.

The deepest level of culture—the deeply held and largely implicit assumptions the people hold about reality—is much more difficult to access, and it usually takes several years for an outsider to begin to understand. A people's assumptions about reality are often expressed through their creative arts such as poetry, dances, songs, proverbs, and stories, and in rituals and ceremonies surrounding birth, coming of age, marriage, and death. Assumptions help people to understand and accept why things are the way they are. As people imbibe these implicit understandings through experiences, they do not usually analyze or reflect on them. An example of an assumption in EDG cultures is that a girl will be saved (or found) by her Prince Charming

---

22   Marjory Foyle, *Honourably Wounded: Stress among Christian Workers* (London: Monarch Books, 2001), 69–82.

and that they will "live happily ever after." This assumption focuses on the guy finding and winning the girl but does not reflect on the relationship after the wedding day.

Included among the deep-level assumptions that form the worldview of a group are their assumptions about logic, or the process by which ideas and arguments are accepted as being worth considering. EDG people are convinced by linear and dialectic logic. The Millet people we worked among in Bulgaria circle around an issue to arrive at their point. Arabs argue by analogy. None are convinced by the alternative approaches, and in fact they can become frustrated and even offended when other approaches are used. Some cultures are not interested in the content of the argument at all, only the feelings aroused by the interaction.[23]

Cultures differ in how they evaluate whether something is true. An example of an assumption held by most EDG people is that things that are tested and proven by scientists are true and reliable. An example for the Millet is that if you are a relative, you are reliable and trustworthy. These values are largely unexamined and tend to be upheld regardless of evidence to the contrary.

HOW LANGUAGE DIFFERENCES AFFECT MULTICULTURAL TEAMS

Part of the behavior that is at the surface level of every culture is language. Language differences are a key factor contributing to communication problems in multicultural teams. We found that the ability of multicultural church planting teams to communicate was markedly hindered by having members who lacked proficiency in the team language.[24] Languages embody the assumptions and structures of the cultures they represent. This is why different languages do not have a one-to-one correspondence between words and meanings. In order to communicate effectively in another language, we

---

23   Duane Elmer, *Cross-cultural Connections: Stepping Out and Fitting In Around the World* (Downers Grove, IL: InterVarsity Press, 2002), 150–59.

24   R. Hibbert, "Church Planting Teams," 190.

need not only to learn its vocabulary and grammatical structures, but also to learn about the social structures, values, and assumptions of the culture.

Team members' proficiency in the team's common language profoundly affects the quality of their interaction with each other. Nonnative speakers of the team's common language can feel excluded from discussions if their lack of fluency prevents them from expressing their thoughts quickly or clearly enough. It is all too easy for native speakers of the team language to think that when nonnative speakers do not participate in discussions, they are not interested in the topic or cannot grasp the issues. Another reason why nonnative but relatively fluent speakers of the team language can face communication problems is that even subtle differences in pronunciation or grammatical structuring can result in native speakers misunderstanding what they are saying or thinking they are rude.[25]

Even when every team member feels free to contribute, misunderstandings can easily occur as team members and leaders from different cultural backgrounds tend to use words and concepts in different ways. Leaders from Kuwait, Turkey, and Qatar, for example, use words like "consultation" and "participation" primarily to induce feelings of belonging to the group with the understanding that the leader will still make the final decisions.[26] Leaders from EDG cultures, in contrast, usually understand these words as implying involvement in a decision-making process that will result in a shared plan of action.

HOW CULTURAL DIFFERENCES AFFECT MULTICULTURAL TEAMS

Underlying differences in behavior between cultures are different sets of values and assumptions. We have found that six dimensions of cultural

---

25   Stephen Chen, Ronald Geluykens, and Chong Ju Choi, "The Importance of Language in Global Teams: A Linguistic Perspective," *Management International Review* 46 (2006): 679–96.

26   Selda Pasa, Hayat Kabasakal, and Muzaffer Bodur, "Society, Organisations, and Leadership in Turkey," *Applied Psychology: An International Review* 50 (2001): 559–89; Ikhlas Abdalla and Moudi Al-Homoud, "Exploring the Implicit Leadership Theory in the Arabian Gulf States," *Applied Psychology: An International Review* 50 (2001): 506–31.

values and assumptions are particularly significant in multicultural teams and often cause misunderstandings:

1. Individualism versus collectivism

2. High-context versus low-context communication

3. Task orientation versus people orientation

4. Direct versus indirect communication

5. High power distance versus low power distance

6. High uncertainty avoidance versus low uncertainty avoidance[27]

The dimension of individualism versus collectivism describes the degree of importance people attach to their group and the degree to which they prefer to act as individuals or as part of a group. Collectivists are group oriented. They are closely linked to their groups and view themselves as part of lifelong groups such as their extended family, their tribe, or their nation. They base their identity primarily on the groups they belong to and make decisions by considering what will be best for the group. They are motivated by the norms and duties imposed by the group. Individualists, in contrast, define their identity much more independently, make decisions on the basis of what will be best for the individual, and give priority to personal rather than group goals. They stress personal achievements and individual rights and choose which groups they are part of.

---

27   Individualism and collectivism have been described in great detail in Harry Triandis, *Individualism and Collectivism: New Directions in Social Psychology* (Boulder, CO: Westview, 1995). This dimension is also described in Hofstede, Hofstede, and Minkov, *Cultures and Organizations*, 89–134. High- and low-context cultures were first described in Edward Hall, *Beyond Culture* (New York: Anchor, 1976), 85–103. Task and people orientation are described in Elmer, *Cross-cultural Connections*, 125–34. Direct and indirect communication are described in Sarah Lanier, *Foreign to Familiar: A Guide to Understanding Hot- and Cold-climate Cultures* (Hagerstown, MD: McDougal, 2000). Power distance and uncertainty avoidance are described in Hofstede, Hofstede, and Minkov, *Cultures and Organizations*, 53–86, 187–233.

People from high-context cultures are aware of the many nonverbal cues in the context such as the room the communication is happening in, the ways the people they are with are dressed, how people are sitting or standing, their tone of voice and gestures, and other things going on in the room. They place as much or more value on these nonverbal elements in the communication as they do on the words themselves. People from low-context cultures, in contrast, pay attention almost exclusively to the words of the communication and ignore many of the elements in the wider context, such as nonverbal cues. This difference causes endless problems in multicultural situations. If something has been said or written down, low-context people expect that it will be adhered to. High-context people are much more sensitive to the nonverbal messages around the words, such as the low-context person's impatience, and care much less about what was written down. For low-context people, words are binding. For high-context people, relationships are binding and words are largely irrelevant.

In situations where written agreements are used, such as many teams and business partnerships, people from low-context cultures (such as EDG cultures) consider that everything has been settled when a signature is put to paper. Although they may have invested several hours or even days communicating with their partners in order to get the paper signed, once it is signed they consider it completed. They are oblivious to the eye contact going on between the people from the high-context culture, the restlessness, the signaling to other people outside the room, or even the protocols of interaction, except in terms of achieving the goal of the signature on the document. When, after signing, it seems that the other signatories ignore the document, they get angry and frustrated. For the high-context partners, the paper was just part of the relationship-building process and of little importance to the other things being communicated.

People from high-context cultures are usually also people oriented rather than task oriented. They want to help low-context people overcome their impatience and frustration and relax and enjoy their time with them. They consider the task of secondary importance compared to the quality of relationships between them. However, they often have some difficulty coping, because the low-context people are very direct and seem rude when communicating. The low-context people do not display any consideration for their feelings or the complexity of the situation. The high-context people keep hinting indirectly, but the low-context people seem oblivious to what they are saying. Low-context people think they have communicated clearly because they have said the words as simply and clearly as possible. The high-context people also think they have communicated clearly because they have gently referred to a few of the things that might be affecting what they think the low-context people want to achieve. In fact, the low-context people seem to be getting quite hot and agitated, and the high-context people think that the low-context people just need to cool down and so suggest they have something to eat.

Cultures also have different ways of structuring their hierarchies. Power distance refers to the degree to which followers expect and accept that their leaders will have more power than they do.[28] Different cultures are comfortable with different degrees of power distance. The major way this affects multicultural teams is in decision making. People from high-power-distance cultures are much more comfortable with leaders making unilateral decisions on their behalf. Those from lower-power-distance cultures expect leaders to involve them equally in decision making. They expect to participate in the process. This difference is virtually irreconcilable in many teams. Higher power distance may also be associated with leaders being expected to extend their responsibility over the personal lives of team members, even to the extent of being a patron who provides for their personal needs.

The final aspect of cultural difference that causes issues in multicultural teams is uncertainty avoidance. This is the degree to which people tolerate uncertainty and ambiguity. In cultures that have high uncertainty avoidance people try to minimize risk and anxiety by doing everything they can to plan for every contingency. In their cultures there are culturally defined rules and procedures for every circumstance. Those who come from low-uncertainty-avoidance cultures, in contrast, are comfortable in unstructured situations and changeable environments and try to have as few rules as possible. They are reluctant to waste time and resources on things that may never happen. Team planning for the future can be significantly affected by tension between these two perspectives. This is particularly likely to be relevant to compliance with bureaucratic requirements for team activities. Team members from

---

28   Hofstede, Hofstede, and Minkov, *Cultures and Organizations*, 53–86.

high-uncertainty-avoidance cultures will want to get all the government permissions and paperwork sorted out before they do an activity, even if the process takes many months or even years. Low-uncertainty-avoidance team members will prefer to just get on with the activity and will be ready to deal with any problems if and when they arise.

These different dichotomies are not either/or categories but spectrums of possibilities. They help team members working with culturally different teammates to realize that there are many different variations of difference and that difference is not wrong but simply different. For team members who have not previously encountered or reflected on cultural difference, understanding these dimensions of cultural difference can also help them to realize that their cultural orientation is simply one possibility on a spectrum. The incredible creativity of humanity means that cultures can vary in myriad dimensions, including subtle variations on common themes.

Team members from different cultures perceive the world around them, including their team's task, in different ways. Just about every aspect of team process, life, function, and communication will be perceived and managed differently by people from different cultures. They will have different ways of communicating, different sources of motivation, different views of what effectiveness looks like, and different views of integrity and trust. If these views cannot be successfully integrated, the team will be unable to function to its full potential.[29]

THE DEEP INFLUENCE OF CULTURAL DIFFERENCES ON EMOTIONS

Our cultural values and assumptions are so deeply embedded in us from birth that they evoke strong emotions in us, even though we cannot articulate why. A particularly clear example of this is found in comparing approaches to babies and children between individualist EDG cultures and collectivist Millet culture. EDG parents bring their babies home from the hospital

---

29   Martha Maznevski and Mark Peterson, "Societal Values, Social Interpretation, and Multinational Teams," in *Cross-cultural Work Groups*, ed. Cherlyn Granrose and Stuart Oskamp (Thousand Oaks, CA: SAGE, 1997), 62.

and place them in their own rooms to sleep, separate from their parents, in their own beds that are surrounded by rails, and put them in playpens surrounded by walls. These rails and walls are there to protect the babies, but they also create a very clear boundary between the baby and other people. If babies object to being left on their own, there is an elaborate system of psychological training to teach babies that they must be alone in the world and be quiet so that the other people in the babies' world can get on with their own lives. As babies grow they will be placed on the floor and surrounded by toys with which the babies are expected to occupy themselves. Toys are deemed to belong to the individual child, and although major efforts might be made to teach the young child to share, it is acknowledged that the toys belong to the individual, and the child has the right to retain the toys if he or she so chooses. It is no surprise, therefore, to discover that adults from EDG cultures prefer homes in the suburbs, surrounded by gardens and fences, and do not appreciate their boundaries being crossed except by explicit invitation. It is also no surprise that these cultures are champions of individual human rights.

In major contrast, Millet babies never leave the arms of people. They sleep in their mother's bed for many years, and during their days are passed from relative to relative. They are continually part of human interaction, and rarely, if ever, are they given toys. Children are ever present wherever adults gather, and it is unthinkable that a child would retire to his or her own room for individual activity. For Millet, loneliness is an unknown concept and very difficult to understand. They live in extended family housing with a central area for communal gathering, eating, and working. Anyone's problem is everyone's problem. They continually visit each other and move around in groups. Children are always taught to share. Even if children have one small biscuit, they must either give it away or break it and share it with others. It is inconceivable that food or possessions be kept to oneself; they must always be shared. In this culture, debt is an honor, especially to a number of people, because it indicates that others value you enough to loan money to you. As the Millet are a poor minority people, money is usually in short supply for everyone, so they will often go into debt in order to provide a meal for a visitor, which not only affirms the worth of the host (who receives the loan) but preserves the honor of the group before the visitor.

It should now be easy to imagine the potential for major conflict when EDGs and Millet attempt to work in a team together. Even if an EDG and a Millet team member have both studied cross-cultural communication and understand intellectually individualism and collectivism, many of their teammates' actions will feel wrong and evoke powerful emotional responses. Collectivism is a nice, and even more biblical, concept than individualism until a Millet teammate's child takes your child's new, expensive toy that you had specially sent over from your home country. Individualism, so quaintly symbolized by those weird, prison-cell beds for babies, is fine until your teammate rudely turns you away at the door because he needs "family time." Each team member feels offended by the other's actions and feels that the other's culture is simply wrong. They feel angry and hurt, even though they intellectually understand intercultural dynamics.

It is difficult for us to understand how much of what we think, feel, and value is determined by our culture, especially if we are from a dominant or majority people group and have not had extended exposure to another culture. Awareness of our own culture usually develops only when we personally encounter another culture over an extended period. When we have not had this deep exposure to other ways of seeing the world, we do not see culture as an issue, because our culture's ways are all we see, and they are the right way. Because of this, we unconsciously assume superiority in interactions with people from other cultures and try to impose our culture's way of doing things on others. Christian workers, missionaries, and mission agencies can behave in this ethnocentric way without realizing it and think that the way things are done in their home churches is the only way that really pleases God.

Each of us makes judgments about things based on our assumptions about what is good, right, and beautiful. Our concepts of what is good, right, and beautiful are a complex mosaic founded on a lifetime of stories, images, and experiences that we have experienced together with members of our cultural community and that have been continually reinforced and affirmed to us by important people from within our community. This mosaic of assumptions differs from culture to culture. People from every culture have a unique way of ordering their world by classifying things as good or bad, right or wrong, and beautiful or ugly.

Some of the more obvious differences between cultures at the behavioral level are in what people wear and the music they listen to. Even though these differences are relatively superficial, it is often difficult for people from one culture to appreciate the music of another culture, as the music is constructed with unfamiliar instruments, sounds, and rhythms. It is not uncommon for people from one culture who have to listen to music from another culture to describe it as "wrong" and to feel like they cannot stand it. Recently we heard a member of one culture refer to another culture's dancing as "hideous." The same applies to clothing. People from one culture often do not like the colors and styles of another group's clothing and refer to them as garish or even ugly. On a deeper level, people from cultures that highly value the independence of women can be quick to condemn cultures that ascribe beauty and honor to marriage, childbearing, and keeping house. When people encounter these differences, they feel driven to change the "wrong" in the host society, such as when a missionary feels compelled to teach new converts to sing "properly"—meaning they must sing using the musical style the missionary is comfortable with.

People from one culture can easily judge the actions of the people from another culture as bad, wrong, or ugly based on their assumptions. In collectivistic cultures, for example, the way people behave towards each other, and their ability to preserve harmony, is seen as good and beautiful. When individualists lose their temper and lash out at people, animals, or objects, collectivists perceive this as particularly ugly behavior. When a local Lengua Indian saw a North American missionary beating a horse for damaging his vegetables, for example, the Indian concluded that the missionary must be subhuman. What the missionary had done was, according to Lengua assumptions about the need to preserve harmony inside yourself and in the world around you, completely inappropriate and ugly.[30]

When we make negative judgments about culturally different practices, we are essentially defining our ways of doing things as clean and the other culture's as dirty. Anthropologist Mary Douglas argued that dirt is fundamentally "matter out of place."[31] Earth, for example, that is useful and good

---

30   Jacob A. Loewen, *Culture and Human Values: Christian Intervention in Anthropological Perspective* (Pasadena: William Carey Library, 1975), 142–43.

31   Mary Douglas, *Purity and Danger* (London: Routledge, 1966), 37.

in its right place in the garden, becomes dirt when it is trodden inside the house and onto the carpet. Things that we see as bad, wrong, or ugly offend our sense of order and are therefore in this sense dirty. Where dirt, in whatever form, intrudes, it is not right and has to be dealt with; we feel compelled to clean it up. In intercultural interactions, even among highly trained missionaries, it is not uncommon for people to consider that their colleagues might not even be Christians because of the "dirt" that has blemished their shared context.

Team members from collectivist cultures tend to be much more concerned about preserving group harmony and avoiding loss of face than individualists. They may avoid saying things that might upset that harmony or cause loss of face, such as reporting damage to a car or the unacceptable behavior of a colleague. Team members from individualistic cultures who observe this behavior may consider their collectivist teammates unreliable. They may see them as liars and possibly question whether they are even Christians. The collectivist, on the other hand, may see the individualist who reports negatively on a teammate's behavior as disturbing the group's harmony and threatening relationships, and they may wonder if the individualist can be a Christian.

The feelings associated with the judgments we make can be very strong. Some cultures are more aware of these feelings and have well-developed language to identify and explore emotion. Most Koreans, for example, share an underlying emotion called *han*. *Han* is a widely shared feeling of pain and inward frustration, a "wounded heart" that results from abuse, exploitation, and violence.[32] People from EDG cultures, in which overt emotional expression is seen to muddy the ordered world, find it difficult to identify with or understand emotions like *han*. Team members who come from cultures in which emotional expression is considered bad often do not have the skills to identify or relate to these kinds of emotional expression in their teammates. Koreans and many Chinese people, in contrast, are often much more aware of the emotions of others. We have found that Korean team members often recognize and understand the anger or hurt of an offended team member more readily than EDG team members.

---

32   Dongsoo Kim, "The Healing of Han in Korean Pentecostalism," *Journal of Pentecostal Theology* 15 (1999): 125–26.

When someone from our own culture contravenes the accepted way of doing and seeing things, everyone is offended, but our emotional response is relatively minor as immediate steps are taken by everyone to bring the offender back in line and restore right order to the world. However, when our way is contravened in an intercultural interaction, the rules are completely different. If your group is dominant, you can insist that your version of the order of the world is restored by forcing the offender to behave like you. If you are in the minority and powerless, your worldview is threatened, which can be highly distressing. Even if you conform, or allow the people from the other cultural group to do it their way, you still have to resolve the internal cultural dissonance and its associated negative emotions. We have often heard multicultural mission team members say of their fellow team members, "They can't possibly be Christian if they act that way." David Greenlee gives a good example of this:

> In the early days of Operation Mobilization's ministry through its ship Doulos, "Hans," from northern Europe, was the supervisor of "Ray," from Southeast Asia. Ray's task was to serve customers on the ship's large bookfair and make sure his shelves were stocked and in order; Hans oversaw the shift of workers to which Ray belonged.
>
> As I recall the incident, Hans dropped in to visit the ship's director one day. "I don't think Ray can be a Christian," he eventually said. "He spends so much time talking to people that he rarely has his shelves stocked and in order."
>
> Shortly after that, Ray came for an appointment unaware of Hans' earlier visit. "There is no way that Hans is a Christian!" he insisted to the director. "All he cares about is work and schedules, not about spending time with people."[33]

---

33   David Greenlee, *One Cross, One Way, Many Journeys: Thinking Again about Conversion* (Tyrone, GA: Authentic, 2007), 7

IMPLICATIONS OF CULTURAL DIFFERENCES FOR TEAM COMMUNICATION

All communication is deeply influenced by culture. We miscommunicate when we do not take into account both our own culture and the culture of the person we are communicating with. The difficulties of communicating cross-culturally are not so much due to the cultural differences themselves but due to our unhelpful and inaccurate interpretations of those differences. This is why understanding cultural differences and how these differences affect communication is so important for multicultural teams. As we begin to understand the cultural values of others in our teams, we will also begin to interpret their communication more accurately and understand them more fully.

William Gudykunst explains that when we communicate with people from other cultures we experience uncertainty and anxiety, and that we need to manage these so that they are at an optimal level—neither too high nor too low. If our uncertainty is too high, our ability to interpret others' messages or accurately predict their behavior decreases. If our anxiety is too high, we interpret others' behavior according to our own frame of reference or by stereotypes rather than thinking through what that behavior means in the other person's own frame of reference. Similarly, if our uncertainty or anxiety is too low, we tend to interpret the other person's actions using our own familiar framework, ignoring cultural differences and being unmotivated to explore alternative perspectives. What we need to do, according to Gudykunst, is to become "mindful." When people communicate mindlessly they tend to use broad categories and stereotypes to interpret the behavior of others. Becoming mindful involves consciously working at our ways of communicating to maximize understanding. It means that we think about how our actions and words will be interpreted by our teammates and also that we work at interpreting their actions in terms of their frame of reference.[34]

---

34   William Gudykunst, "Applying Anxiety/Uncertainty Management (AUM) Theory to Intercultural Adjustment Training," *International Journal of Intercultural Relations* 22, no. 2 (1998): 227–50.

It is important for multicultural team members to realize that language is only a small part of any message that they or their teammates communicate. One of the major difficulties in cross-cultural situations is our inability to "read" the nonverbal communication signals of team members from other cultures. In the same way, team members from different cultures than us may be "reading" our signals as meaning things we did not intend to communicate. A study comparing the ability of people from the USA and Jordan to perceive deception across cultures provides a good example of this: within-culture judgments—that is, judgments made by Americans about Americans, and judgments made about Jordanians by Jordanians—were relatively accurate, but cross-cultural judgments were extremely inaccurate and little better than flipping a coin.[35] Since nonverbal communication is such an important part of communication, especially for people from high-context cultures, becoming aware of and learning how to interpret nonverbal communication accurately across cultures is a vital skill for multicultural team members and leaders to work on.

IMPLICATIONS OF CULTURAL DIFFERENCES FOR TEAM LEADERS

Multicultural team leaders need to develop intercultural competence—the ability to respond and relate effectively to team members from a wide variety of cultures. Intercultural competence enables the team leader to recognize the expectations that various team members have concerning leadership, to foster effective team communication, and to enhance relationships between team members. By understanding other cultures, the team leader becomes more aware of how their words and behavior can be misinterpreted and is more capable of accurately interpreting individuals' responses in discussion and decision making. Intercultural competence can prevent the team leader from unnecessarily offending team members and feeling personally offended by cultural differences. Leaders who have some knowledge of the specific cultures represented on their team are also better able to discern

---

35   Charles Bond, Adnan Omar, Adnar Mahmoud, and Richard Bonser, "Lie Detection across Cultures," *Journal of Nonverbal Behavior* 14, no. 3 (1990): 189–204.

which problems are culture related and which are a result of other differences such as individual personalities. Intercultural competence helps the leader facilitate the team's negotiating a mutually agreed-upon approach to managing conflict. It also helps the leader to manage interethnic rivalries on the team.

An interculturally competent leader can help their team communicate more effectively. Cultural differences mean that communication in a multicultural team is a complex minefield. Each culture represented on the team will bring to the communication process different cultural assumptions, contextual interpretations, nonverbal behaviors, and approaches to preserving the face of participants. It is unrealistic to expect team leaders to continually adjust their communication style to suit the culture of each team member simultaneously in the context of team meetings. The interaction is too complex and rapid for them to do this. While multicultural team leaders do need to have the intercultural competence to be able to understand and manage communication with each individual team member, in the context of the whole team they need to help team members themselves develop the intercultural competence to communicate with each other.

The complexity of communication in a multicultural team is one reason why team formation usually takes longer in multicultural teams than it does in monocultural teams. Much of the foundational work of building a multicultural team is done in the early stages of forming and storming. In these early phases the team leader needs to help the team explore cultural values and the meanings of nonverbal behaviors. The leader should encourage the team to make explicit as many cultural assumptions as possible. Assumptions related to the dimensions of cultural difference discussed in this chapter are a good place to start.

Intercultural competence is also needed to understand and appropriately respond to team members' expectations of their leaders. Culture affects these expectations. People from different cultures have different ideas about what good leadership looks like. They have different views of the importance, value, status, and influence of leaders.[36] These different views of leadership mean

---

[36]   Robert House, Paul Hanges, Mansour Javidan, Peter Dorfman, and Vipin Gupta, *Culture, Leadership, and Organizations: The GLOBE Study of 62 Societies* (Thousand Oaks, CA: SAGE, 2004), 5.

that team leaders will only have credibility as leaders in the eyes of team members when they lead in a way that matches the team members' cultural expectations, at least in some key aspects. Members of multicultural teams do not generally expect leaders from other cultures to become completely like leaders in their own culture.[37] They make allowances for leaders from different cultures, but nevertheless still have unconscious expectations of their leaders that are shaped by their own backgrounds.

In her research into multicultural mission agencies, Lianne Roembke found that European and North American missionaries were often offended by what they saw as the authoritarian leadership style of African and Asian team leaders. On the other hand, Asians and Africans questioned the competence of leaders who wanted to involve everyone in all decisions. Many Asian team members reported being bored and frustrated by Western-style participative decision-making meetings and that they just wanted to get on with the task.[38] In our research into church planting teams, we found that Asian members of multicultural church planting teams were much less positive about their leader's style than EDG members. Many Asian team members felt that their team leaders were indecisive. These team members also had higher expectations that their leaders would give clear direction, clarify roles on the team, and provide pastoral care.[39] Other researchers have found that team members from Asia, the Middle East, and Africa are more likely to prefer an autocratic leadership style and that they are more concerned with harmony in the team than with performance.[40] The greater the difference in concept of leadership between leaders and followers, the less influence the leader is likely to have.

Another way in which leadership expectations differ across cultures is in how much of their lives team members allow and expect their leaders to influence. North Americans, for example, expect there to be a strong

---

37   David Matsumoto, *Culture and Psychology: People around the World* (London: Wadsworth, 2000), 476.

38   Lianne Roembke, *Building Credible Multicultural Teams* (Pasadena: William Carey Library, 2000), 130–31.

39   R. Hibbert, "Church Planting Teams," 166.

40   Kamel Mellahi, "The Teaching of Leadership on UK MBA Programmes: A Critical Analysis from an International Perspective," *Journal of Management Development* 19 (2000): 297–308.

distinction between work time and personal or family time. They do not expect their leaders to have any say over what occurs in their personal or family time.[41] In contrast, in Japan and India workers often expect that their leaders will be involved in their personal lives, even to the extent of helping them find marriage partners. A first step for leaders of multicultural teams is to grow in their understanding of these differing expectations.

There are two main ways of developing the intercultural competence necessary to being a good multicultural team leader. The first of these is to become familiar with the general categories of cultural differences such as those described in this chapter and to gain experience observing how these are expressed in a wide variety of cultures. The second way is to learn the values of each of the team members' specific cultures, including their values concerning leadership. Leaders can develop this more specific intercultural competence by asking team members about their values and expectations of leadership. These discussions could be included in some of the team's meetings during its first year of operation. Examples of questions that leaders can ask their team members about their cultures' views of leadership are listed in appendix 1.

It is unrealistic to expect that multicultural team leaders will be personally familiar with all the cultures represented in their team. Multicultural team leaders need to become lifelong students of culture. By continuing to learn about other cultures, they become increasingly aware of the variety of ways in which humans order and make sense of their world and relate to one another within it. Becoming more aware of this variety also means that leaders are more sensitive to the differences between value systems in different cultures and more capable of predicting possible issues that might arise. Open-mindedness makes leaders more able to accept practices, interpretations, and approaches of team members that are different from their own and to make these differences explicit in a way that helps the team either accept the differences or negotiate a compromise. If team leaders are unaware of the cultural bases of these differences, they may judge them as wrong and inhibit discussion rather than open discussion up as a path to negotiation.

Team leaders who have lived in another culture have a great advantage, because they have at least a general understanding of cultural difference

---

41   Matsumoto, *Culture and Psychology*, 473–74.

and have personally experienced the challenge of adapting to a new culture and the degree of effort needed to really connect with people from other cultures. The sense of inadequacy, the emotional stretching and trauma, and the development of self-awareness through experiencing hurt in previous intercultural interaction all enable the interculturally experienced team leader to appreciate and empathize with team members from other cultures. There is no substitute for this kind of practical experience of extended immersion in and face-to-face interaction with people from another culture.

CHAPTER 3

A VISION FOR MULTICULTURAL COMMUNITY

The most compelling reason for us to appreciate diversity—especially cultural diversity—is God's creation. God delights in diversity. In all creation, not even one snowflake or blade of grass is exactly the same as another. There is a strong emphasis in the creation narrative on all living things being created "according to their kinds" (Gen 1:11,12,21,25 NIV), and the account concludes with the summary, "Thus the heavens and the earth were completed in all their vast array" (Gen 2:1 NIV). In contrast, ever since the Tower of Babel, human beings have been expending a great deal of energy trying to create conformity. Monolithic factories produce thousands of products that are exactly the same. Suburbs are filled with house after house built to exactly the same plan, and politicians and lawyers work hard to define laws and policies that ensure that societal procedures are followed with exacting reproducibility. Marriage counselors commonly have to advise husbands and wives to stop trying to change their spouses to behave like themselves.

Difference seems dangerous to us because it is unpredictable and out of our control. Difference, or "otherness," with its inherent "out-of-control-ness," makes us anxious. In intercultural encounters we attempt to manage our anxiety using one of two strategies towards culturally different others. Miroslav Volf uses the terms "embracing" and "excluding" to describe these two strategies.[42] Embracing others means accepting and including them.

---

42   Volf, *Exclusion and Embrace.*

Excluding others, in contrast, creates an us/them dichotomy in which some people are deemed unacceptable and are kept out of the group. In order to exclude or embrace, we create boundaries between ourselves and others. Boundaries act as identity markers, and members of each ethnic group maintain the boundary of their group by controlling who can cross the boundary to be included and what they must do to cross it.[43]

Control is the most common strategy that people use to manage cultural difference, and it is often used in multicultural teams. Control is really a conditional embrace. When there is a power difference between the cultural groups in a team, the more powerful group usually sets the conditions for the less powerful to be embraced. The conditional embracers are really saying, "You can join us if you either become like us or hide your difference where we can't see it." As the less powerful group must play by the rules of the dominant group, the dominant group's anxiety is eased because they have made difference manageable by bringing it under their control. The suppressed or oppressed group(s) become anxious because they feel that their identity is being threatened; they feel they must deny something of who they are in order to be accepted and reap the benefits of belonging to the more powerful group. The dominant group's use of exclusion or embrace is mostly unconscious. Exclusion and conditional embrace are automatic human responses to a threat to our sense of group identity or to our group's well-being.

In this chapter we explore the dynamics between different cultures when they live and work closely together; one of the greatest challenges occurs when one cultural group is more dominant or powerful than others. We also provide an outline of what the Bible teaches about diversity in general and cultural diversity in particular. Lastly, we describe how organizations and team leaders need to adapt their thinking and approaches in order to create healthy multicultural teams.

---

43   Barth, *Ethnic Groups and Boundaries*, 9–38.

THE CHALLENGE OF ETHNOCENTRISM

We all tend to assume that our ethnic group's ways of doing things are right and true and that other groups are uncivilized or somehow less human. This is known as ethnocentrism. Ethnocentrism affects the way we feel about culturally different others and often leads us to dislike them or feel contempt towards them. It is common to all ethnic groups. In Irian Jaya, for example, the Dani people looked on the Western missionaries who were trying to reach them with the gospel as ghosts, while the missionaries considered the Dani to be uncivilized. Each group considered the other to be less than fully human.[44]

The perception that "our way is right" leads us to assume that we have a monopoly on truth and to think that other ways of doing things are deficient or abnormal. Any group that is in the majority in a society or a team tends to impose its way of doing things on others. But it is not only majority groups that can do this. A group may dominate even when it is in the minority, such as when a minority group gains political power in a country and attempts to fashion the country in its own image. In a multicultural team, the leader may be from a minority group in the team but nevertheless feel he can dominate others because his cultural group is the most powerful in the organization.

When a dominant (majority or minority) group defines the actions or values of other groups as deficient, it is easy for that dominant group to assume that they should fix up those deficits. Although members of the dominant group have good intentions, their attempt to fix others' behavior is based on the idea that the others' ways are inadequate. Their efforts are usually ignored or rejected by the members of nondominant groups since they see the interventions as detrimental to their well-being and as reinforcing the impression that they are deficient compared to the dominant group. This common problem occurs when groups with more money, resources, and power try to intervene to fix up what they perceive as deficits in less privileged groups. Development projects among the poor or among indigenous peoples often suffer from this deficiency mindset.

---

44   Charles Farhadian, "Comparing Conversions among the Dani of Irian Jaya," in *The Anthropology of Religious Conversion*, ed. Andrew Buckser and Stephen Glazier (Oxford: Rowman & Littlefield, 2003), 58.

When people are defined as being deficient in relation to the dominant group, they can easily feel devalued and subhuman. They have no way of changing the dominant group's opinion or of gaining respect for what they have to give. It is as if a room full of people is discussing them but they have no opportunity to contribute to the discussion. Edward Said gives a poignant example of this kind of discussion in his book *Orientalism*. He describes how a whole field of scholarly study and popular discussion arose in the Western world about the Middle East and Islam but failed to include the viewpoints of Middle Eastern people. As a result, Westerners held on to a wildly distorted view of the Middle East and Islam, strongly colored by Western ethnocentrism. The Orientalist view of the Middle East and of Muslims became a way of controlling otherness and a conditional embrace that communicated, "You can be part of our discussion as long as we set the agenda."[45]

In multicultural situations, unconscious discrimination occurs when members of the dominant ethnic group do not take the time to listen to and understand the perspectives of culturally different others. Instead, assuming that everyone thinks like they do, they take over decision making. When the other group or groups express alternative opinions, the dominant group attributes negative motives to them. An example of this is an African American church and a European American church that attempted a merger in the mid-1990s. Though they shared the same beliefs, after two months of shared worship meetings they voted to abandon the merger and go back to their separate congregations. But not everyone wanted to separate. The more dominant European-background church members believed the merger had gone well. They were blind to the differences that caused the African American church members to vote against the merger. African American worship practices were not appreciated by the dominant group, and the values that they held dear were ignored.[46]

This kind of problem is frequently encountered in multicultural teams. Dominant-group members can tend to talk about team members from

---

45   Edward Said, *Orientalism* (London: Penguin, 1995).

46   Kersten Priest and Robert Priest, "Divergent Worship Practices," in *This Side of Heaven: Race, Ethnicity, and Christian Faith*, ed. Robert Priest and Alvaro Nieves (Oxford: Oxford University Press, 2007), 275–91.

other cultures rather than including them in conversations. When they do include them, it may be only to fix up the problems their group is causing or experiencing rather than to genuinely work together to reach collaborative solutions. Dominant team members can be afraid to allow nondominant team members to have too much say, fearing that their suggestions might threaten the way things should be.

CULTURAL DIVERSITY IS GOD'S DESIGN

Diversity is God-created. Inherent in God's design of the world is infinite variety. Although everyone emerges from DNA, and 75 percent of everyone's genes are identical, there are myriad variations created from the same building blocks.[47] No two people, not even identical twins, are exactly the same. Difference is normal; we should expect and accept it. We first see this in Genesis chapters 1 and 2. God creates a rich and colorful variety of forms and creatures. In addition to day and night, land and seas, sun, moon, and stars, the Lord creates many kinds of plants, birds, fish, and animals.

When God created humans, he created them diverse in the sense of being male and female (Gen 1:27). In order for humanity to fulfill God's mandate to fill the earth, subdue it, and rule over all the animals (Gen 1:28), people needed to adapt to diverse environmental conditions. Just as Adam was given freedom in how he approached the tasks of taking care of the garden of Eden and naming the animals (Gen 2:15,19,20), the whole of humanity was given freedom about the specifics of how it went about the task of ruling over the earth. As people spread out across the earth and faced different environments, they generated different ways of solving problems and different approaches to family life, relationships, work, and play. This generated different ways of life; in other words, different cultures. Even before the Fall, then, God envisioned cultural diversity, and he enjoys that diversity.[48]

---

47   Noah Rosenberg et al., "Genetic Structure of Human Populations," *Science* 298 (2002): 2381–85.

48   Frank Chan, "Biblical Materials for a Theology of Cultural Diversity: A Proposal," in *Understanding Diversity: Theological Views on Diversity* (Dubuque, IA: Kendall Hunt, 2005), 140–41.

The mystery of synergy through diversity is inherent in God's creation design. This synergistic effect, where difference complements and increases the impact of individuals, is a common theme in the Bible. It is a mystery because we cannot easily explain or measure it. The mystery of this synergy is expressed in the Trinity, in the four living creatures who look different but serve God together (Ezek 1; Rev 4; 5), in marriage, in families, and in the body of Christ. It is man and woman together who reflect the image of God and who together make one unit (Gen 5:1,2). God said that it was not good for Adam to be alone and created a helper who was just right for him. She was made from Adam, but she was different from him. In her difference from him she made whole the incompleteness of man on his own (Gen 2:18–24). In the same way, no individual Christian can adequately express who Jesus is. It is the body of Christ, with all its different parts, that together reflects Jesus (1 Cor 12). Paul writes to the church in Corinth, "All of you together are Christ's body, and each of you is a part of it" (1 Cor 12:27). There is something about togetherness in difference that empowers and creates something new. Effective teams have synergy. This occurs when the effect of working together interdependently is greater than the sum of what each individual on the team could achieve by working alone.

Humanity's rebellion against God came to a climax at the Tower of Babel when, as one people speaking the same language, they started building a city and a tower. They said the reason for doing this was "so that we may make a name for ourselves [and not] be scattered over the face of the whole earth" (Gen 11:4 NIV). When God confused their language, the consequence was that "the LORD scattered them from there over all the earth" (Gen 11:8 NIV). Rather than simply a punishment for sin, this was God's way of correcting them and getting his purpose for humanity back on track.

The primary issue at Babel was the people's refusal to obey God's command to spread out across the earth. As they spread out they would encounter different physical environments and diversify in lifestyle and language. The people decided instead to build a monolith extending up to the heavens. They were demonstrating the human predilection for uniformity—not many communities, but one; not many lifestyles, but one; not many governments, but one. All human ingenuity was focused on one object, instead of being applied to the challenges of the vast physical diversity of the world. What happened to those who did not want to live in the city? What options were there for those who had skills better suited to sailing across oceans than baking bricks for a skyscraper? God saw what the people were doing and was not pleased. He had made people for creativity and diversity, and they wanted monolithic conformity in opposition to his will. He saw they needed help to scatter, so he ensured they could not enforce sameness by making sure they could not understand each other. From this perspective, difference—especially difference in languages—is a blessing. The story of the Tower of Babel explains not only how and why people spread out across the world speaking different languages, but also the development of the different nations and clans that are described in Genesis chapter 10. The Tower of Babel "explains why empire building always involves a drive towards linguistic and cultural uniformity."[49]

God continued to affirm ethnic and cultural diversity after scattering the people over the world. Immediately following Babel, God introduced his redemptive plan to bless all the peoples of the earth (Gen 12:1–3). He planned to do this through Abraham, by making him into a nation that would be a channel of blessing to all other nations. Yet the way God chose to redeem the world was not for Israel to subsume other nations into itself. People from other nations that God blessed through Israel continued to be identified by their ethnic background, even though some of them married Israelites and lived among them. A few of the many examples of this are Rahab (Josh 2), Ruth the Moabite (Ruth 1:4), Ittai the Gittite (2 Sam 15; 18), the widow of Zarephath (1 Kgs 17; cf. Luke 4:24–26), and Naaman the Syrian (2 Kgs 5).

People from other nations were not required to become Jews to receive God's blessings. Naaman was not condemned for being an enemy general with an Israeli prisoner of war in his home, and Jesus emphasized that God healed a Syrian rather than one of many Jewish lepers in his synagogue talk at Nazareth (Luke 4:27). The Old Testament laws concerning foreigners in Israel did not require them to become Jews but still protected and cared for them and guaranteed justice (Lev 19:33,34; Num 15:15; Deut 24:17–22).

---

49 Dewi Hughes, *Ethnic Identity from the Margins: A Christian Perspective* (Pasadena: William Carey Library, 2011), 50.

Foreigners were included in the community without having to be subsumed into it. They could participate without having to give up their non-Jewish identity. They were able to participate in the people of God even to the extent of being included as ancestors of the Messiah, as Rahab and Ruth were (Matt 1:5).

The nations were not condemned for being different from Israel but for worshiping other gods. The Bible records different customs and seems to delight in giving examples of when people from other nations seek God. God urged the Egyptians in Moses' time, the Ninevites in Jonah's day, the Babylonians and especially king Nebuchadnezzar in Daniel's time, and the Persians to listen to and obey God, but he did not require them to become Jews. Isaiah predicted that "many peoples" would stream to God to worship and learn from him, but that they were still identifiable as other nations (Isa 2:2–4), and that there would be a highway from Egypt to Assyria so that Egyptians and Assyrians could worship God, but that they would continue to be Egyptians and Assyrians (Isa 19:23–25).

When Jesus came, he modeled care for and inclusion of people from all nations into God's family. A particularly poignant example of this is his going out of his way to extend God's salvation to the Samaritan woman and the people of her village (John 4). His last command to his disciples was to make disciples of all nations (Matt 28:19). In the process of fulfilling this command, the early believers wrestled with how to include Gentiles into the people of God. Some were convinced that Gentiles should be circumcised and effectively become Jews in order to become Christians. But Paul fought for Gentiles not to have to be circumcised, and the church's leaders eventually agreed (Acts 15). Gentiles did not have to become Jews in order to become followers of Jesus, and in the same way, Jews did not have to eat Gentile food in order to prove their conversion to Jesus' Way. Neither Jew nor Gentile had to change their culture in order to become a Christian.

The Bible is clear that pushing one particular cultural approach as the only right way of doing things is contrary to God's desire. Jesus is the only fixed point in Christianity. Clustered around Jesus, the radiating center of our faith, is a huge diversity of culturally shaped and God-honoring ways of living for Christ. God affirms difference, and he appointed an extraordinary apostle—Paul—to ensure that cultural difference was preserved in the early church. God has no favorites. He cares for everyone in the same way.

The New Testament strongly affirms that people do not have to adopt another culture in order to become Christians. God's purpose in making the nations and determining their boundaries, Paul told the Athenians, "was for the nations to seek after God and perhaps feel their way toward him and find him—although he is not far from any one of us" (Acts 17:27). Paul emphasizes that God's purpose was that each nation would seek him, because God is not far from any one of us in all our diversity, individually or as nations (Acts 17:26–28). Jesus brought together Jews and Gentiles (Eph 2:11–22) in such a way that Jews could still remain Jews and Gentiles could stay Gentiles. They had to learn to accept one another because Christ had accepted them (Rom 15:7). Paul fought hard, and successfully, to protect the cultural integrity of the Gentile peoples against assimilation into Jewishness (Acts 15; Gal 2:1–10; 3:28). It was not just a fight against legalism, but about who had the right to determine what being a Christian looked like.

From its origins, Christianity has been a faith that, as it is taken into each new context, becomes expressed in new ways. Believers from every culture are free to create indigenous expressions of Jesus' body.[50] Pentecost and the crowd around the throne of the Lamb affirm cultural and linguistic differences. At Pentecost the ability of "devout Jews from every nation" to understand without the painstaking process of language learning was temporarily restored (Acts 2:5). Each of them heard their own language being spoken by the believers (Acts 2:1–12). Language differences were not removed—the people were amazed because they were able to hear the wonderful news about God in their own languages (Acts 2:7,12). At this beginning point of the church, God reaffirmed his intent, earlier expressed in creation and at the Tower of Babel, that people are to be diverse. The same picture of diversity is found in the crowd around the throne of the Lamb, which is not a homogenous mass of conformity but a dynamic throng from every nation and tribe and people and language (Rev 5:9; 7:9).

---

50   Andrew Walls, *The Missionary Movement in Christian History: Studies in the Transmission of Faith* (Maryknoll, NY: Orbis, 1996), 43–54.

UNITY MEANS HARMONY NOT CONFORMITY

The drive to make other people like ourselves is a consequence of sin. It represents our desire to make everything in our own image, or at least to control other people's image so it does not disturb our image of ourselves. This is in distinct contrast to the harmony within diversity of God the Father, Son, and Holy Spirit. Sin has affected our relationships with others in many ways. It causes breakdown in relationships through lack of trust and a tendency to attribute negative motives to others. The sin of pride causes us to assume that our way is right and therefore others' ways are wrong. Pride leads us to assume that the world revolves around us and that we do not have any need to learn from others. Sin corrupts the power to influence and change for good into a desire to dominate and control. Sin also distorts the concept of unity. Instead of unity promoting harmony, sin makes us feel like everyone needs to sing my tune, my way, in unison with me.

Christians have a tendency to think that diversity is a threat to unity and that that means eliminating difference, especially cultural difference. As a result, churches and Christian organizations often try to make their members conform to common norms. The New Testament emphasizes that Jews and Gentiles, slaves and free people, men and women, and the "civilized" and "uncivilized" have been brought together in the body of Christ (Gal 3:26–29; Eph 2:11–22; 4:1–6; Col 3:11). Some people use this wonderful reality to enforce conformity by accusing anyone who questions the status quo of attacking the unity Christ died to establish in his church. We have a tendency to use biblical proof texts on unity to ward off any suggestion that cultural differences should be embraced.[51] This approach enables members of the dominant cultural group to control their anxiety over difference, but it also has the unwanted side effect of suppressing the diversity that God created and crushing the spirits of those who do not naturally fit into what has been defined as the norm. Biblical texts like these are sometimes used as battering rams to force everyone to conform to the patterns of those in power and to keep the control of resources and power in their hands. While this theology protects the comfort of the dominant group, it alienates and

---

51   Hughes, *Ethnic Identity*, xvii.

excludes nondominant groups and is used as an excuse to blame the non-dominant groups when relationships break down and they leave to form their own separate groups.

We are usually attracted to other people who are like us. These feelings of attraction cause us to intuitively trust people who are similar to ourselves and be wary of those who are different. This also means that we tend to trust information from people from our own culture more than information from members of other cultural backgrounds.[52] Arguments against promoting cultural diversity are often a response to an unspoken fear that power holders will lose their control of power and resources if people from other cultures are really included.[53] Because we are afraid of difference, we try to obliterate it. In some parts of the world this fear and need to obliterate the other has led to genocide. In multicultural teams this same fear can lead team members to try to force their colleagues from other cultures to do things differently, simply because they are not comfortable with, or feel like they cannot cope with, the difference. A North American might try to make a Korean team member wash dishes in an American way, a Brazilian might try to make an Englishman be more physically expressive, or an Australian might try to force a Chinese team member to be more assertive in group discussions.

It is very hard to overcome our fear of really including others who are different. But it is possible because of Jesus. He has made us one in his body (Gal 3:26). This oneness is not one amorphous mass, and does not mean we all look or behave the same way. Instead it is like a functioning human body with different parts, all looking different, all doing different things, but all connected to the head, which is Jesus (1 Cor 12). We so quickly forget that Jesus is our head rather than any one of us. His Holy Spirit provides us with the power to forgive and mend relationships, even in the face of seemingly irreconcilable conflict. He pours into our souls the balm that heals the hurt and soothes the frustration and anger (Heb 4:15,16). He also provides us with the ability to trust when trust seems impossible, through the discipline

---

52   Carley Dodd, *Dynamics of Intercultural Communication*, 5th ed. (Boston: Abilene Christian University, 1998), 64–65, 209–14.

53   Gerald Bates, "Missions and Cross-cultural Conflict," *Missiology: An International Review* 5 (1977): 195–202.

of attributing right motives rather than projecting our own fears onto the actions of others (Phil 4:8).

If team members from nondominant ethnic groups are made to feel that the only way to belong to the team is to conform to the dominant group's ways of thinking and doing things, they can be wounded in their inner being, and their sense of who they are can be deeply disturbed. Yet every person has been created in the image of God (Gen 1:26), and each individual is unique and precious just as they are. Destroying people's sense of personal worth and their unique identity according to how God has made and developed them within their own particular social context is very serious. God wants us to build fellow Christians up, not tear them down (Eph 4:29; 1 Thess 5:11). The cost of "unity" should not be the destruction of its participants. The Apostle Paul understood unity in Christian community to mean respect for one another, which includes respect for others' cultural ways of doing things, including their ways of serving God. In his book on ethnic identity, Dewi Hughes writes: "To object to a fellow Christian's desire to worship and serve God within their cultural heritage is the exact opposite of what Paul is saying. . . . This unity that we have is to be expressed in mutual love and respect and not in destroying each other's identity."[54]

The desire of any group to impose on others what they see as Christian culture presupposes that there is a Christian culture that is distinct from and above all other cultures. But the truth is that there is no single Christian culture, only Christian ways of doing things in many different cultures. A common example of ascribing a specific cultural orientation to a presumed supraculture is when Westerners insist on democratic approaches to decision making as if there were no other God-endorsed ways of arriving at decisions in groups. Another very common example is when dominant-group members dismiss biblical interpretations that do not fit with theological formulations that have been developed in their own culture. In doing this they see their own interpretation as being the only truth rather than seeing it as a culturally shaped interpretation. This is significant, because in Christian contexts theology can be a very powerful tool for controlling others, especially when those with less power assume that those with more power must be right.

---

54   Hughes, *Ethnic Identity*, 100.

In order to live in harmony in multicultural teams, we must treat our teammates as truly equal with us. Hughes has called this completely equal treatment "risky generosity."[55] Old Testament law required Jews to treat foreigners living among them as if they were Jews, loving them as they loved themselves. It said: "Do not take advantage of foreigners who live among you in your land. Treat them like native-born Israelites, and love them as you love yourself" (Lev 19:33,34). It also said: "Native-born Israelites and foreigners are equal before the LORD and are subject to the same decrees" (Num 15:15). The same risky generosity that God wanted Jews to show to people from other ethnic groups can guide us in relating to people who are different from us.

The best way of thinking about unity is as harmony. Psalm 133 emphasizes this central characteristic of unity:

> How wonderful and pleasant it is when brothers live together in harmony! For harmony is as precious as the anointing oil that was poured over Aaron's head, that ran down his beard and onto the border of his robe. Harmony is as refreshing as the dew from Mount Hermon that falls on the mountains of Zion. And there the LORD has pronounced his blessing, even life everlasting.

Harmony is not a choir singing in unison, which occurs when all voices sing exactly the same tune. Harmony occurs when each group in the choir sings its own part and together all parts produce a beautiful sound. If one part is missing or weak, the music is tainted by that part's absence. However, just as it can take an inordinate amount of time and a great deal of effort for choirs to learn to produce beautiful sounds, so it can take Christians a long time and strenuous effort to learn to reflect God's glory and experience his blessing through harmony. It is possible, however, if we are willing to humbly persevere.

Getting on with people who are different from us is hard work. Paul emphasizes this when he writes, "Make every effort to keep yourselves united in the Spirit, binding yourselves together with peace" (Eph 4:3). When the

---

55   Ibid., 131.

ces extend beyond superficial behaviors to deep assumptions about the world, relationships can break down at unpredictable moments for apparently incomprehensible reasons. Including others in a church or a team means including them in the control of resources and decision making. When those people are unfamiliar to us and unpredictable, it is not surprising that we are afraid of including them.

The Bible is full of examples of conflict between people. Beginning with Cain's killing Abel, and continuing through the conflict between Esau and Jacob, between Joseph and his brothers, between the peoples of Canaan and the Israelites, between King Saul and David, between Jesus and the Jewish leaders, between Paul and Barnabas, between Paul and Peter, and between Euodia and Syntyche, interpersonal conflict can be found in almost every book of the Bible. Conflict is a normal human experience. If conflict is normal between people from the same culture, how much more is it likely to occur between people who have different values and views of the world! The reason the Bible is so full of exhortations to get on with each other is because harmony is so difficult. Harmony is something that has to be worked at. Harmony is learned through practice in the crucible of experience. The pain of conflict is like the cutting of a diamond that enables its beauty to shine through. God can use conflict to help us deepen our understanding of him and of each other. The focus in multicultural teams needs to be on learning to embrace conflict and developing effective strategies to manage it.

THREE WAYS OF APPROACHING MULTICULTURAL COMMUNITY

There are three main approaches to different cultures living and working together: assimilation, cultural pluralism, and multiculturalism. In assimilation, one culture dominates and the different cultures merge with the dominant culture. In cultural pluralism, the cultures mix as a set of parallel subcultures. In multiculturalism, there is a complex interweaving of the separate but distinct cultures into a new and distinctive pattern. Below we assess how appropriate each approach is for enabling team members to feel valued and empowered in a multicultural team.

Assimilation

Assimilation is often referred to as the "melting pot" approach. Assimilationists expect people from other cultures to adopt the dominant group's culture and to essentially become one of the dominant group's members. The assumption is that when the minority group members are mixed with the majority, they will lose their distinctiveness and adopt the values and ways of the dominant group. One of the major problems with the assimilation approach is that the cultural group with the greatest power defines the cultural norms, including the definitions of difference, and all others are forced to comply with the dominant group or be alienated. The dominant group assumes that their ways are universally right and is unwilling to consider the viewpoints of others.

When one group has dominated for a long time, the members of that group often do not realize that there are other ways of understanding the world, as they assume their way is the right way. They are culture-blind in the sense that they do not realize their way is just one culturally shaped way of doing things.

The assimilation model assumes that everyone should think, feel, and act the same way. It excludes people who are culturally different, seeing them as childlike or inferior. Difference is viewed as a deficit from the norm that must be managed or corrected. Assimilationists look for faults in those who do not assimilate and want to change them so that they will fit in.[56] Although people of other cultures may do their best to adapt, they start from a position of disadvantage and discrimination, which often makes it impossible for them ever to fully assimilate. They are faced with the no-win situation of having to deny their own identity in order to become something they will never fully be allowed to be.

We have often heard native English-speaking members of multicultural mission teams, who are part of the dominant group, complaining about other team members talking with each other in their own languages. They

---

56   Stella Nkomo, "The Emperor Has No Clothes: Rewriting 'Race in Organizations,'" *Academy of Management Review* 17 (1992): 487–513.

see this behavior as divisive and subversive. They are frustrated that they cannot understand what is being said, as if it is their right to always know what others are thinking and saying. They seem unaware of the strain that constantly listening and communicating in a second (or third or fourth) language puts on people. This demonstrates an unconscious assumption on the part of the dominant-group members that the nonnative English speakers should adopt EDG language and cultural ways. If nondominant-group members show their difference (through speaking in other languages), they are assumed to be doing something wrong.

Effective and healthy multicultural teams are established on the foundation of valuing and respecting every team member. Assimilation is not an appropriate approach for a healthy multicultural team. Assimilation is built on the pervasiveness of just one culture; it prevents the valuing of other cultures and denies people from other cultures an authentic voice. An assimilationist team essentially functions as a monocultural team, in which one culture provides all the norms for team life, even if there are people from other cultures in it.

Cultural pluralism

The second possible way to approach multicultural community is cultural pluralism, which is often described as a "salad bowl" approach. In this model, different cultural groups are allowed freedom to express their various cultures, but the boundaries between the cultural groups are defined and maintained. The major difficulty in this model occurs at the boundaries where the different cultures have to interact. In practice, people from the various cultural groups do their own thing when relating to people from their group, but they have to use the cultural norms of the greater power group when relating to other groups. When this model is applied to organizations, minority groups are allowed to exist but are usually underrepresented in leadership. The majority culture, or the culture with the greatest power, is also implicitly understood to be superior. The performance of minority groups in areas such as education and health tends to be compared with performance in the more dominant culture, and differences have to be managed in order to bring the nondominant groups up to the standards of the dominant group. There is an implicit assumption that the minority groups should be like the majority.[57]

Cultural pluralists are more realistic than assimilationists in that they focus on managing diversity rather than expecting it to disappear. In this model, boundaries between cultures are well maintained and there is less likelihood than in the assimilation model of the whole group developing a collective identity. Minority group members hoping to cross into the dominant group are unlikely to be accepted. But this approach, like the assimilation model, is incompatible with effective multicultural teamwork. It prevents synergy developing in the multicultural team because boundaries between groups are maintained and team members of different cultural backgrounds are unable to value each other and work together closely. Cultural pluralism would be well suited to a working group in which members of different cultures work in parallel on different tasks without developing the interactive synergy inherent in an effective team.

Multiculturalism

The third way of approaching multicultural community—multicultural-ism—is sometimes referred to as a mosaic model. All the individual parts mesh together to create a new picture that is both a single new entity but is also dependent on the equal and unique contribution of all the different parts. Relationships are negotiated rather than coerced. The new entity is constructed by the participants rather than outside powers. Every mosaic will look different according to its members and context. This model offers flexibility, adaptability, and participation. When this model is applied to an organization, members are more likely to feel like they belong. It also enhances the organization's ability to adapt and be flexible.

Multiculturalism is often only an ideal rather than a reality in practice. On the rare occasions where it can be found in organizations, cultural difference is fostered and valued. The presence of many cultures does not make an organization multicultural. Instead multiculturalism describes a society where everyone feels valued, whatever their culture.[58] Valuing other cultures

---

57   Ibid.

58   Alberto Canen and Ana Canen, "Multicultural Leadership: The Costs of its Absence in Organizational Conflict Management," *International Journal of Conflict*

means engaging with them on their own terms rather than through the lens of our own values and experience.

Multicultural teams have to aspire to the multicultural model if they are to be successful in achieving synergy. There is no other way to become an effective unit than for team members to learn to value each other and want to encourage each member to contribute from the richness of their diverse backgrounds.

Multicultural teams that enable all members from different cultures to feel valued and to have a voice need to find a way to create a culture-neutral space for team formation in which the natural tendency towards conforming to the most powerful group can be overcome. Even where there is balance of power and resources between a number of groups in a multicultural society or team, choosing to base the ways of doing things in a team on only one of the cultures will automatically disrupt the balance and give the chosen culture more implicit power.

THE NEED TO CREATE A NEUTRAL SPACE

For a team to be healthy and truly multicultural, it needs a neutral space to negotiate its own unique approach. Homi Bhabha, a Harvard professor who has thought deeply about multiculturalism, calls this space a "liminal space."[59] *Liminality* is an anthropological term that describes a state of transition between one stage of life and another.[60] As people leave one stage of life, such as childhood, they commonly pass through a ritual experience that first separates them from their original state and prepares them for the next stage. Although the term was first used to describe initiation rites, it has been applied to Christian activities such as retreats, pilgrimages, and camps, in which people withdraw from the world for a time, expecting to be changed through spiritual renewal.[61]

Management 19 (2008): 6.

59   Homi Bhabha, "The Third Space: Interview with Homi Bhabha," in *Identity: Community, Culture, Difference*, ed. Jonathan Rutherford (London: Routledge, 1990), 209.

60   Arnold van Gennep, *The Rites of Passage* (London: Routledge & Kegan Paul, 1960).

61   Victor Turner and Edith Turner, *Image and Pilgrimage in Christian Culture:*

To create this neutral or liminal space, multicultural team members need to partially distance themselves from their own cultures in order to develop a new and unique team approach. Although it is not possible to completely separate ourselves from our own cultures, as they are too deeply ingrained, in order to participate effectively in a multicultural team we must hold our own ways of thinking and doing things lightly and become open to new ways. The phase of team formation then becomes like a liminal state in which the team transitions from being a group of individuals who each have fixed, culturally shaped conceptions of how things should be done to being a synergistic group that has together established a shared set of team values which they own together and which defines them as a group. One of the major tasks of the multicultural team leader is to create and preserve the liminal space that allows cultural power imbalances to be corrected and every member to feel safe and free to contribute to the development of the team's unique identity.

IMPLICATIONS FOR MULTICULTURAL TEAMS

Every member of a multicultural team has to interact with multiple cultures simultaneously. The greater the number of cultures in a team, the greater the diversity, complexity, and ambiguity will be. Multicultural teams need extra help, compared to monocultural teams, to cope with the added factors influencing team dynamics. Team leaders need to help team members understand their teammates' cultures.

It is important to accept that total agreement on everything and never having any conflict is unrealistic and that even the idea of achieving it is unhelpful. A problem that can develop in organizations where there is a high value on multicultural and diverse teams is that team members avoid conflict and make unnecessary compromises for fear that the team unity will be undermined. It is important to recognize that intercultural misunderstandings are inevitable. Cultural differences need to be made explicit so that problems are openly aired rather than left to develop into interethnic grievances.

Anthropological Perspectives (New York: Columbia University Press, 1996).

One of the major challenges to building effective multicultural teams occurs when the team exists within an organization dominated by one ethnic culture, or when there is a majority group of one culture on a team. Teams in this situation often default to the norms of the dominant culture because this path seems easier.[62] If the team leader is also from the majority-culture group, equity will be more difficult to achieve.[63] In such a situation it is imperative that the team leader's behavior reinforces the value and full involvement of everyone in the team and that power discrepancies are intentionally addressed. If the leader does not do this, major strains in team relationships are likely to develop. Members of nondominant groups may become angry when forced to conform and may feel excluded. This can cause them to wonder whether it is worth being part of the team.

It is critical for members of dominant cultures who want to work in multicultural teams to examine their attitudes and assumptions. It is particularly helpful to do this in a group with people from other cultures who are confident in sharing their own opinions. In a truly multicultural team, every member's assumptions will be challenged. This may be particularly confusing and disorienting for dominant-group members who are not used to questioning their own culture. A multicultural team needs to be a safe enough place that members feel free to challenge each other's assumptions and attitudes and query why they do things the way they do without feeling that one culture will necessarily overrule.

If team members who come from the dominant culture have not experienced living in another culture, they will find it hard to overcome their ethnocentrism. Organizations can help address this challenge by selecting personnel, and especially leaders, for multicultural teams who have intercultural experience. Intercultural experience does not always mean that dominant-group members have understood the issues associated with dominant-group privilege, however, and they may need help to identify their assumptions and be able to allow people from other cultures to have equal voice and access to resources.

---

62   Claire Halverson, "Group Process and Meetings," in *Effective Multicultural Teams: Theory and Practice*, ed. Claire Halverson and Aqeel Tirmizi (Dordrecht, The Netherlands: Springer, 2008), 111–33.

63   Roembke, *Building Credible Multicultural Teams*, 111–12, 153.

The choice of team language often carries an unconscious message about the cultural orientation of the team and may subtly reinforce assumptions of the superiority of a dominant culture. Where there are varying levels of fluency in the chosen team language, it is important for the team to establish processes that address this imbalance, such as speaking slowly, asking for clarification, allowing the use of team members' languages with translation, using summaries and visual records, and allowing discussions outside the team-meeting context. It is important that team members all have the sense of being listened to and also that their contribution is acknowledged. Multicultural teams need to have nonthreatening ways of discussing difference, developing a common vocabulary and processes that promote understanding of issues and incidents within the group.

The leader must facilitate the creation of a safe space for team members to speak and a genuine sense that each person's opinion and experiences are valued. However, as ways of speaking are culturally shaped, by only having one style of interaction the team or its leader may inadvertently reinforce a pattern of cultural dominance. The leader should create multiple contexts and ways for team members to interact, including different physical settings and modes of communication, so that equal participation can develop.

The complexity of multicultural teams means that they do not lend themselves to simplistic approaches to team formation or leadership. Beware the entrepreneur who offers a one-day seminar that has all the answers and a three-step plan that will solve all problems! Multicultural team leaders need to be reflective practitioners who view the task of leadership as a continually developing set of skills built on some successes but also many mistakes. They need to continually reflect on what is happening and what they are doing in response. They are constantly monitoring their own actions and reactions, as well as those of the people they are interacting with, learning from others on the team and external to it (including reading and attending more formal learning experiences), experimenting with different approaches, and adjusting what they do in response to what happens. They also hold their own values and approaches lightly, being willing to adjust and flex in relation to what they learn from others and from the experience of the team.

CHAPTER 4

BUILDING HEALTHY MULTICULTURAL TEAM COMMUNITY

A healthy team community is one in which its members respect and trust each other. They feel safe and communicate openly with each other. They feel they have equal voice and influence. They feel safe to talk about anything, including things that make them feel uncomfortable. They plan, decide, and evaluate their work together. They care for each other and feel that they belong together, need each other, and fit together.

The period of team formation is the most critical period for a team's leader. The leader has to win the respect of the team members and enable them to relate well to each other. During team formation, patterns for team interaction are set up that will greatly affect how well team members interact with each other and work together in the future. Multicultural team formation takes much longer and requires a bigger investment of the team leader's energy and focus than formation in monocultural teams. Multicultural team leaders generally need to specially focus their attention on the relationships in the team for the first three to six months of the team's life. This focus on relationships includes several elements: proactively fostering a liminal space in which members learn to hold their own cultures lightly and forge shared team values, learning about the team members and their cultures, learning to learn together, preparing the team for conflict, and helping it to learn from conflict when it occurs.

CREATE EARLY OPPORTUNITIES FOR SUCCESS

The rest of this chapter focuses on building relationships. While teams are engaged in the relationship-building process, it is important that they do not lose sight of their task. During the early relationship-building process the team also needs to be doing things together that contribute to its task. As team members work together, they learn about each other and will have their cultural values confronted. The process of finalizing the team's vision, goals, and strategies (which we focus on in chapter 5) can take several months, but meanwhile the team should work on a few short-term goals that are readily achievable in the first few weeks or months of the team's life. These early goals ideally focus on researching the context and finding resources that may be appropriate for future ministry. Achieving something together helps to create a team "script" for working together. It also boosts morale as team members experience the success of overcoming the challenge of diversity together.[64] Success helps team members to believe that they can achieve together and to want to stay together to achieve even more.

BUILD A SINGLE TEAM IDENTITY BY FORGING STRONG EMOTIONAL BONDS

Becoming a team involves a transformation from many "I's" to "we." This transformation is not just in language or policy but involves the development of a deep emotional connection that binds members together into a new collective identity. This emotional bond is based on shared experiences and a commitment to common values that cause members to want to work together and care about each other's welfare. This bond develops by spending time together to get to know each other better and by overcoming challenges together. There is no single approach to doing this that will suit all situations. The specific activities that will most help the team develop community will depend to some extent on the specific individuals in the team and their backgrounds. But some activities have been found

---

64   Richard Hackman, "Creating More Effective Work Groups in Organizations," in *Groups That Work and Those That Don't: Creating Conditions for Effective Teamwork*, ed. Richard Hackman (San Francisco: Jossey-Bass, 1989), 503.

to be especially helpful in this phase, including eating together and taking time out to do enjoyable, fun things such as playing games together, going out for the day, or sharing different cultural celebrations. Another possible activity is to work together on a community project unrelated to the team's work, such as a school clean-up day. These activities all help to contribute to building a sense of "we." The leader should explain the purpose of these activities, because they may seem a waste of time to team members who are particularly task focused. For other team members, investment in these activities will be crucial to their developing sense of belonging and connection with the team.

The common sense of identity—of being "we" rather than "I"—is particularly forged through experiencing challenges, difficulties, and conflict together. The process of having to work through difficult issues, being vulnerable with each other, and communicating deeply, can create strong bonds between members. These experiences can be emotionally draining, but they are invaluable. It is helpful for the leader to remind the team of this potential benefit of going through difficult times when they are in the middle of them. When the team manages to negotiate difficulties and resolve conflict early in team life, this creates a sense of confidence among members that they can do anything together. This confidence, also known as team efficacy, has a close relationship with teams becoming effective in their ministry.[65] Each experience, each conflict resolved, each day out together (and especially the mishaps and amusing things that make everyone laugh together) creates a team history that people can remember, refer to, and relate to as part of what makes the team what it is.

The development of emotional bonds helps team members to overcome their anxieties about difference and build intimacy and mutual understanding. Doing fun things together and creating a shared history helps to transform strangers into friends. When the team enters the storming phase, team members will have a sufficiently strong trust in each other and willingness to give the benefit of the doubt to their teammates in order to weather the storms.

A helpful way of seeing the development of this emotional bond is in terms of a positive "emotional bank balance." Stephen Covey describes an emotional bank account as "a metaphor that describes the amount of trust

65   Michael Campion, Ellen Papper, and Catherine Higgs, "Relations between Work Team Characteristics and Effectiveness: Implications for Designing Effective Work Groups," *Personnel Psychology* 46 (1993): 823–50; R. Hibbert, "Church Planting Teams," 147, 206.

that's been built up in a relationship. It's the feeling of safeness you have with another human being."[66] Strong investment in building team relationships early in the team's life helps to develop a large and positive emotional bank balance. When things go wrong or team members are hurt, it is easier for them to forgive because they have built a high level of trust in and care for one another. The bigger the team's emotional bank balance prior to the storms, the more team members will be willing to make the effort to communicate with and forgive each other in the midst of the storm. In other words, the team leader needs to help the team to invest in the emotional bank balance of the team in the early stages of team life so that their relationships are able to endure the storms ahead.

FOCUS ON THE CENTRAL CORE OF VISION AND VALUES

Paul Hiebert's "centered-set" model can helpfully be applied to multicultural teams. This model suggests that a group such as a team can find its definition in its center rather than its boundaries.[67] If the team is seen as a centered set, the vision of a team sits at the center, with the team values arranged around that center. This is portrayed in figure 5, in which each of the different shapes arranged around the team's vision and values represents a team member.

Everything in a team should be focused and oriented around its center or core, made up of its vision and values. All other boundaries and definitions are relatively fluid. Team members are part of this centered set and are in the process of discovering how the team's vision and values impact their lives and affect their personal and corporate growth and development. It does not matter how far away each member is from the center, in the sense of how much they have internalized the team's vision and values. The important thing is that they all focus their attention and energy on the vision and values and commit themselves to them. While one team member

---

66   Stephen Covey, *The 7 Habits of Highly Effective People* (New York: Free Press, 1989), 188.

67   Paul Hiebert, *Anthropological Reflections on Missiological Issues* (Grand Rapids: Baker Books, 1994), 122–31.

may appear closer to the center, the time that team member takes to reach the center may actually be longer than a team member who seems further away. It is not the distance that matters but the importance of the center to each team member. As agreeing on vision and values is so important to team cohesion and success, it is critical to invest time and effort in agreeing on shared vision and values.

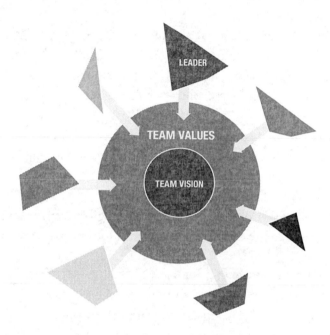

Figure 5: Diverse team members all oriented towards the central team vision and values

BUILD A SAFE CLIMATE

In a healthy community everyone feels safe to be who they truly are.[68] In a healthy team, members feel free to be themselves and to express their thoughts, feelings, concerns, opinions, ideas, and disagreement without fear of rejection, censure, judgment, or punishment. They feel safe enough

---

68   Scott Peck, *The Different Drum* (London: Arrow Books, 1987), 67.

to risk embarrassment. They feel able to share freely and are not afraid of being hurt. They feel free to disagree and to express their opinions, doubts, and uncertainties. One team member we interviewed said that feeling safe meant that everyone was able to "be themselves and say what they really think." A supervisor put it this way: "It's a safe environment, a place where you can say what you really think, reveal what you really think, what you really feel, what you really believe. So a good multicultural leader creates a space where folk can really do that."[69]

The leader contributes to a safe climate by making every team member feel at home. The result is, according to one team member, that teammates are "not afraid of each other and they're not afraid of the reaction of the others. They're actually safe to express themselves and not worried about what happens when they say what they really think." People in this kind of team feel safe to express disagreement: "In a certain situation I was the only team member that disagreed with a decision that was being made, and because the team leader had created that community, I felt safe to express that I disagreed even though everyone else felt the same way."

Creating a safe environment in the team also gives team members the ability to evaluate difficult experiences together. One interviewee explained:

> Even though we went through a really bad stage, there was the safety to actually talk about how people felt about everything that had gone on and to work that through. . . . As we came through it, "safety" in team meant we could talk about how the crisis had been dealt with, how we each felt, and this led to restored relationships, greater appreciation for each other, and team bonding.

In a safe team climate, mistakes are accepted as inevitable and normal. One multicultural team took this a step further and created a ritual to cel-

---

69   This, and other comments and quotations attributed to various team members, leaders, and supervisors we interviewed, come from Evelyn's doctoral research. For more details about this research, see the beginning of chapter 8. Individual interviewees are not identified in order to preserve their anonymity.

ebrate mistakes.[70] This helped the team to accept mistakes as an essential part of the team's development.

To build and maintain a safe climate the team leader needs to be able to handle emotion in the team. This includes helping team members to deal with emotion so they can really hear what others are saying and also express it constructively.

Leaders need to guard team members' personal integrity and not try to force them to do things that go against who they are. When team members feel forced to act against who they are, it places great stress on them and makes them question their personal worth. Leaders need to find ways of encouraging participation but also find creative or alternative processes for communication that make team members feel safe to communicate. One way of doing this is to lengthen the consultation and discussion process for making decisions so that individuals' views can be collected outside team meetings, rather than requiring everyone to speak up in group meetings. If team members appear upset in a team meeting and do not want to share, they should be given permission to communicate at another time, and the team meeting should be sensitively halted until all are ready to move on. If team leaders consistently communicate that people are more important than agendas and that they are willing to truly listen to dissenting views and adjust processes out of respect for who people are, communication will become easier with time as team members become more assured of safety, and team processes that ensure respect for each other will be established.

Part of building a safe climate is resisting the temptation to oversimplify issues. Multicultural teams can often seem chaotic and confusing. To build a safe climate in the middle of confusion requires the leader to have a high tolerance for ambiguity.[71] The leader needs to avoid black-and-white thinking and develop a "paradoxical mindset" that accepts opposing interpretations

---

70   William Loewen, "Participation and Decision-making in a Changing Workforce," in *Cultural Diversity and Employee Ownership*, ed. Margaret Showers, Cathy Ivancic, William Loewen, Anthony Mathews, and Pamela Stout (Oakland: National Center for Employee Ownership, 2002): 59–74.

71   Janet Bennett, "Transformative Training: Designing Programs for Culture Learning," in *Contemporary Leadership and Intercultural Competence: Exploring the Cross-cultural Dynamics within Organizations*' ed. Michael Moodian (Los Angeles: SAGE, 2009), 97.

as plausible and does not view paradox as needing to be removed. This ability to negotiate complexity and paradox is intrinsic to good leadership, especially when dealing with cultural differences. While a simple problem-solving mindset is overly focused on finding a final resolution, a paradoxical mindset views paradox as a lens for greater understanding and a catalyst for change.[72] A leader who is able to resist the temptation to oversimplify team members' comments and concerns and who promotes open discussions of issues enables the team to develop robust decision-making processes.

AVOID UNWRITTEN RULES

Unwritten rules are expectations that have not been made explicit. They are quite common in organizations and are generally destructive.[73] Unwritten rules are usually enforced by leaders, and newcomers are often oblivious to them until they break them. As the rules are not documented or mutually agreed on, newcomers feel powerless to query or challenge them, especially as it is rarely clear what the rules' origins are, which means they cannot identify who to appeal to about them. It is this lack of transparency about unwritten rules that undermines safety and trust. Unwritten rules are "the way we do things" and may not be what newcomers thought they were signing up for, because they add to or even contradict the organization's written policies.

Unwritten rules can be avoided by making expectations explicit. When an issue comes up and the leader (or another team member) thinks this is "how things should be done," then the team needs an open enough climate to talk through the issue rather than assume the leader's, or a particular team member's, way will prevail. Unwritten rules are also prevented when there is a transparent culture in the team and organization. This means that there are no secret documents, and information about discussions and processes is made accessible to all members. No group or individual should hold a

---

72   Jeffrey Yip, "Leading through Paradox," in *Leading across Differences: Cases and Perspectives*, ed. Kelly Hannum, Belinda McFeeters, and Lize Booysen (San Francisco: Pfeiffer, 2010), 171.

73   David Johnson and Jeff VanVonderen, *The Subtle Power of Spiritual Abuse: Recognizing and Escaping Spiritual Manipulation and False Spiritual Authority within the Church* (Minneapolis: Bethany House, 1991), 67.

monopoly on power, and their decisions and processes should be open to scrutiny by anyone who chooses to look. Transparency and accountability are also aided by having people other than the leaders documenting decisions and managing money and other resources.

DEVELOP EFFECTIVE TEAM COMMUNICATION PROCESSES

The multicultural team leader needs to focus more on the team's communication processes than on its products, especially in the early stages of the team's life. Building community involves establishing what individual team members believe, value, and enjoy. This requires lots of time, active listening, and working to integrate what people say into a shared set of team values. It can be helpful for team members to try to take the perspective of their teammates and then for the team to try and construct a collective view taking into account all perspectives. It is sometimes helpful to extend the decision-making process beyond team meeting times by meeting with team members individually and discussing issues with them. Taking this extra time gives nonnative speakers of the team language some time to think through and understand the issues better and prepare their responses. This may mean that communication is slower, but it also provides opportunity for better reflection on the issues being explored.

Poor communication results in confusion and frustration for the team. In our research, team members we interviewed consistently wanted their leaders to help them to talk with each other, especially in cases of conflict. As one team member commented, "It would have been good if the team leader would have helped us to communicate with each other, to talk about the conflict, and to come to resolution."

When members of a team do not all share a common first language, there is great potential for misunderstanding, as well as a risk of excluding nonnative speakers of the team language. The team and its leader must accept that communication will take more time and develop an ethos of forgiving mistakes in communication and clarifying what other people mean. Strategies for clarifying communication include

- writing up position papers in the team language and giving these out in advance of a meeting to give everyone time to think through the issues,
- making sure that the meaning of spoken communication is clear by asking clarifying questions,
- encouraging and drawing out participation from quieter team members in group discussions,
- simplifying the way language is used to aid communication,
- adjusting the way the group functions to allow opportunities for team members to discuss things in their first language, and
- preferentially using face-to-face communication over electronic media.

The potential usefulness of position papers was illustrated by one team leader who said it helped their team "jump-start the conversation and gave us the time to really understand what the other person was really trying to say." A member of another team enthused about how helpful it was for people on her team to check what their teammates meant in order to ensure "that they were all on the same page."

It is ultimately the team leader's role to ensure that team members are communicating effectively with each other. Helping to clarify communication can involve asking clarifying questions, reinterpreting or articulating what one team member says to another, or checking that you have understood correctly to ensure that meaning is correctly conveyed. One team member explained that the leader should "extract the meaning of what one member says and explain it in different words to other members." In another multilingual team situation, a team member described how sometimes her leader "would communicate for me to explain my issues or difficulties to the rest of the team or the other way around, and that was helpful."

When there is misunderstanding, the team leader has to help team members articulate what is wrong so that they can deal with the problem. Conflict and misunderstanding can only be solved when communication breakdowns are explicitly dealt with and someone makes the team talk about it with a view to improving communication in the future. The team leader should encourage team members to take the initiative to go to others who have made a hurtful comment and work it through with them.

One of the roles of the leader can be to help team members identify and express emotions that may be preventing them from hearing what others are saying. A team member expressed her appreciation for the way her team leader helped her to cope with her emotional responses in the team: "There've been many times during team meetings where I've felt emotional or upset, and I always appreciated the fact when the leader would see that I was uncomfortable and ask me about it rather than me having to initiate my feelings."

A challenge encountered on many multicultural teams is the difference between team members who speak a lot and those who are quieter. This can be due to personality, culture, or lack of language proficiency. In order to develop effective communication, leaders must draw out quieter members in discussion to help the team hear their ideas.

Many interviewees talked about the importance of language in multicultural teams. For many multicultural teams, varying degrees of proficiency in the team's language among the team's members is a major cause of miscommunication. In one interviewee's team, everyone was using a second or third language to communicate, so misunderstandings were very frequent. Interviewees stressed that mistakes are inevitable in multicultural teams due to misunderstanding. The team leader has a special role in helping to resolve miscommunication. One leader helped the team navigate through a major misunderstanding by patiently translating "from English into English, translating from one person's understanding of the phrase into another person's understanding of the phrase." As a result, eventually "the light bulbs went off and people said, 'Oh!' Then the issue wasn't an issue anymore—it was just misunderstanding."

Getting team members to simplify the language they use is another helpful strategy that aids effective communication. One team leader had to specifically train his team members to adjust their language use:

> [I] try to train my other staff that haven't been exposed to that culture to just change their language ever so slightly to make sure they're getting the right information out and they're interacting as a team. Adapting your language, normal Australian slang, changing the tone, changing the speed, writing it down . . . it seems to work. Some of the staff don't like to do it, but they end up seeing more positive results. It works well.

Team leaders also need to make a special effort to keep on explaining things until they are sure they are understood. One leader explained:

> Sometimes you've got to be really patient and explain things as well, and also if they don't understand or have a language barrier, or they don't quite fully understand the tone that you're delivering it or the words you're using, you've really got to show a lot of patience to make sure they understand.

Giving preference to face-to-face communication allows for immediate feedback to be given and clarification to be asked for. It has the added advantage of including nonverbal elements of communication like tone of voice and body language. A leader explained why she preferred face-to-face interaction: "If it's misinterpreted face-to-face, you can resolve it there and then, because you can see the misinterpretation in their eyes and you can challenge it."

BUILD TRUST

Establishing trust is critical to team function. If trust is not established very early in a team's life, it is unlikely to be developed later on. High trust provides a sense of confidence, optimism, and efficacy in team performance, whereas low trust is associated with skepticism and a feeling that things are not going to work.[74] Once team members have become skeptical, their skepticism

---

74   Sirkka L. Jarvenpaa and Dorothy E. Leidner, "Communication and Trust in Global Virtual Teams," *Journal of Computer-mediated Communication* 3, no. 4 (1998): 0.

can become a self-fulfilling prophecy. When team members do not expect something to work, they do not try to make it work. Then when it does not work, they use this as proof that they were right to believe it would never have worked in the first place.

Trust is one of the main foundations for team functioning. It does not prevent problems from occurring but provides a basis on which they can be solved. It allows for vulnerability, sharing, caring, and feeling safe to be oneself. Trust does not judge or keep tabs on other team members. Trust is both a gift and something that has to be earned. It is also easily undermined. It is fostered by investing time in relationships, valuing individuals, embracing difference, giving responsibility, and forgiving mistakes. If team trust has broken down, it is the leader's responsibility to identify the cause and seek to restore it.

One interviewee believed that trust is "one of the main foundations for a team being able to function" and that "if you don't have [it], that's the beginning of the end of the team." Another interviewee stressed that trust did not take away the misunderstandings and miscommunication, but it provided a foundation that enabled them to be dealt with. He said that trust "opened us up to a whole other level of vulnerability and sharing, because I knew that my teammates cared for me and I cared for them."

Trust gives space for doing things differently. It allows team members to do tasks in different ways while pursuing a common vision. It helps the team to embrace the differences rather than forever fighting them. A supervisor explained that trust lets "people run with what they do well."

Three types of trust have been described: (1) trust based on belonging to the same group, (2) trust based on predictable expectations of behavior developed through relationship building, and (3) trust based on reciprocal self-interest.[75] Although all three forms of trust will operate in a team, trust based on belonging is what the team leader is aiming to build between members.

An example of trust based on reciprocal self-interest in a team situation can be found in one approach to resource sharing. I choose to give team money to a teammate to buy a motorcycle to go to the villages, trusting that

---

75   Debra Shapiro, Blair Sheppard, and Lisa Cheraskin, "Business on a Handshake," *Negotiation Journal* 8, no. 4 (1992): 365–77.

when I need something for my ministry, that teammate will be happy to give for my cause. This type of trust might particularly apply in gift-giving cultures, where there is an expectation that gifts will be balanced reciprocally between people over time.

When trust is built on predictability, it is related to knowing how people will behave based on their prior behavior and demonstrated values or attitudes. Whether or not the relationships are positive, it is the predictability that is relevant. When you can predict how people will behave, you can trust them to act that way and therefore plan how you will manage it. If, for example, a team member always talks more loudly and aggressively when he gets stressed or upset, you can work to identify the stressors that cause this to happen and not get upset by what that team member says when he gets stressed.

The strongest and most enduring kind of trust is that which comes from belonging. To a large extent, this trust will stand regardless of what you do. It means that people are more willing to forgive you or be patient when you act in unpredictable ways, and you can be confident that they will always work for your best interests, because they know that you have the team's best interests at heart. This kind of trust is built on relationships and emotional bonds.

Where trust is low, poor communication and misunderstanding often result, and this can lead to a spiral of declining trust. Following is an example of how the spiral of declining trust can occur. A low-context team leader may not trust a high-context team member to manage team money well, at least by the standard of his or her own low-context values and accounting practices. The leader may then retain control of the money and give a small allowance to the team member. The team member then has to always ask the leader for money for extra expenses, even for team business. The team member sees that the team leader does not trust him, as the leader's nonverbal communication makes his or her lack of trust very explicit. The team member is at first confused, then hurt, and eventually angry. Why should he always have to ask for money, as it is a shared team resource? When he confronts the leader about this, the leader is evasive and talks about the organization's or donors' accountability requirements. When the member asks to learn these requirements, the leader grudgingly agrees to teach him. When the member sees the records, he is amazed to discover just how much money is available and angry about how difficult his work has been made by lack of funds. He approaches the donors directly and secures their direct support for his own work. The team has already divided into different factions supporting the leader, the member, and those who want to avoid conflict. Inevitably, the team fails and there is destructive relationship damage. By not applying risky generosity and trusting all members of the team in the first instance, mistrust has now become endemic in the relationships, not just between member and leader but between everyone who knows them. Not only has the leader's original fear of losing control of the money been fulfilled, but the leader has also lost the team itself.

As with unwritten rules and as shown in the above example, any lack of transparency will also diminish trust. A lack of transparency is also evident in the example of declining trust given above. Secrecy, or even the hint of secrecy, must be avoided in teams. Until the team has reached the stage of all team members feeling like they belong, team members will rely on reciprocity and predictability, which are undermined when actions and motives are not transparent. It is very important that the team leader helps team members to talk with each other and models the discipline of thinking positively about teammates so that the spiral of declining trust does not develop.

Part of the process of building trust is developing a perception of shared boundaries between people.[76] Instead of having boundaries that exclude the other person, team members have to actively work together to build common boundaries. This can only occur when team members feel safe. When we feel safe, we are less worried about being hurt and are therefore more easily able to communicate. We naturally trust people that we identify with, so the more the team leader can do to create shared experiences that build a common team history and identity, the more team members will be able to trust each other. For multicultural teams, this means that community-building activities and discussions are imperative from the earliest stages of the team's life.

---

76   Jenai Wu and David Laws, "Trust and Other-anxiety in Negotiations: Dynamics across Boundaries of Self and Culture," *Negotiation Journal* 19, no. 4 (2003): 329–67.

INSIST ON THINKING WELL OF TEAM MEMBERS

Thinking well of others and giving them the benefit of the doubt is key to developing and maintaining good relationships. When a teammate has done something we do not understand, it is all too easy to attribute negative motives to them. Insisting on thinking well of teammates is a habit we can develop by meditating on and applying biblical teaching such as this: "Fix your thoughts on what is true, and honorable, and right, and pure, and lovely, and admirable. Think about things that are excellent and worthy of praise" (Phil 4:8). The leader must be careful to continually interpret teammates' actions positively to others, refusing to speculate on motives and unknowns and insisting that team members talk with each other about issues rather than make assumptions. It is normal in human interaction to attribute negative motives to behavior and words that we do not understand. This is called negative attribution.[77] The only way to overcome negative attribution is to refuse it and to speak with the other person to understand better what they are thinking and doing. Team leaders must not allow themselves to make negative attributions about other people and must refuse to allow team members to do so. The team leader needs to model and encourage this insistence on thinking well of others and communicating well with them.

DISCUSS AND CELEBRATE INTERCULTURAL DIFFERENCES OPENLY

Cultural differences on the team should be discussed openly and a consensus reached about culturally sensitive group norms and practices. At the same time, team members need to realize that everyone's preferences cannot always be honored. Whether or not their preferences are accepted, team members still need to be comfortable with what is chosen. It is important for all team members to be aware of the values, assumptions, and behaviors of their own culture and those of their teammates. Good groundwork can be

---

77   Duane Elmer, *Cross-cultural Servanthood: Serving the World in Christlike Humility* (Downers Grove, IL: IVP Books, 2006), 50.

laid by discussing these together at the beginning of the team, but the team needs to be aware that value conflicts will arise as they start doing things together and that these cannot be avoided.

Teams need to make the most of their diversity. Leaders can help this process by specifically affirming to the team and others how a diversity of cultures, personalities, and roles has helped the team to achieve what it has accomplished. Celebrating differences can also be helped by incorporating the cultural celebrations of everyone on the team into team life. One team member in our research commented, "I think it is really good to celebrate great differences, to laugh about differences, because laughing gives space for appreciation, takes tension away, opens the mind to understand one another and to realize the differences and accept the differences in one another."

LEARN HOW TO LEARN TOGETHER

Teams need to learn how to learn together and become reflective practitioners. Reflective practitioners reflect on what they do in the light of what other people have written about and experienced in similar situations.[78] Steps in the process of learning to reflect together include describing the situation from the perspectives of everyone involved, interpreting it in the light of cultural information and theory gained from books and other sources, and using an inclusive process in formulating solutions. Once a solution has been formulated, it is implemented for a period of time, and then what has been done is evaluated. Through evaluation, new issues are identified and the learning cycle begins again. Encouraging team members to do further study or to attend relevant seminars and workshops related to the work of the team and then getting them to share what they have learned with the rest of the team is a valuable way to help the whole team to learn.

In order to be open to learn, team members need to be willing to change. To model this, a good leader must be a lifelong learner who takes time to reflect on practice, and then changes and adapts in the light of that reflection. Innovation and change can be stimulated by allowing freedom

---

78   Donald Schön, *The Reflective Practitioner: How Professionals Think in Action* (Aldershot, England: Arena, 1995).

to explore new ideas and by encouraging experimentation. This means having a team climate that allows for taking risks and in which mistakes are forgiven. Failure is not perceived as negative but as a collective opportunity for learning. Edgar Schein stresses the emotional role of the leader, especially during periods of learning and change. The leader must provide stability and emotional reassurance and cope with the uncertainty and risk that is entailed in reflecting, experimenting, and making changes.[79]

BUILD A SHARED UNDERSTANDING OF LEADERSHIP

As different cultures have different expectations of leadership, the multicultural team leader needs to facilitate team members' acceptance of and adjustment to unfamiliar leadership styles.[80] Highly effective teams usually share leadership around the team according to the expertise of members. For this to work well, the team needs to develop a shared mental model of leadership.[81] The leader also needs to be able to develop leadership capacity in others.

As shared leadership begins to develop on a team, the direction of influence grows from being not just from leader to members, but also from member to member. The team becomes more interdependent and interconnected. It is not possible for leaders to keep trying to adjust their leadership style according to each individual culture represented on the team. Everyone on the team must compromise and adjust. Ideally a complex, netlike dynamic of mutual understanding, compromise, and adjustment develops in which leaders foster and facilitate the development of a healthy team dynamic, including shared leadership.

---

79   Edgar Schein, *Organizational Culture and Leadership*, 4th ed. (San Francisco: Jossey-Bass, 2010), 375.

80   Peter Dorfman, Paul Hanges, and Felix Brodbeck, "Leadership and Cultural Variation: The Identification of Culturally Endorsed Leadership Profiles," in *Culture, Leadership, and Organizations: The GLOBE Study of 62 Societies*, ed. Robert House et al. (Thousand Oaks, CA: SAGE, 2004), 671.

81   Katzenbach and Smith, *The Wisdom of Teams*, 45.

Highly effective teams are characterized by shared leadership.[82] As a team develops, the gifts, abilities, and roles of each team member are discovered and clarified, and as this process unfolds, different members take responsibility to lead in areas relevant to their expertise. In a church planting team, for example, a team member with expertise in Bible storytelling might take the lead in training and encouraging their teammates in telling Bible stories to local people. Another member who has a special burden for getting others to pray could coordinate the collection and sending out of prayer information to supporters and perhaps also organize prayer meetings for the team. In the same way, each of the other team members takes up an area of special responsibility in which they lead the team. This kind of shared leadership helps to foster cohesion, trust, and a sense of collective ownership of team vision. Through shared leadership, team members have increased control over processes and outcomes, and this also increases their sense of efficacy as a team.[83] The team still has an overall leader, but his or her role is to facilitate and encourage this development of shared leadership in specific areas rather than feeling threatened by it.

DEVELOP A BALANCE OF ROLES AND PERSONALITIES

There needs to be a balance of roles and personalities on the team. Any imbalance needs to be actively solved either through recruiting new personnel, relocating team members, or helping team members develop in areas the team is weak in. It is important for the leader to not only understand the interpersonal dynamics on the team but also help the team understand these dynamics. As one interviewee commented, "Any team leader should understand each different team member and what are their talents and what are their skills and how you balance with the other. You won't put two people strong in one thing in one group, so understanding interpersonal dynamics is very important."

---

82   Ibid., 80.

83   Stephanie Solansky, "Leadership Style and Team Processes in Self-managed Teams," *Journal of Leadership and Organizational Studies* 14 (2008): 332–41.

Chapter 6 provides a more detailed exploration of how the leader can develop this understanding of team roles and personalities and how leaders can work towards a good balance among them.

EMBRACE CONFLICT

Conflict is an opportunity for growth and development. Embracing conflict and managing it well leads to better decisions and the development of new ideas and approaches. Leaders can help their teams to embrace conflict by ensuring that potential conflict is addressed early and, when more major conflict does occur, making sure the team perseveres until the conflict is fully resolved. In and through the process, the leader can make sure that the team's agreed-on conflict management process is consistently applied and reviewed, and that after conflicts are resolved the team takes time to learn from the process. The team leader should reinforce the idea that conflict is normal and that the team's ability to persevere through to resolution is an indicator of its strength. Conflict should not be a secret or ignored. It should not be a "no go" area, nor should those in conflict be ashamed. When conflict occurs, everyone on the team may be dismayed, but they should be determined to work through it and rejoice in the outcomes it brings. The refusal of the team leader to allow conflict to fester is a key factor in the team's success in managing conflict. We will explore conflict and how to manage it in more detail in chapter 7.

CONTINUALLY PROMOTE AND PRESERVE THE TEAM'S FOCUS

Team leaders have the primary responsibility for helping the team internalize and keep working towards the team's vision and goals. They do this by keeping the team accountable to their vision and goals, by helping the team review its progress towards their goals, and by enabling team members to make any necessary adjustments to the way they work.[84]

---

84   Nick Nykodym, Sonny Ariss, Jack Simonetti, and Jean Plotner, "Empowerment for

Good team leaders consistently act according to the team's vision and values. This vision- and value-driven style of leadership enables leaders to respond flexibly to the needs of team members and to changes in the context. Rather than leading from a set of fixed prescriptions or rigidly imposing approaches that have been developed in different contexts and for different teams, good leaders base their decisions on what the team has already decided—the team's shared vision and values. Leaders like this are seen to be acting not according to their own idiosyncrasies or a desire to control but according to what is best for the team and its accomplishing the vision.

An essential function of a good team leader is to help the team focus and to minimize distractions. If the members of a team are not aligned in focus according to a shared vision, empowering individuals will result in chaos. If there is a lack of congruence between individual and group goals, or there are distractions from internal or external forces, the team will be unable to focus well enough to be productive. For team leaders to enable the team to focus, they need to be personally focused and committed to the vision and goals of the team, and they must take care not to dilute the team's efforts with too many priorities.

Team leaders should be "consummate team members," as they must provide a model of teamwork for the team.[85] A team will reflect its leader. For this reason, leaders must embody and model the vision and values that they are influencing people to follow.

ENABLE THE TEAM TO MAKE DECISIONS TOGETHER

The processes of how a team works together, including the quality of interpersonal interaction between its members, cannot be separated from the product the team is aiming to achieve. From the very first meeting of the team, the leader works to build a healthy team community. In order to build a collaborative climate on the team, the leader needs to help the team to make decisions together. A team begins to achieve high performance

the Year 2000 and Beyond," *Empowerment in Organizations* 3, no. 4 (1995): 36–42.

85   Ron Cacioppe, "An Integrated Model and Approach for the Design of Effective Leadership Development Programs," *Leadership and Organization Development Journal* 19 (1998): 37.

when leadership is shared among its members. This does not mean that the leader abdicates his or her role. Instead, it means that the responsibility and authority for decisions becomes collectively owned and shared. Leadership in a highly effective team is not so much a person as a dynamic communal process where everyone in the team is working out what is important together and then implementing their decisions. Communal decision making does not mean that everyone has equal amounts of time that they speak, nor even that the decisions are made in a single meeting together. It means that the team has developed its own effective way of deciding together, which draws on the strengths and backgrounds of each member and maximizes their contribution to the decision-making and implementation process. The role of the leader in developing this collective efficacy—the confidence the team has in itself to achieve its vision—is to empower the group to decide and act rather than to direct or decide for it. This concept of leadership is embodied in the saying that great leaders are those who cause those they lead to say, "We did it ourselves."[86]

PROTECT THE TEAM FROM NEGATIVE OUTSIDE INFLUENCES

In order for the team to be a safe place where team members are willing to take risks for the sake of the team and its vision, team members need to know that their leader will always stand by them even when they fail. This brings a security to the team and a sense of common identity. The leader provides a protective boundary within which everyone belongs together, and there is no fear of outside influences that might tear them apart.

The leader stands between the team and the world outside. Feedback about the team from the organization and others will tend to come to the leader more than team members. When the feedback is good, the leader should not hesitate to pass it on to the team. But when the feedback is negative or unhelpful, the leader should use discretion about passing it on to team members. In many cases it is more helpful for the leader to absorb the

---

86   Peter Senge, *The Fifth Discipline: The Art and Practice of the Learning Organization* . (New York: Doubleday, 1990), 431.

criticism and protect the well-being of the team. If change needs to occur, the leader can address this without passing on negative feedback that may harm the team's or an individual team member's morale.

In this way, the leader acts as a gatekeeper to protect the team from outside influences that might harm it, concentrating instead on building up the team members and their interactive synergy. An example of this is when some team members have given a presentation to others outside the team and feedback comes back to the leader that the presentation was poor. It is usually not helpful to tell the team members involved that the presentation was poor. The leader should take note of the criticism and focus on helping the team to approach their presentations in a different way next time. In many cases, the leader is already aware of team members' weaknesses, and passing on criticism will only harm them rather than build them up.

CHAPTER 5

CLARIFYING THE TEAM'S PURPOSE AND APPROACH

DEFINING VISION IS THE FIRST TASK OF A TEAM

Every team exists for a specific purpose and is focused on accomplishing a specific task together. This is the major difference between teams and other kinds of groups that work together. In a working group, for example, individuals work alongside each other in parallel rather than working together interdependently.[87]

A team's purpose drives it to overcome the challenges of working together to create strong group cohesion and achieve synergy, in which the performance of the team is greater than the sum of individual members' efforts. Many groups refer to themselves as teams but do not have this singular focus. Calling a group a team when it does not have this clearly defined and shared purpose often leads to frustration and confusion among team members who are looking for the greater cohesion and effectiveness that teams promise. If there is no clear focus, everyone ends up doing their own thing. This prevents the group from developing a clear sense of group identity or enough common focus to be productive together. Since having

---

87   Katzenbach and Smith, *The Wisdom of Teams*, 88–91.

a shared purpose is so fundamental to effective teamwork, the team leader must first focus on clarifying the team's purpose.

One of the best ways for team leaders to think about the team's purpose is in terms of vision—the picture of what the future would look like if God poured out his blessing on the team and its work and the team were completely successful. Once the team's vision is clear, the goals, which act as signposts on the way to the vision, can be established. When the goals have been agreed on, strategies to achieve those goals can be discussed. If this order of approach is not followed, the team's purpose easily becomes confused with the ways in which it might be achieved, and the team may start doing things that work against its purpose.

Defining vision can take many hours of discussion, but this time is an essential investment in the team's success. For multicultural teams, the process of defining vision may seem endless, as team members are not only trying to decide on things together but also learning to understand each other and working through their differing cultural expectations of leaders, decision making, and conflict management. The leader and team must steadily persist in this task, however, so that the vision becomes crystal clear and healthy team processes are established.

In some multicultural teams, when vision is discussed during the formation phase of the team's life—in what has been called the "honeymoon phase"—the decision-making process can seem easy. Team members in the initial weeks of team formation are usually excited about the team's task and working together on a new project. Everyone is trying hard to get on with each other and avoiding any conflict. However, if different expectations about team vision are not discussed early on, some components of the vision may not be fully accepted by some team members or may not have been fully understood. This means that in the first year of a multicultural team's life, while the overall purpose of the team should be clear, specific components of the vision may need to be held more loosely and frequently revisited to ensure that the vision truly reflects what all team members want and believe they can achieve together.

A team is defined by the commitment of its members to a commonly agreed-on vision, goals, and strategies to achieve the goals. This is the primary distinguishing feature of a team as opposed to other kinds of groups that work together. Helping a team to define its vision, goals, and strategy is the first task of a multicultural team leader. The rest of this chapter outlines how to lead the team through the process of clarifying vision and deciding on goals and strategies.

TEAM EFFICACY

The one factor that consistently predicts whether a multicultural team will achieve its goals is its members' belief that it can.[88] Team members' belief that their team can succeed is called team efficacy. In our own research into multicultural church planting teams, we found that team efficacy was the most useful predictor of effectiveness in starting new churches.[89] There appears to be a creative power built into people who believe in something enough that they are willing to work together to achieve it. Believing that an apparently impossible task is achievable seems to generate the capacity to think creatively about obstacles and the commitment to persevere through challenges. If some team members become discouraged, the rest of the team is able to encourage them. As the team's efficacy is focused on its vision, having a clear vision helps team members articulate what they believe in, remind each other of their vision when they are discouraged, and encourage each other to keep pursuing their vision when faced with obstacles.

A diverse team has the capacity to be more effective than a nondiverse team. This is because the diversity of experience and viewpoints in the team brings a richer perspective to decision making and team approaches to challenges. Diverse teams face greater difficulties, however, and these often prevent them from achieving the required degree of togetherness. It is the believing together that constitutes team efficacy. This is the quality God referred to at Babel: "The people are united, and they all speak the same language. After this, nothing they set out to do will be impossible for them!" (Gen 11:6). For this reason, the leader of a multicultural team needs to continually affirm the value of diversity in team life and function.

---

88   Campion, Papper, and Higgs, "Relations," 823–50.

89   R. Hibbert, "Church Planting Teams," 147, 206.

The team leader can help the team grow in its belief that it can succeed by ensuring that the team's goals are clear and measurable. When each goal has been achieved, success should be celebrated. Every goal's fulfillment is a milestone on the road to the vision. By marking each milestone with a celebration, members learn to value their collective achievements and feel their success. They can then refer to each celebration as proof of their ability to succeed when faced with new challenges, and look forward to the feeling of accomplishment in the future. Teams that get onto a good track by setting clear goals and celebrating their achievement early on in their work together tend to keep working effectively in the long term.[90]

Having clear and measurable goals also enables the team to continually monitor its progress, evaluate its actions in the light of outcomes, adjust its approach, and reevaluate. This process is part of becoming reflective practitioners. Monitoring, evaluating, and adjusting what the team is doing builds efficacy as it increases the team's confidence in its ability to tackle larger and more complex challenges. The team gains confidence because their prior experience has been positive. It is important for the leader to continually highlight to the team that the processes they use to achieve their goals are as important as the products of their work.

As the process of team building can be long, multicultural teams need to set a few initial, short-term goals that are easily achievable. This is important for the team to develop a sense of being able to accomplish things together. If, for example, the team's purpose is expected to take more than three years to be fulfilled, it would be good to have initial goals that can be achieved in the first and third months while the team vision is being more clearly defined. These short-term goals must be meaningful and involve everyone working together. This builds the team's belief that it can work together and also creates opportunities for early successes that the team can celebrate together.

A church planting team in Eastern Europe exemplified this early goal-setting process. During the three months that this team took to work out its vision, goals, and strategies, it also set the goal of visiting every town and village in their region by the end of this period and for each member to meet and begin to get to know at least five new people per week during this

---

90   Hackman, "More Effective Work Groups," 481–82.

time. They found having these clear and achievable short-term goals very helpful. The goals were focused simply on getting to know their context, and they did not compromise any elements of vision or strategy that the team was discussing during the same period, but the research still provided valuable information for the team's decision making. As the goals were clearly measurable, team members were able to gauge their progress towards its fulfillment and celebrate when they had achieved them.

CLARIFYING TEAM VISION AND PURPOSE

If you aim for nothing, you will certainly achieve it. Vision defines what a team is aiming for. Vision articulates a dream. The vision of a team may be broader than what the team aims to achieve, but must contain specific elements that are attainable within a specific time frame.

Vision is visual. It begins with a picture, which then may be articulated into a statement. Vision must be sufficiently clear that it can be hung on a wall, frequently referred to, and easily shown and explained to others. It is the defining feature of the team and pulls the team towards its fulfillment. It also serves as a constant evaluative tool for any activity the team considers engaging in.

Without vision, people just do. They do anything that seems good to them at the time but does not necessarily lead anywhere. Without constant reference to the vision, especially when faced with challenges, team members can become overwhelmed with the tasks surrounding them and forget what they are trying to achieve. A helpful adage says, "When you are up to your neck in crocodiles, it's hard to remember that your vision was to drain the swamp." The swamp will never get emptied if you are continually battling crocodiles, but if you drain the swamp, the crocodiles will disappear. Vision enables the team to keep things in perspective and not become exhausted doing things that may be good but actually prevent it from achieving what it set out to do.

FROM VISION TO ACTION: STEPS IN STRATEGIC PLANNING

Step 1: Research the context

As vision is specific to the team and its context, the first step in defining vision is to develop an understanding of the context in which the team will be working. The team's understanding of its context should be continually developing throughout its life. However, the more thoroughly the team investigates where it will be working and who it will be working with at the start of its life, the more robust and relevant its vision will be. Beginning with research also builds into the team's DNA an orientation to continual learning.

The process of examining the context and analyzing the task of the team is also one of the first steps in team building. In this early phase of team life the leader should give members freedom to pursue the research tasks in ways that make sense to them and affirm these different ways of doing things. The leader should also help the team to reflect on and debrief every activity of the team. By doing this, team members become aware of their own assumptions and those of their fellow team members about how things should be done, and these assumptions can be explored and made explicit. Engaging in reflection together at this early stage of the team's life, when there is usually little conflict, helps team members get used to the process of reflective learning before it becomes emotionally charged.

It is unhelpful to pretend that the obstacles the team faces are minor or to exaggerate them. Realistic analysis of what the team faces enables the team to plan effectively and makes it more likely to succeed. The process of examining the challenges should also enable team members to express their fears and hesitations without censure. This sets a climate of openness and safety in the team. If team members' concerns are dismissed, ignored, or ridiculed, they will feel devalued as people and will not feel safe to participate in future team discussions. The team leader should encourage honest expression of concerns and ensure that those concerns are respected by all members of the team and addressed realistically and compassionately. Teams that address concerns thoroughly at the outset and do not ignore things that may be difficult to talk about will have a greater ownership of the team's vision.

Step 2: Get and communicate some idea of the possibilities

As leaders are responsible for initiating the process of clarifying vision, it is good for them to have some idea of vision as a starting point. If they are more visionary themselves, they can start with their own formulation of a vision, which can then be discussed by the team. Team members from high-context and higher-power-distance cultures (see chapter 2 for explanations of these terms) may be reticent to contribute to the vision if the leader's opinion is seen as definitive. Team members from low-context cultures may object to any suggestions by the leader that seem prescriptive. This means it is important that team leaders stress the tentative nature of the vision they outline and that the vision outline serves as a template or starting point for team discussion and development. In some contexts, the objectives of the organization that the team is part of provide components of the basic vision outline.

Leaders who are more concrete, detailed, and present oriented in the way they think (rather than abstract, big-picture, and future oriented; see chapter 6 for more explanation) often find it difficult to imagine future possibilities. It may not be possible for them to consider or propose possible vision options. In this situation, the leader needs to identify team members who have this ability and empower them to initiate or even lead the process. If there is nobody on the team who can do this, the leader may need to invite a facilitator from outside the team to help with the process.

Step 3: Clarify the vision together

A team's vision defines the endpoint of the team's work and makes sure everyone on the team is heading in the same direction. In the picture on the next page (fig. 6), vision is depicted as a star in the far distance beyond many mountains. The mountains represent the challenges and obstacles to achieving the vision. The team members are gathered together at the bottom left of the figure, facing the vision, but not yet having defined their route to reaching it.

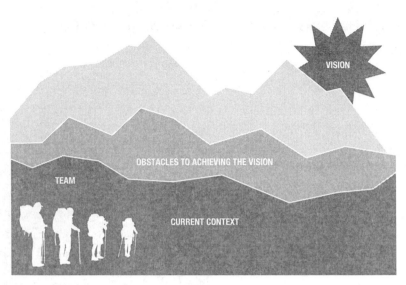

Figure 6: Define the vision

We recommend that vision be defined by individual team members sharing their dreams for the future, negotiating these, and putting them together into a corporate picture. This does not mean superimposing individual pictures on a big canvas. Points of similarity need to be noted, discrepancies and conflicts discussed, unrealistic proposals sensitively discarded, and a simple, clear single picture incorporating all agreed-on elements created. The final picture also needs to be evaluated to ensure it is consistent with the organization's objectives.

If the team has a majority of concrete thinkers, or members are not familiar with thinking about vision, it may be helpful to start with a brainstorming exercise. This helps people start thinking about possibilities. Brainstorming is a special, disciplined activity where everyone on the team is completely free to suggest any idea, even ideas that seem ridiculous. Every idea is written down, preferably on a large board or piece of paper that everyone can see. During the brainstorming time, people are not allowed to discuss the ideas. They may ask for clarification simply to understand what is meant, but discussing any idea's feasibility is forbidden. In brainstorming even the most outrageous ideas can be suggested. These ideas sometimes prove to be the most productive. The process of brainstorming together is valuable because it reinforces that all members' suggestions are valuable, encourages creative thinking, and helps the team to learn how to listen to each other without being negative and to consider alternative perspectives and possibilities.

Once members are comfortable with thinking about the future, the leader should give everybody time to create their own pictures of what the fulfillment of the team's purpose might look like. Team members from collectivist cultures may prefer to do this task together rather than individually. The approach should be flexible but ensure that each team member has the opportunity to contribute to the end picture.

The question the team is trying to answer is, "If God poured out his blessing on the life and ministry of our team, what would the result look like?" Team members should be encouraged to be specific in terms of the things they think would happen if God poured out his blessing. The team is considering the end result of their task. Another way of putting the question is to ask, "How will we know whether we have been successful?"

Each individual or group should prepare a creative way of expressing their answer to this question—a picture, model, poem, drama, song, or story—that communicates all the elements of what they believe will have come into existence if the team has been successful in its task. Expressing the vision in creative ways helps to broaden team members' thinking beyond the measurable goals that will eventually be adopted. It also creatively engages team members who are not so focused on words or are less fluent in the team's language. Finally, it encourages people to think from unusual perspectives and engages emotions that help team members to connect with the team vision.

The next step is to ask team members to present and explain their creative expressions of vision to the whole team. Then the process of drawing out common elements and negotiating a collective picture can begin. As this analysis and negotiation process can be complex and difficult, it may be helpful to have a facilitator from outside the team present, such as a team coach (see chapter 10 for further explanation of the team coach's role). Having a team coach present takes the pressure off the leader and helps the leader become part of the "we" of the team as his or her picture is merged with the whole group's.

Team vision is not the combination of all the activities team members are involved in or want to be involved in. A conglomerate of activities is not vision. Vision is the outcome of activities and should indicate when it is time for activity to cease. A clear vision will help the team to determine which activities are appropriate and relevant to achieving the team's purpose. Some of the activities team members are involved in may help to achieve the vision, but many will not. If these unhelpful activities are enshrined in the vision picture, the achieving of the vision will be compromised before it starts.

If the process of defining vision has been done well, team members will be passionate about their vision, continually communicate it, and passionately defend it. It will be constantly referred to and used to evaluate all team decisions and activities. It is the single most important element in defining the team's identity and helping the team change from a group of individuals to a collective "we." This step in team formation is essential, and the leader must ensure that sufficient time is invested in it. It does not matter whether this is done at a team retreat over a concentrated number of days, or whether it is done gradually over weeks or months. Each approach has advantages and disadvantages. Whatever is in the vision picture becomes precious to the team members. It is vital to ensure that the right things are in that picture!

Once the vision in picture form is clear, the next step is to articulate the vision in a statement of as few words as possible. Some people have suggested that it is helpful to aim for twenty-five words or less, as this will be easier to memorize. It must answer (in words) the question, "If our team has been successful in its purpose, what will the result look like?" The work of putting the picture into words helps the team to identify clearly the vision's focal elements and provides the team with a statement that helps them to quickly explain to others what the team is all about. As this vision statement will be constantly quoted in team discussions, it should be phrased in a way that makes it easy to remember, understand, and apply to decision making.

Step 4: Clarify and articulate team values

The values statement outlines the way the team will work to fulfill its vision in terms of ethos, principles, and values. Many outcomes of the team's work will depend on how the team does things and what it models by these patterns of working together. Articulating a values statement helps the team to work through how it needs to do its work in order to ensure that its vision is achieved.

This process of creating a values statement can be kick-started by getting team members to think of statements that they are sure every team member will disagree with or feel extremely uncomfortable with when they hear them, and then discussing these statements to see whether everyone does feel uncomfortable and what it is about them that creates the discomfort. If the statements are written anonymously and drawn out of a box, they can be discussed without people feeling embarrassed if not everyone agrees. Below are some questions that can help with discussing these statements and eliciting team values.

- How did it feel to consider and write down ideas like this?
- Why did team members choose the statements they did?
- What common themes run through them?
- What do these statements show about how the members view the team?
- What blind spots or biases might the statements indicate?
- What taboos on the team emerge from the statements?
- What do the statements imply about the goals of the team?
- What do the statements imply about the way the team works?
- Does any statement differ significantly from the rest? Why is that?

It may be helpful for team members to fill in, individually or in small groups, the following diagram (fig. 7), identifying overlaps between personal, team, and organizational values. Their filled-in diagrams can then be presented and discussed with a view to finding those elements everyone on the team can agree with. It can also be helpful to discuss why differences exist between the three circles.

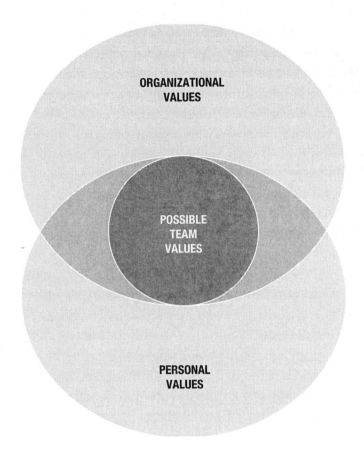

Figure 7: Areas of value overlap

When the team is discussing its values, it is helpful to insist that team members illustrate each of the values they suggest with specific examples from experience that demonstrate what those values mean in practice. Doing this highlights what the words really mean to each team member and makes potential areas of conflict clearer.

In the initial stages of the formation of a multicultural team, it is unrealistic to expect a values statement to be more than a list of generic principles about how people should get on with one another. The real values of team members will usually only emerge through conflict. It is still important to initially discuss values together, as every interaction helps to build relationships and understanding. Experienced team leaders and team coaches will also be able to raise issues that other teams have struggled with. In this early

stage of the team's life, team members are usually too focused on not offending each other to be able to grasp the practical implications of articulating
shared values. It is relatively easy to agree on principles in general terms,
but it is only as the team begins to "storm" and experience conflict that the
significance of values becomes clear.

As team members begin to conflict with one another, values should be
revisited, refined, and illustrated with specific examples of what they mean
in the team's context. It is good to then illustrate the values with specific,
mutually agreed-on procedures that help the team to enact their values. For
example, a team may have a value such as "people are more important than
programs." To help team members understand what this means, the team
covenant might include an explanatory comment that if a person is late to a
meeting, everyone on the team will still intentionally welcome them, or that
team members will wait for everyone to arrive for a meeting before starting to work on the meeting agenda. These procedures may be recorded in a
document like a team covenant or memo of understanding. This document
is a record of the team's commonly agreed-on vision, values, and procedures.

Step 5: Determine goals

Goals are progress indicators. They define the steps that are needed to achieve
the vision and provide opportunities to celebrate team achievements on
the way to the endpoint. In order to determine whether or not they have
been achieved, goals must be very clearly defined and specifically measurable. Goals are determined by careful analysis of the task the team faces,
identification of the specific elements of the vision that must be achieved,
and agreeing together on the essential things that must be in place and in
what order and time frame. If a goal cannot be measured, it is not a goal.
It should be so clearly specified that no one, team member or outsider, can
question whether or not the team has achieved it.

Goals draw the team towards its vision. To do this well, they must be
both realistic and push the team a little beyond what seems likely to happen. This extra push is a response to faith in God's unlimited ability, and it
generates team efficacy, synergy, and creativity. It is admittedly a difficult
balance to achieve. If the goals are too easy, teams achieve them with little
effort and are not stimulated to achieve the impossible (therefore missing

out on the creative synergistic energy of "teamness"). If goals are consistently unrealistic and too difficult, team members will become discouraged and disillusioned and are likely to give up. It is fine for a team to fail occasionally, as this stimulates reflection, evaluation, review, and change of practice, but repeated failure is likely to destroy the team's morale and lead eventually to team failure.

As goals are milestones along the path to the vision, they also act as points for rest and reflection. When goals are achieved, the team should celebrate. Even if they are not achieved or only partially achieved, the team can still celebrate their arrival at the milestone. These milestones also provide an excellent opportunity for the team to review how far it has come, to reflect on the team processes that have helped them get there, and to look ahead to the next goal and work out any adjustments that may be needed now that they have a closer view of the vision. The team should make the most of these opportunities to celebrate, rest, and reflect as they build team community and a collective sense of accomplishment.

The picture below (fig. 8) adds the goal signposts into the strategic plan. Goals indicate progressive elements that need to be in place if the vision is to be achieved. At this point in strategic planning, people often get sidetracked onto discussions of how the goals could be achieved and whether they have the necessary resources. The absence of a road in the picture at this stage is an intentional reminder that thinking about the road unhelpfully distracts the team from setting goals. In this step of goal setting, the team asks the question, "If the vision is to be achieved, what must be set in place to ensure it happens?"

It is not possible to predict the future, and rarely possible to predict exactly how the team's work will unfold. This is even more the case when the team is working in unpredictable environments. This means that while it is important to set goals that progress in a logical manner towards the vision, team progress or events outside the team may change the situation, and the team may then have to review and adjust their goals. Vision is fixed. Goals are as fixed as is possible, given how changeable the situation and work of the team might be. Teams need to be certain about the next one or two goals and fairly sure about the ones after that. As they reach each goal post, they evaluate the goals ahead in the light of the vision and agree together on the route to the next few goals.

Figure 8: Determine your goals

Step 6: Agree on strategies to achieve the goals

The following picture (fig. 9) traces a single road from where the team starts to the vision. This road represents the strategies that the team uses to take them from one goal to the next. The path that the road takes is rarely straight. Instead it must negotiate many obstacles that are represented in the picture by mountains. These obstacles mean that not all of the path can be seen by the team. Unless the team has a very simple or short-term task, the route to the vision is rarely straightforward.

Figure 9: Agree on strategies

Strategies are the most flexible aspect of planning. There are many different ways in which goals can be achieved. Often the most obvious way of doing something is not the most effective for achieving the vision or honoring the values of the team. Too often teams default to the way things have always been done, or the way the loudest or most powerful voice on the team wants to do things, rather than taking the time to think through different approaches and evaluate their relative value or probable effectiveness. When a team defaults to familiar methods without thinking through their potential effectiveness in their particular context, they can end up with outcomes that hinder or even prevent the fulfillment of the vision.

Strategies should always be evaluated according to the vision and values of the team. The team should never assume that there is only one way to fulfill a goal. There are always several ways to achieve a goal, but the alternative approaches may not have been thought of.

Creativity is especially valuable at this stage of the planning process, and brainstorming is a good way to start the discussion. This is an area where, if everyone on the team is truly respected and valued, its diversity is a great strength. The range of experiences and perspectives of team members from different cultures can generate many more useful ideas and approaches than a monocultural team could ever conceive of. It is good to set a specific time limit to the brainstorming time (e.g., twenty minutes). After the time is up, the ideas should be grouped together to see if any common themes appear, and then the team can start discussing the possibilities. The experience that team members bring from different contexts can also help them in working out how to adapt alternative approaches to fit the local context.

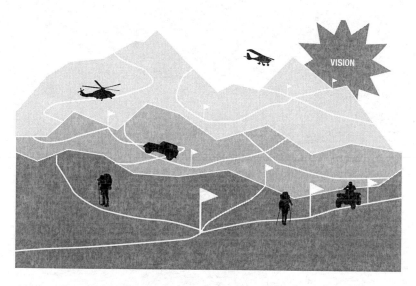

Figure 10: There are always many different ways of achieving any specific goal

As there are many ways to achieve different goals, not every team member needs to use the same strategy. The goal that is just ahead of the team is nonnegotiable and fixed, but the way of reaching it is not. Team members can experiment with using a range of approaches. By doing this the team will develop a broader and deeper understanding of their context and of the effectiveness of various methods. When the team leader allows different strategies to be used, the diversity of team members' gifts and strengths can be harnessed, as different team members can work in ways that suit their strengths, and this also helps them to feel valued. In contrast, forcing everyone to use the same approach can be damaging to team members' self-concept. This does not mean that team members should have permission to do whatever they want. All strategies need to be evaluated and accepted by the whole team before they are employed. The picture on the previous page (fig. 10) shows how several alternative strategies, represented by alternative paths, can be used to arrive at the team's goals.

Figure 11: Goals may not be achieved one after the other, although they often are

Regardless of how well a team plans, team members cannot know every eventuality before it happens. People and circumstances change for multiple reasons. Even the most thorough research will not reveal all the issues that the team will face in working on its task. Because circumstances may change and progress may not be as predictable as expected, the team should set goals but be prepared to review them regularly. Teams should be crystal clear on where they want to end up (their vision) and the way they want to do things (their values), both of which are fixed. However, teams need to be willing to be somewhat flexible about their goals if necessary. Goals may also be fulfilled in surprising ways, so team members should be ready to adjust their planning and approach if goals are fulfilled in an unexpected order. Figure 11 represents the unpredictable order in which goals may be achieved. This means that although teams may have a general approach to strategy that is articulated in their values, specific strategies should be decided for the short term only (e.g., for six months at a time), and teams should be ready to review and choose new strategies in response to goal progress.

Step 7: Start work (and keep communicating the vision)

Strategic planning, if done well, is a lengthy and exhausting process. It will usually take days or even weeks to do it thoroughly. Some team members may become frustrated by the hours of discussion and find it difficult to see the point of the process. It is important for the leader to keep explaining why the process is essential, as well as to make sure there are sufficient breaks so that all members are able to really engage with the process. Once the vision, values, goals, and initial strategies have been defined, there is no need to plan for such lengthy team discussions. They are an essential, initial feature of the team that does not need to be repeated. The focus of the team can then shift to the work itself.

Once the vision and values have been set, they should be frequently re-iterated and revisited. If the strategic planning process of the team has been done well, others in the team will have sufficiently internalized the vision and values to keep reminding the team of them. But the leader should also schedule specific times for revisiting the vision, values, and goals so team members are continually aware of what they are aiming for. With a clear vision to aim for, measurable review points (goals) along the way, and clarity about how to proceed (strategies), team members can confidently start their work knowing that they are all agreed about what they will do and how they are going to do it. The process of having invested so much time and energy in agreeing together will also ensure that they believe they can achieve the impossible together (efficacy).

CHAPTER 6

APPRECIATING TEAM MEMBERS' PERSONALITIES, ROLES, AND GIFTS

When a team is working well, the results of the team members working together and applying their different skills to their task are greater than if each individual had worked alone. This characteristic of teams is called synergy. Synergy in teams is the interaction or cooperation of team members to produce a combined effect that is greater than the sum of their separate, individual effects. It is the result of team members working on their tasks collaboratively and interdependently, and it enables them to achieve so much more than they would have if each person had simply been working in parallel.[91] If, for example, there were three major tasks to accomplish and three team members worked on each of these tasks separately from the others, they would be less effective and produce fewer results than if the three members worked collaboratively on these tasks. This synergy—the extra effect of working collaboratively—is portrayed in the diagram (fig. 12) on the next page.

---

91   Jon Katzenbach, *Teams at the Top: Unleashing the Potential of Both Teams and Individual Leaders* (Boston: Harvard Business School Press, 1998), 115.

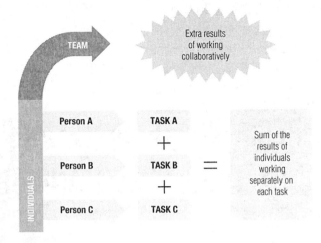

Figure 12: Teams versus individuals working together (adapted from Katzenbach, Teams at the Top, *115)*

Synergy and the extra results of working collaboratively are part of God's design for his people. The Apostle Paul explained that God has formed his people into one body and that each person has been given gifts to use for the benefit of the whole body. God's purpose is that each individual or part of the body uses the gifts given to them to help the others (Rom 12:3–8; 1 Cor 12:1–11; Eph 4:1–16). Apostles, prophets, evangelists, pastors, and teachers, for example, are to use their God-given gifts to equip the people to do their God-given work by each using their own abilities. The result is that the body of Christ grows in maturity and Christlikeness (Eph 4:11–15). This growth in maturity cannot be achieved by individual Christians living and working on their own.

For synergy to develop, team members need to develop a good understanding of their own skills and abilities as well as the skills and abilities of their fellow team members. When they have this understanding, they can work in a way that complements each other.

One of the team leader's key roles is to help team members develop this understanding of their own strengths and those of others. Building on this mutual understanding of each member's abilities, the leader then needs to help the team clarify the roles of each member. There are many ways that the leader can help team members develop this foundational understanding. Two tools that we have found to be especially helpful in this process are the personality types described by Katherine Briggs and Isabel Myers and the team roles described by Meredith Belbin.[92] Most of this chapter is focused on explaining how these two tools can help teams come to an understanding of the strengths and abilities of each of their members.

Synergy is dependent on each team member feeling respected and valued because their unique contribution to the team is recognized and valued. Each team member's unique personality brings an essential perspective to the team. The value of each perspective needs to be understood and appreciated by the whole team. Similarly, each team member's role in the team needs to be clarified so that the team's expectations of each member are clear and the way in which each team member's roles interact with and complement each other's is made explicit. The leader is responsible for guiding this process of clarification. Leaders also need to ensure that the distribution of personalities and roles on the team is as balanced as possible.

Some people object to using tools to understand personalities and roles, as they feel the tools are too simplistic, or they object to being put into boxes. The purpose of using these tools, however, is not to make a final categorization of ourselves or our teammates but to create a doorway through which to begin to understand and appreciate our fellow team members. Conflict often occurs due to personality differences (sometimes referred to as personality clashes), which are further complicated by different cultural backgrounds. Each tool for understanding personality or a person's role in the team is a doorway to getting to know someone better. It helps us to begin to understand them. Using these tools can help us to see why people do things the way they do, and this can help us stop jumping to negative conclusions about our fellow team members. When team members understand how they and others "tick," they are better able to support, encourage, and communicate with one another, and they are more able to work effectively together.

---

92   The foundational theory and history of the Myers-Briggs Type Indicator (MBTI) are explained in Isabel Myers, *Gifts Differing: Understanding Personality Type* (Mountain View, CA: Davies-Black, 1995); team roles are explained in Meredith Belbin, *Management Teams: Why They Succeed or Fail* (Oxford: Butterworth-Heinemann, 2010), and in Meredith Belbin, *Team Roles at Work* (Oxford: Butterworth-Heinemann, 2010).

THE MYERS-BRIGGS PERSONALITY TYPES

The Myers-Briggs Type Indicator (MBTI) is a self-report questionnaire designed to help people better understand themselves and others. It is based on Carl Jung's theory of psychological types, and describes people's preferences about how they perceive the world and make decisions. The MBTI results describe important differences between people—differences that are common sources of misunderstanding and miscommunication in multicultural teams. One excellent aspect of MBTI is that it frames differences in positive terms and does not include a negative personality dimension. In a team situation this is particularly good, as it means differences can be discussed as strengths and there is no discussion of character faults.

According to the Myers-Briggs model of personality, there are four primary ways people differ from each other. Isabel Myers called these "preferences" and likened them to the preference people have for using one of their hands over another.[93] These four preferences can be put in the form of four questions, which are given below, each with two alternative answers. Each of the questions represents a spectrum, and each person's personal preference can fall anywhere from one extreme to the other.

Where do you draw your primary energy from: the outside world of people (Extraversion [E]) or the inner world of thoughts and ideas (Introversion [I])?

How do you prefer to take in new information: as clear, tangible facts and details about the here and now (Step-by-step thinker [S]) or as abstract concepts and big-picture possibilities (New-possibilities thinker [N])?

How do you prefer to make decisions: by feeling for people and the effects decisions will have on them (Feeling [F]) or by thinking about principles in an objective, logical manner (Thinking [T])?

How do you prefer to organize your life: by judiciously planning, organizing, and working for closure (Judicious [J]) or by playfully and flexibly exploring the world in an open-ended way (Playful [P])?[94]

---

93   Myers, *Gifts Differing*, 193.

94   We have renamed some of the MBTI categories so they have names that are easier to relate to team dynamics. In the MBTI schema, S stands for Sensing, N for Intuition, J for Judgment, and P for Perception.

The MBTI types are preferences or tendencies towards a particular way of thinking or of doing things rather than fixed "either-or" boxes. Each person is best understood as being somewhere along a spectrum on each preference, so it is possible for one person to be on one end of the extraversion spectrum and another to be only mildly extraverted. We have also observed that, in general, different cultures tend to fall at different places on the spectrum, so that an introverted Romany [I] from Bulgaria might look very extraverted to an introvert from Germany, or a strong judicious planner [J] from a Turkic culture may seem like a playful explorer [P] to an English person. So although there is considerable research evidence that personality type is consistent across all cultures,[95] the way each trait is expressed in different cultures varies.

Whether or not you fill out the Myers-Briggs questionnaire, the real value of the Myers-Briggs model of personality is in working out your Myers-Briggs type for yourself. Often we find that, when people use questionnaires, they answer as they have been trained to answer according to the expectations of their family, school, or church, and these are often biased towards particular traits. We will give examples of how this happens when we discuss the individual preferences.

We learn who we really are in the process of interacting with other people. In the Western world people are becoming more isolated and have often not had extensive experience in deeply relating to others before they join a multicultural team.[96] This means that many Westerners do not know themselves very well. For these reasons, if you are new to ministry, you should be aware of the various traits but hold your initial assessment of yourself lightly. In fact, working in a team is one of the most valuable ways of learning about yourself. As you see the contrasts between yourself and fellow team members, you will start to discover who you really are. One of the tasks of multicultural team leaders is to ensure that there is an open climate on the team that enables team members to explore their own and others' personalities and that affirms the discoveries people are making about themselves

---

95   Isabel Myers et al., *MBTI Manual*, 3rd ed. (Mountain View, CA: Consulting Psychologists Press, 1998), http://www.myersbriggs.org/more-about-personality-type/international-use/multicultural-use-of-the-mbti.asp.

96   Sherry Turkle, *Alone Together: Why We Expect More from Technology and Less from Each Other* (New York: Basic Books, 2011).

and their teammates. This open climate helps the team value the different strengths people bring to the team and avoids the unhealthy alternative of focusing on the things team members see as negative.

There are many books and websites that can help you to work out your Myers-Briggs type. Some of the most useful ones are listed at the bottom of this page.[97] Rather than discuss all the dimensions of personality in depth, we will now explore the aspects that most often cause tensions in teams.

A healthy team needs a balance of the four personality preferences to function well. If there is a particular imbalance in the team, the team will need to find ways of addressing the imbalance. This is good to remember, as it stresses how much we need each other to be able to gain a well-rounded perspective on what the team is facing and in order to be able to tackle the task effectively.

Approach to people and thinking: Extraverts [E] and Introverts [I]

Although everyone has been created to be able to relate to other people, not everyone has the same capacity to continually relate to others. This is a reflection of the introversion/extraversion dimension of personality. Introversion and extraversion do not determine how well people can relate to other people, but how widely and for how long they prefer to interact with others. Introverts can be highly skilled at relating to others, and extraverts can sometimes be completely oblivious to what others are saying. The focus of this dimension is on where individuals get their energy from and how they do their thinking.

A strong extravert [E] loves interacting with people. This does not just mean sitting quietly in the presence of other people. It especially means

---

97   One of the most helpful websites is http://www.keirsey.com, in which David Keirsey provides a good online test, the Keirsey Temperament Sorter (http://www.keirsey. com/sorter/register.aspx), which gives a personalized report with your four preferences/ letters and also provides an explanation of each type (http://www.keirsey.com/4temps/ overview_temperaments.asp). Particularly useful books that explain the personality types in more detail include: David Keirsey, *Please Understand Me II: Temperament, Character, Intelligence* (Del Mar, CA: Prometheus Nemesis, 1998); Jean Kummerow, Nancy Barger, and Linda Kirby, *Work Types* (New York: Warner Books, 1997); and Otto Kroeger, Janet Thuesen, and Hile Rutledge, *Type Talk at Work: How the 16 Personality Types Determine Your Success at Work* (New York: Dell, 2002).

talking with them. Extraverts are those people who cannot help talking whenever they are in the presence of others—in a queue, on the bus, at a meal table. They do not really care what they are talking about. They just enjoy talking. Extraverts actively seek others out. After spending time talking with others they are generally buzzing with energy, even if they are physically tired. For extraverts, people are exciting! An extravert will burn out if they are prevented from relating to people for more than a short period of time.

A characteristic of extraverts that can cause problems in teams is that extraverts often need to talk to think. They process ideas by exploring them with others. In team planning, extraverts must be provided with opportunities to discuss ideas in order to work through them. Major misunderstandings can occur when team members assume that the extravert's enthusiastic discussion of an idea means the extravert agrees with it. In fact, the extravert's enthusiasm is as much for talking as it is about the idea itself. Often, the next day, the extravert will just as enthusiastically discuss or advocate an opposite perspective. We have seen team members become confused, frustrated, and even angry when this occurs. The extravert can be accused of being changeable, uncommitted, or even lying. Extraverts will eventually make up their minds, but they need talk time to do it.

Extraverts are a great asset to teams, because they will always seek out people, both within the team and outside it, and will help draw introverts out of their shells. Particularly in ministry teams that have a people focus, extraverts are essential to help pull the team out into engaging with the local community. Another major advantage extraverts bring to the team is their lack of fear of saying what they are thinking. This means that they will tend to say what everyone else is thinking but may be hesitant to express. It also means that, as a leader, you can be fairly confident that you know what is going on inside extraverts, because they will have told you.

In contrast, an introvert [I] draws their personal energy from inside themselves. Spending time with other people, and especially having to talk with other people for extended periods, will drain the introvert's personal energy and leave them feeling exhausted. Strong introverts will burn out quickly if they are in a ministry situation where they have little break from people, whether the people involved are teammates or others. Introverts need time out to recharge their internal batteries. If introverts are accepted for who they are, many will be able to cope with time with people as long as they are not forced to speak. In collectivistic cultures especially, introverts will happily be continually part of a group because they do not feel the same pressure to talk in the group that individualistic cultures often exert.

Introverts tend to think before they speak, and usually need a little time to think before responding to others. They process ideas internally and do not necessarily feel the need to discuss the ideas before they are fully formed. In fact, for the strong introvert who has not learned the value of refining ideas by discussing them with others, challenging their ideas can make them feel that their integrity is being threatened. This is because introverts' ideas often come from deep within their being and they have often invested a lot of time and energy in formulating them, so it is difficult for the introvert to separate the idea from their identity.

Team members may treat teammates who do not speak much as if they do not have any ideas, especially if there are dominant extraverts in the team who tend to monopolize decision making. Introverts may need to be empowered to express their opinion, and speaking may not always be the best way for them. Introverts may find it easier to express their opinion through another team member. They often appreciate being given a written agenda and drafts of ideas before team meetings to give them time to think through the ideas and formulate a response either in written or spoken form. Well-intentioned attempts to force introverts to give verbal responses to issues in meetings may result in their feeling alienated and continually stressed.

Introverts are needed on teams as they bring stability and carefully considered responses to ideas, issues, and situations. They tend to take more time than extraverts to observe the reactions of people around them to what is being said and to think of appropriate responses. As introverts are happy with their own company, often for extended periods of time, they are often more comfortable than extraverts with desk or creative work that they can do on their own, or with detailed strategic planning or other administrative or evaluative work that is focused more on documents than interacting with people. As most teams will have tasks that require engaging with people and other tasks that require more individual work, it is good to have a balance of team members to manage both kinds of tasks.

Introversion tends to be more valued than extraversion in traditional, conservative churches in individualistic cultures. There are several expressions of this valuing of introversion. For example, it is directly taught and modeled that a personal faith is cultivated by a "quiet time" (where individuals read the Bible and pray on their own); people are taught to be quiet in meetings and trained to exert self-discipline by guarding their tongue (cf. Jas 3:1–12) and thinking before they speak (cf. Prov 21:23). In Western Bible colleges and seminaries, individual study is reinforced with competitive individual exams and written assignments that students usually work on alone and, in the vast majority of cases, a lecture-style approach where students learn and think quietly on their own. Consequently, Bible college graduates in ministry can find it difficult to rediscover their extraversion and accept it as a positive trait.

An imbalance between introverts and extraverts on the team will affect the team's ability to relate to the world outside itself, build a coherent team identity, reflect on its team processes, and manage its time together. Strong extraverts on the team may place inordinate pressure on introverts to spend time together or to speak out before they are ready. Strong introverts may inhibit the team's ability to communicate and may shackle extraverts from doing what they do best—going outside and relating to other people.

When the team's task requires relating to or building networks with other people, a team without extraverts will find it very difficult to reach out to people in their surrounding community. Even if introverts force themselves to do this, they will very quickly become exhausted. Even if a team's work is to examine document archives in a bunker, it will still need those who are able to build bridges with the people who control and manage those archives and possibly also to relate to those who are mentioned in the archives. Extraverts are the team members who can most easily build bridges between the team and the world outside. If a team has no extraverts, it should actively recruit for them and meanwhile encourage those who are less introverted to focus on developing their extraversion.

If there are few or no introverts on a team, the team will continually focus its energy outside the team. While this is good for activity and relating to people, team processes will tend to suffer and team identity may dissipate. Introverts help the team to reflect on what it is doing and are happy to maintain desk-based activities that fulfill organizational and bureaucratic requirements. Introverts are more likely to be the people on the team who monitor the team's progress towards fulfilling its goals and who ensure that the team's strategies and processes are consistent with its vision and values.

Approach to information processing: Step-by-step thinkers [S] and New-possibilities thinkers [N]

The S/N dimension of personality describes how people prefer to receive and structure new information in order to process it. Step-by-step thinkers [S] start with what is in front of them and build up to a whole. New-possibilities thinkers [N] start with the whole and then identify the necessary components.

Step-by-step thinkers start with what is in front of them—the concrete facts or objects—and arrange these carefully one after the other until they reach a final conclusion. They do not need to know the outcome until they get there. They like the process of making decisions to be consistent, predictable, and well controlled. They distrust imagination, intuition, and hunches unless the person who uses them has a proven track record of being correct. It is not that they particularly dislike intuition; it is simply that they cannot understand the basis for it. It makes no sense to them. They are not usually able to make decisions by intuitive leaps, but instead reach their conclusions step by step. It is as if the step-by-step thinker is in a closed box and cannot imagine the world outside the box. In order to get out of the box, the step-by-step thinker systematically cuts a door through the wall of the box or builds steps over the side of the box. Once they are outside, they start to examine the details of what they see. They must focus on the detailed realities of the present time and context in order to gradually build up a picture of the whole situation.

In contrast, new-possibilities thinkers are intuitive and imaginative. They tend to be focused on the future. For some new-possibilities thinkers the future can seem more real than the present. These people do not feel restricted by the realities of what is confronting them. New-possibilities thinkers need to know what the end point of any decision-making process will be in order to consider how that point should be arrived at. They are not able to process information without knowing what the purpose of the processing should be. For them the end picture determines what information should be considered and how it should be approached. The important thing for new-possibilities thinkers is the vision. They are not concerned with the details of how the vision might be accomplished, as they see these as being contingent and changeable. Because they strongly believe that the present must flex for the sake of the future, they may become very frustrated with step-by-step thinkers, whom they perceive as trying to set in concrete things that might have to change as the situation develops.

As the church becomes more established in any society, it becomes more and more concerned with preserving and promoting good conduct. A certain way of doing things becomes established, and the leadership develops a vested interest in keeping things the way they have always been. The church, like other older institutions in society, finds it difficult to change, because change threatens the status quo. As like attracts like, the membership of older institutions, including the church, tends to select leaders who are step-by-step thinkers who are skilled at maintaining values and traditions and who concentrate on the details of their immediate context rather than the discomforting consideration of the world outside and the new questions and possibilities for change that it evokes. New-possibilities thinkers who ask difficult questions and consider new ways of doing things tend to be considered difficult or even rebellious and are often sidelined.

An imbalance in this area of personality on the team will especially affect its strategic planning and monitoring of progress. It may also affect the team's ability to make decisions together due to differences in approach to information processing.

When most team members are step-by-step thinkers, the team will spend most of its energy fortifying its own "box" (maintaining the status quo and refining the details of it) rather than determining whether it needs to adapt or modify its box in order to fit its environment or achieve its vision. The team will have a tendency to become obsessed with details and forget the bigger picture. When faced with challenges, the team may become overwhelmed by the mass of new details and be unable to find any solutions to their dilemma. In the classic example of a team's task being to drain a crocodile-infested swamp, it would typically be the step-by-step thinkers who would not be able to see beyond the crocodiles snapping at their ankles in order to focus on how to get rid of the water.

Wildly unrealistic vision is also a risk on a team, and it can develop when a team has an oversupply of new-possibilities thinkers. Without the grounding in current reality that step-by-step thinkers bring, imagination may take the place of vision. In some cases, strongly intuitive thinkers may even act as though the vision has been achieved before it has become reality. As new-possibilities thinkers are more concerned with goals than the strategies needed to achieve the goals, they may sometimes pay little or no attention to strategy. Without step-by-step thinkers to bring strategic planning down to earth, the team's purpose is in danger of becoming wishful thinking rather than reality. If a team's vision is too unrealistic, the team can quickly become discouraged.

Approach to decision making: Feeling for people [F] and Thinking about principles [T]

When people make decisions they tend to prioritize either objectivity, logic, and principles [T], or how the decision will affect people and how people will feel [F]. This does not mean that principle-driven decision makers [T] do not care about the effect on people or that those who prioritize how decisions will affect people [F] neglect principles in their decision making.

Team members who place a higher priority on the effect of decisions on people care about how people will feel and what the impact of the decisions will be on the lives and work of others. They think about the reactions of those who will be affected by the decision and give their emotions and responses value and credibility. Team members who consider the effects that decisions will have on people will tend to consider all groups of people who are affected, including the wider community. They will also consider the long-term impact on team members and team relationships.

Team members who prioritize principles in decision making do not ignore the effect their decisions will have on people, but they consider people's reactions less important than what is right or wrong, or logically best, in the situation. These team members may still care deeply about how people feel but are ready to weather their reactions for what they consider to be the greater good. People who make decisions based on principles will not only choose general principles but will also strongly uphold the vision and values of the team and organization.

The church in the Western world, until recently, has been comprised mainly of people from EDG cultures and has employed a very low-context way of communicating (see chapter 2). A major aspect of this low-context orientation is that Western churches tend to be focused on the written word, law, and systematic theology.[98] Systematic theology, which underpins doctrine, embodies a rational, logical, systematic, and intellectual approach to faith, which has often tended to downplay emotion and subjective experience. New believers are taught to ignore their feelings and rely on truth that is defined as propositional statements derived from the written word of God. While there is some validity in this position, it does represent the bias of low-context cultures. High-context cultures, in contrast, very quickly understand that Jesus, the person, is the truth (John 14:6) and that truth is a relational concept based on our relationship with the person who is truth, rather than a list of laws.

Truth, based on the person of Jesus, focuses on preserving relationships according to how Jesus would think and act in any situation. Sometimes, rigid application of laws (defined as truth) can cause damage to relationships in ways that dishonor Jesus and grieve the Holy Spirit. A simple example of this is the "relational yes" used in high-context cultures, which often confuses and offends missionaries from low-context cultures. For example, if a missionary invites a person to church and that person perceives that the missionary will be very disappointed if they don't turn up, the invitee may say, "Yes, I will come to the meeting." In the context, all local people would understand that the invitee will not come to the meeting. It is obvious to them, but not to the missionary, that the invitee is saying, "I like you as a person and I want to please you. I don't want you to be upset and feel pain or distress." The invitee is expressing love for the missionary and seeking both their well-being and preservation of relationship. However, the missionary's low-context orientation to communication causes him to judge the invitee as a liar. The missionary considers the invitee un-Christlike, because he perceives the invitee to have broken a law. When the invitee sees the missionary become offended and angry and unable to act reasonably towards the invitee, the invitee also considers the missionary un-Christlike, because his actions destroy relationships.

---

98   Richard Hibbert and Evelyn Hibbert, "Contextualizing Sin for Cross-cultural Evangelism," Unpublished manuscript, 2012.

Although it is often argued that feelings can cloud judgment, it is very important for a team to weigh up the effects of their decisions on people (including other team members). The primary problem that an overemphasis on feeling for people causes in team decision making is paralysis. The situations teams face are often so complex and affect so many people that it is difficult to balance all the potential needs, reactions, and responses of everyone involved. Usually the only way to overcome this paralysis is to evaluate the options in the light of the vision and values of the team. The process of doing this not only reinforces the vision and values of the team but also helps the team to make a more considered decision and to be ready for any reactions. Being able to give a reasoned response to people's concerns helps team members to cope with their own reactions and to support each other if they face negative reactions to their decision from others outside the team.

In contrast, those who focus more on logic and objective principles in decision making tend to ignore the human impact of their choices. If people who focus more on logic and principles are in the majority or have the loudest voice, the team is at great risk of hurting others as it goes about fulfilling its task. Team members who are concerned only with what is logical are often not aware of the negative long-term impact of their decisions on people. As theological training tends to select for and reinforce a principles orientation to decision making, it can be very difficult for team members with this background to learn to listen to team members who prioritize human impact. It is critical for a team's health and for the long-term effectiveness of its ministry that team members have a balanced approach to this dimension of personality and that members from both sides of the spectrum are able to respect, listen to, and value each other's insights.

Approach to the outside world: Judicious organizer [J] and Playful explorer [P]

The fourth dimension of personality described by Myers-Briggs concerns how people relate to their environment. Some people need a higher degree of control than others. In a team situation, there are two major environments that need to be managed: the team and the world outside the team. As the people in the team are also part of the environment, tensions can arise as team members try to understand and negotiate boundaries of control.

Judicious-organizer team members [J] are quintessentially those who try to shape and structure the world around them. Conscientious and reliable, judicious team members will invest much time and effort in doing "what should be done" and helping others to do the same. Without them the team's goals would not be achieved, the necessary processes and structures would not be established, and organizational and other bureaucratic requirements would not be fulfilled. They consistently strive to fulfill everything that society requires of them, as defined by respected authority figures such as church or organizational leaders. They like life to be ordered and predictable, and where it is not they will create boxes to live in that protect them from ambiguity and provide a controllable border with the outside world.

Most ministry situations are unpredictable. Many team tasks are uncontrollable. Many judicious organizers, who can cope well in their home situations, where everything is under control or at least seems to be under their own control, cannot flex enough to cope with the unpredictability of their team work situation. In team situations, other teammates do not always respect the judicious organizers' desire for planning, order, and predictability, and they ignore or forget structures and processes. Judicious organizers can experience major stress if they feel they have lost control of a situation or are faced with overwhelming ambiguity.

Playful-explorer team members [P], in contrast, manage the unpredictability of life with relative ease. They like to keep decisions open and enjoy unpredictability. They tend to adapt to the world around them rather than feeling the need to change the world to suit them. This gives them a delightful ability to explore the world, experiment with it, and not be too concerned about rejection or failure. All difficulties and challenges are excuses for more fun experimentation! They are also more inclined to take risks and get distracted. They can frustrate their teammates by being late to meetings and by leading the team off on tangents. On the other hand, they will not hesitate to take risks that might help to more quickly achieve team goals and can save their judicious-organizer teammates from becoming bogged in a mire of predictability. Often it is the spontaneous exploratory act of a playful explorer that reveals an approach or insight that leads the team to do more than they might otherwise have imagined possible. In more risky ministry situations, the confidence of the playful explorer in the face of ambiguity can help to keep the judicious organizers calm and able to cope.

As institutions, including churches and mission agencies, mature, they tend to focus increasingly on the structure and control needed to maintain the status quo.[99] Over time the right way of doing things becomes defined by the people who are more suited to maintaining order—the judicious organizers—because they are willing to invest the time and effort needed to support it. Judicious organizers look at the world around them and construct fences and boxes to keep its unpredictability at bay. Playful explorers climb the fences and rip open the boxes to get back into the unpredictable world. In fact, playful explorers may not even notice the fences in their eagerness to get back outside and enjoy what life has for them. This can lead to severe conflict in teams. Playful-explorer team members are often bewildered by attempts to rein them in and will resist being controlled. Judicious-organizer team members tend to judge the actions of playful explorers as rebellious and label them "unreliable." As the church and society both endorse predictability, playful explorers often find themselves condemned and marginalized. However, playful explorers are critical for teams. Like the extraverts, these team members pull the team out into the world outside and prevent the team from becoming engrossed in itself. Playful team members also help the team to enjoy its work, take risks, and move on from failure.

The development of synergy in a team is a dynamic, unpredictable process that is a result of the interplay between the members of the team and the tasks they have to perform together. In a monocultural team, the expectations of each team member and the interplay between them are relatively predictable. Members of monocultural teams have culturally learned and shared ways of dealing with conflicts over control issues. In general, judicious organizers will be more tolerant of playful explorers from their own culture, perceiving their behavior to be within the bounds of what happens in society, even if it is sometimes annoying or frustrating. But in a multicultural team the unpredictability of other people's behavior is much greater and often feels out of control. Judicious organizers will usually feel quite stressed and feel

---

99   For a very helpful analysis of the strengths and weaknesses of institutionalization in religious groups, including churches, read Thomas O'Dea, "Five Dilemmas in the Institutionalization of Religion," *Journal for the Scientific Study of Religion* 1 (1961): 30–39.

the need to exert control over the situation in order to decrease the stress. To make team dynamics more complicated, what might in one culture seem to be very controlled behavior may, in another culture, seem to be out of control. Examples of this include an Australian who reprimands a Turkish teammate for being over an hour late to a team meeting, or an English team member who bans a Brazilian family from bringing their children to team gatherings because they make too much noise.

If there are too many people from different cultures trying to exert control over the team at the same time, severe conflict is inevitable. When there are too many judicious organizers from one culture on a team, they may force the team to do things in ways that they are comfortable with in order to cope. If this happens, it will inhibit the development of new ways of doing things and may well prevent the team from discussing and establishing its own unique values. Another problem of having too much control in the team is that the team may be prevented from taking risks. Teams need the freedom to take risks and make mistakes so that they can learn from them and experiment with new and potentially very fruitful possibilities.

Teams need to have structures and agreements to build and preserve their collective identity. They need agreed-on procedures to fall back on, especially when there are high levels of emotionally charged conflict. They have a task to achieve and need to have agreed-on strategies for fulfilling it and goals that provide opportunities for collective celebration, reflection, and evaluation. Judicious organizers will ensure that all these things are in place. Playful explorers will either see mutually agreed goals, strategies, and procedures as necessary evils or they will resist them. Either way, playful explorers will not see structures or rules as set in concrete and sometimes have a tendency to destabilize the team by leading it off on tangents. If the playful explorers' voices are too strong, the team may spend so much time on tangents that it never achieves its objectives. An overemphasis on playful exploration will inhibit the team from building the structures necessary to undergird its collective identity. Alternatively, it may waste a lot of time renegotiating agreements or goals because of a new idea that a playful explorer has encountered.

Each dimension of the Myers-Briggs model of personality is essential to teams, but they need to be in balance with each other. Where there are imbalances, the team needs to be aware of them and make an effort to correct the imbalance. One way of doing this is to encourage team members to develop ways of thinking that are less natural for them. For example, if there are not judicious organizers on a team, one of the team members could be asked to adopt that way of thinking. To use Myers' idea, this is like encouraging right-handed people to use their left hand. A second way of addressing the imbalance is to recruit new team members who have the missing qualities. Understanding the importance of each dimension of personality for effective team functioning can help team members appreciate and value each other, as well as make an effort to listen to each other's perspectives. The team leader plays the important role of continually reinforcing the importance of difference for the health and effectiveness of the team.

UNDERSTANDING TEAM ROLES

In order to work together effectively, each member of a team must be clear about what their part is in the process. Conflict and frustration can arise when boundaries are not clear and there is dissonance between different team members' expectations about their role and the roles of others in seeing the team's task fulfilled. Conflict and frustration can also surface in a team when one or more members are perceived as not doing their fair (or expected) share of the work. The team leader must be able to clarify the roles of each member on the team and encourage them to fulfill their role in fulfilling the team's task.[100]

The Belbin Team Role model, developed by Meredith Belbin and his team in the UK, is a helpful tool that the team leader can use to identify and clarify the roles people take in a team. This model focuses on the behaviors that different team members engage in when they participate in a team. Belbin's initial research led him to identify eight clusters of behaviors, which he called team roles. More information about these team roles, the research behind them, and how they can help your team can be found in Belbin's books *Management Teams: Why They Succeed or Fail* and *Team Roles at*

---

100 Carl Larson and Frank LaFasto, *Teamwork: What Must Go Right / What Can Go Wrong* (Thousand Oaks, CA: SAGE, 2001), ??.

Work, listed in the bibliography. You can find out your own preferred roles by completing the questionnaire at the end of Gordon and Rosemary Jones' book *Teamwork*[101] or completing the Belbin Self-perception Inventory.[102] The eight team roles we have found most helpful in working with multicultural teams are described below.

There are two leadership roles: coordinator and shaper. An ideal team would have both a coordinator and a shaper, and it must have at least one of these roles in order to function well. Coordinators have good people skills and are usually mature, confident, and good at recognizing the strengths of other team members. They lead by clarifying goals and enabling the team to work towards those shared goals by motivating and encouraging team members to do things together and by delegating tasks to them. The shaper is very focused on what the team needs to achieve. Shapers are single-minded, determined, and dynamic leaders who have a lot of drive to overcome difficulties and get the task done. They like to lead and push others into action. They ensure that all team activities align with the team vision and will keep the vision constantly before the team. Shapers perceive obstacles as challenges and will help the team to overcome them. They are essential at the beginning of a team's life or when a team loses its focus or becomes paralyzed by indecision or obstacles. Shapers run ahead of teams and plot their course, while coordinators gather the team members and bring them along with them. As the shaping role is so strong and individual, having two strong shapers on one team is usually a recipe for failure, as each shaper feels the need to plot a different course for the team. Where there are two shapers, it is better to have two teams.

There are two kinds of ideas people on teams: resource investigator and plant. Each of these people brings ideas to the team, but they do this in different ways. Plants source ideas from within themselves, while resource investigators find ideas from other people. Plants are creative and imaginative and able to generate many ideas and offer multiple solutions to problems. They are essential to teams. If a team has no plant, they will need to periodically borrow a plant from elsewhere to generate a list of ideas that the team

---

101 Gordon Jones and Rosemary Jones, *Teamwork: How to Build Relationships* (Bletchley, UK: Scripture Union, 2003).

102 Available at http://www.belbin.com.

can then sift through. Many of the ideas that a plant generates are strange or unrealistic, but some of them will contain the spark of genius needed to ignite the team's synergy. In contrast to plants, resource investigators source their ideas from other people. They develop contacts outside the team to find ideas and resources to help the team fulfill its task. They are generally warm, inquisitive, outgoing, and enthusiastic extraverts who are good at communicating with people. They use these abilities to network with others and, in the process, discover ideas, people, and other tools that can help the team get on with fulfilling its goals.

Team workers are the glue that holds the team together. They are concerned about the people and relationships on the team. Highly sensitive to conflict and misunderstanding, they will work hard to ensure that interpersonal problems are resolved and harmony in the team is restored. Not necessarily highly visible on the team, they work behind the scenes to help people get on with each other and do things that help build a good emotional climate on the team, such as making sure there is good food at team meetings. They encourage team members and attempt to defuse tension before it erupts into full-blown conflict. A team without team workers will find it difficult to hold itself together.

The remaining three roles—implementer, monitor-evaluator, and completer-finisher—help the team to fulfill its strategies and goals by focusing on aspects of doing the task itself. Implementers are particularly good at translating ideas into action. They excel in common sense and are good at taking ideas and finding practical ways to make them happen. They conscientiously and efficiently work on what needs to be done, tackling problems in a systematic way. They are also particularly able to suggest routines and structures that the team can use to more efficiently achieve the task. Monitor-evaluators have good analytical skills and make shrewd judgments that take all possible factors into account. They are good at analyzing problems, evaluating suggestions, and weighing up the pros and cons. They also check that what the team does lines up with its vision, goals, and strategies, and they help restrain the team when it is inclined to enthusiastically run off on tangents that might be good but will not fulfill the team's goals or vision. Completer-finishers make sure that tasks are finished well. They pay exceptional attention to detail. When enthusiasm has waned, and the task is almost completed, it is the completer-finisher who will make sure that the final details are seen to. This enables the team to keep moving forward confidently, knowing that all documents are complete, accounts closed, and resources handed over or disposed of appropriately. Completer-finishers are also invaluable when tasks demand a high degree of precision.

The process of clarifying team roles is important for several reasons. First, it enables team members to appreciate and make use of the skills and strengths each person brings to the team. Second, it enables them to enjoy their work and feel valued since their teammates understand and appreciate what they contribute to the team. Third, it helps to prevent burnout, which can result from team members being forced to work for long periods of time in roles that do not suit them.

The team leader should initiate the process of clarifying the roles of each team member. Belbin's team roles are a helpful tool for beginning this process. Once roles are clarified, the team leader can work to ensure that people are given tasks that match their team role as much as possible. Another key task for the leader is to identify any areas of imbalance in roles. Belbin's research showed that each of the roles was essential for enabling teams to accomplish their task. An imbalance in roles—either too many of one role or the lack of any one role—was found to be detrimental to team effectiveness. If there is a serious imbalance in roles, particularly if a role is missing on the team, the team member who scores highest on the missing role should be encouraged to play that role in team meetings and develop their ability in that area.

Most teams spend a lot of time solving problems in one form or other. Each team role is strongest and most useful in one or more phases of the problem-solving process. The following table illustrates how the roles work together to solve problems. Three of the roles—shaper, coordinator, and team worker—are important throughout the process. The shaper keeps pushing for action by saying, "Let's get on with it." The coordinator keeps the team on track and makes the best use of members' strengths at each point. The team worker continually builds harmony among team members.

PROBLEM-SOLVING STAGE	MOST HELPFUL TEAM ROLE(S)
1. Identifying the problem	Whole team
2. Gathering information	Resource investigator
3. Analyzing information	Monitor-evaluator
4. Generating possible solutions	Plant
5. Selecting best solution	Monitor-evaluator
6. Planning for implementation	Resource investigator and Implementer
7. Implementing the solution	Whole team, especially Coordinator and Implementer
8. Testing the solution	Monitor-evaluator
9. Finishing off the details	Completer-finisher

Table 3: Team roles in problem solving

SPIRITUAL GIFTS

Spiritual gifts are another dimension of difference that can help Christian ministry teams identify, appreciate, and employ the God-given abilities of their members. God has given every Christian at least one spiritual gift, and the purpose of each gift is to help fellow Christians grow in Christlikeness and to build up the whole body of Christ so that it becomes mature (Rom 12:4–5; 1 Cor 12:7–11; Eph 4:11–16). A team of Christians who are participating in God's mission is an expression of the body of Christ. Each team member's God-given gift or gifts have been given to help their brothers and sisters in Christ who are on the team to grow to become more like Jesus, to help the whole team mature and fulfill its part in God's mission. It is only as all the gifts on the team are appreciated and being used that they fulfill their purpose of collectively expressing the fullness of the body of Christ in that team (1 Cor 12:12–31; Eph 4:11–16).

Three passages in the New Testament provide lists of gifts—Romans 12:6–8; 1 Corinthians 12:7–10,28; and Ephesians 4:11. All of the lists are important, and it is likely that the lists are suggestive rather than inclusive of all the gifts that God gives. The gifts are diverse and complementary. Just as personalities and team roles work best when there is a balance among them, it is important for a team to have a balance of spiritual gifts and the right balance for the work that it has to do.

It is also important that the team is actively on the lookout for and encouraging the use of gifts that are not generally valued in traditional ministry contexts, as these may be far more important to the fulfillment of the team's task than some gifts that are highly valued in team members' home churches. For example, it may be very difficult for those with spiritual gifts in the areas of helps, wisdom, administration, and discernment to accept that they should concentrate on the development of these gifts for the sake of fulfilling the team's vision, as many Christians consider these of little value compared with, for example, the gift of teaching and preaching. It can be quite a challenge for the team, and especially the team leader, to encourage and affirm the use of spiritual gifts that are not commonly valued in their home churches.

Several tools are available to help people discover their spiritual gifts. Especially helpful resources, which provide tests for and explanations of spiritual gifts, are listed at the bottom of this page.[103] The most reliable way of discovering your spiritual gifts is through ministry experience combined with the feedback of people who know you well, including your teammates. Learning about your spiritual gifts is learning about another dimension of

---

103 Helpful spiritual gift tests can be found at http://www.spiritualgiftstest.com (which only includes the gifts listed in the three main passages above), at http://www.kodachrome.org/spiritgift (which includes a wider variety of gifts than are listed in the three main New Testament passages), and at http://www.churchgrowth.org/cgi-cg/gifts.cgi?intro=1 (which has a focus on team ministry). An excellent overview and explanation of each of the gifts can be found at https://www.abhms.org/resources/church_life_leadership/wcll-101_Spiritual_Gifts.pdf.

self, just like personality. The team leader has the vital role of creating an open climate in the team in which team members can experiment with doing different things, learn about themselves, feel free to make mistakes, and be affirmed and encouraged for all their contributions.

CHAPTER 7

MANAGING TEAM CONFLICT

INTRODUCTION

Conflict is a major issue in multicultural teams, and multicultural team leaders must be competent to manage it. Duane Elmer reports conducting a workshop for mission executives in which he asked them, "What are the most significant needs of field missionaries?" and "What can we do to assist in meeting those needs?" These mission leaders concluded that without question the greatest problem was relational breakdown between missionaries, and that their greatest need was help in dealing with conflict.[104] Studies of multicultural mission teams reveal that conflict in some cases has led to damaged relationships and team disintegration. Two of the five church planting teams we studied reported damaged relationships, and two of the twelve multicultural mission teams studied by Lorraine Dierck had disbanded due to conflict.[105]

Conflict on a team is "a struggle, or a state of disharmony or antagonism, or hostile behaviors, resulting from contradictory interests, needs, or beliefs, or mutually exclusive desires."[106] Conflict occurs wherever human beings

---

104 Duane Elmer, *Cross-cultural Conflict: Building Relationships for Effective Ministry* (Downers Grove, IL: InterVarsity Press, 1993), 33.

105 R. Hibbert, "Church Planting Teams," 169; Dierck, "Teams That Work," 9.

106 John Ungerleider, "Conflict," in *Effective Multicultural Teams: Theory and Practice*, ed. Claire Halverson and Aqeel Tirmizi (Dordrecht, The Netherlands: Springer, 2008), 212.

live or work together. The only place there is no conflict is the cemetery. No conflict means there is no life. Bill Hybels says:

> The popular concept of unity is a fantasy land where disa-greements never surface and contrary opinions are never stated with force. We expect disagreement, forceful disa-greement. . . . Let's not pretend we never disagree. . . . Let's not have people hiding their concerns to protect a false notion of unity. Let's face the disagreement and deal with it in a godly way. . . . The mark of community—true biblical unity—is not the absence of conflict. It's the presence of a reconciling spirit.[107]

Though it is often uncomfortable, conflict is a normal part of healthy teams. If a team never experiences conflict, it suggests that it is not doing much that members strongly value or that team members are not really communicating what they think and feel. Without conflict, differing per-spectives on issues, tasks, and challenges cannot adequately be considered, which means that the best solutions to problems are probably not being found. If a team continues to be as nice to each other as when they were in the initial "honeymoon" phase of team life, it usually means members are deliberately avoiding conflict, and eventually the team will separate into its individual parts—either psychologically, so that it begins to function like a group of people working in parallel, or physically, so that the team literally breaks apart. A Chinese proverb states, "If you have not fought each other, you do not know each other." Storming—the phase in a team's life in which conflict is frequent and normal—is essential to becoming an effective and high-performing team. Storming is good. It feels bad, but only by going through it successfully and consequently developing good communication and team processes can a team negotiate shared team values and cement a common identity.

If conflicts are managed well, the group becomes better able to manage future conflicts and avoid damage to relationships. The ability of the team

---

107 David Goetz and Marshall Shelley, "Standing in the Crossfire: Interview with Bill Hybels," *Leadership: A Practical Journal for Church Leaders* (Winter 1993): 14

to embrace and manage disagreements is associated with its eventual success in achieving its task, as well as its ability to make good decisions and develop new ideas.[108] If team members recognize that past conflict resulted in a good decision, they may even embrace conflict in future interactions. The process of resolving conflict well involves clarifying areas of confusion, overlooking mistakes people have made, and giving accurate feedback on performance. When conflict is managed well, teams become more ready to make changes in the way they do things, relationships are restored, and team members gain a greater appreciation for each other and for the team leader. The process of resolving conflict together is a formative team experience that helps the team to bond.

The majority of interviewees in our research (65 percent) described conflict in their multicultural teams. A significant proportion (27 percent) said that the leader's being "committed to work through conflict to reach resolution" was one of the five most important characteristics of a good multicultural team leader. One interviewee commented,

> In every multicultural team there will be conflict, because
> we bring so many different colors and flavors to the table
> and ... obviously there would be some situations where ...
> there would be a clash of ideas. . . . A multicultural leader
> should be committed, should be driven to work through
> that conflict towards resolution rather than leave it fester-
> ing within the group, because that will absolutely bring the
> downfall of the group.

Another interviewee observed that a good multicultural team leader has to believe in the value of multicultural teams. Otherwise it is doubtful that he or she will be able to persevere when confronted with the continual challenge of helping a multicultural team to overcome conflict and function effectively.

Team members expect their leaders to be able to deal with conflict, and many team members believe that the leader has the primary responsibil-

---

108 Karen A. Jehn, Gregory Northcraft, and Margaret Neale, "Why Differences Make a Difference: A Field Study of Diversity, Conflict, and Performance in Workgroups," *Administrative Science Quarterly* 44, no. 4 (1999): 741–63.

ity for resolving the conflict. The team leader needs not only to personally mediate to help resolve conflict but also to help the whole team talk about the issues that are causing the conflict.

This chapter presents how and why conflict develops, how culture influences conflict, and how different people resolve conflict in different ways. These topics are illustrated by comments from team leaders and members we interviewed and by our experience as team leaders and coaches. Practical suggestions are given for how team leaders can manage conflict in multicultural teams and for dealing with different cultural methods of conflict management.

CAUSES AND POTENTIAL CONSEQUENCES OF CONFLICT IN MULTICULTURAL TEAMS

Conflict has many causes, and an analysis of any specific conflict will often reveal multiple factors that were involved in its development.[109] One of the main reasons for conflict in multicultural teams is differences among team members arising from their different cultural backgrounds. These differences range from varying values and perceptions of appropriate behavior through to different expectations of their own and other team members' roles. In our research, an important source of conflict was team members' different cultural styles of communication. Team members differed in things like how expressive they were and how they interpreted body language, and this led to misunderstandings.

A second cause of conflict in multicultural teams is different expectations about life and teamwork. Some of these are culturally shaped, but others are due to individual differences. One team member said, for example, "I expected the team to be more organized and more unified." There were also different expectations about how much support team members would give each other. Another interviewee commented, "I think I was expecting to have

---

109 Carlos Cortes and Louise Wilkinson, "Developing and Implementing a Multicultural Vision," in *Contemporary Leadership and Intercultural Competence: Exploring the Cross-cultural Dynamics within Organizations*, ed. Michael Moodian (Los Angeles: SAGE, 2009), 27.

someone to share our burdens in the ministry with—both the problems and the responsibility. I was expecting the opportunity to pray and share with each other quite closely, not just a superficial sharing of ministry needs."

Different expectations also emerged about how much time off was needed for family commitments. Some team members were unhappy with other members' lack of engagement with the team's task and their pursuit of their own agendas at the expense of the team's purpose.

A third major cause of conflict in multicultural teams is poor communication. This leads to misunderstandings between team members and is compounded when the team's language is not spoken fluently by some team members. One team member we interviewed commented, "With different situations where there was misunderstanding, the greatest hindrance was lack of communication. Something was said, and then the misunderstanding was allowed to fester. The mistrust takes root, and then either you clear it up or it continues to grow."

Team leaders contribute to conflict by failing to communicate clearly and being unwilling to discuss problems. Other attitudes and behaviors that trigger conflict are the desire to gain or maintain power, frustration or distress, a perceived threat to territory, dysfunctional personal or group processes, and change.[110]

There is great potential for growth through conflict. Conflict is a powerful force for positive change. Through conflict, creativity can be unleashed and team members' needs and desires are brought out into the open. If handled well, conflicts can lead to renewed motivation, clarification and strengthening of vision and values, venting of frustrations, and personal growth and maturity. Conflict is also an opportunity to bring glory to God by trusting and obeying him through it.

Conflict also has the potential to cause serious damage to teams. If conflict is not handled well, the team and its work suffers. It can lead to teams disintegrating. There are two main ways that conflict is mishandled. The first of these is to ignore it and "sweep it under the carpet." This often leads to a buildup of resentment, gossip, and backbiting. The second way conflict is mishandled is to allow it to turn into an aggressive and uncon-

---

110 Gregory Tillett and Brendan French, *Resolving Conflict* (Melbourne: Oxford University Press, 2010).

trolled explosion of frustration and anger. Both of these scenarios can lead to at least some of the team leaving. Even if the team stays together, it can suffer emotionally and its effectiveness can be markedly reduced. Conflicts that are not addressed tend to escalate. Bill Hybels comments, "Conflict that goes underground poisons the soul and hurts everyone eventually. We would rather have conflict within community than the mask of unity."[111] Whether team conflicts will turn out to be constructive or destructive depends to a significant extent on team leaders and their ability to guide the team towards healthy resolution. Figure 13 illustrates two alternative outcomes that conflict can have depending on which route the team leader is able to guide the team along.

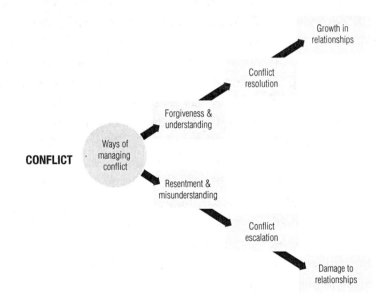

Figure 13: Alternative paths in conflict management

When conflict is not addressed, it tends to escalate. The earlier conflict is dealt with, the easier it is to get to resolution without participants being hurt. A conflict that began with just two team members, if not resolved, can

---

111 Goetz and Shelley, "Standing in the Crossfire," 16.

spread to the whole team as other team members take sides. Team conflict can then spill outside the team to affect other people.

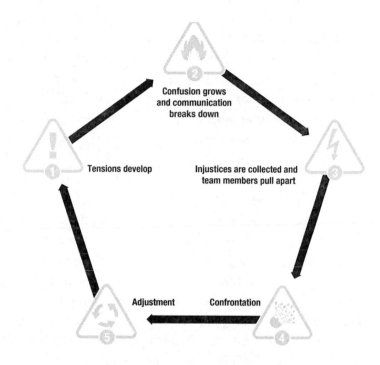

Confusion grows
and communication
breaks down

Tensions develop

Injustices are collected and
team members pull apart

Adjustment

Confrontation

Figure 14: Conflict escalation cycle

Some typical stages in the development of a conflict that is left to escalate without attempts at early resolution are shown in figure 14.[112] In the early stages, before the conflict comes out in the open, team members start to feel tension developing. People are not sure what is wrong and are embarrassed to say anything. But this is the best time to address conflict, as there is still trust and communication is freely flowing. If the early tensions are not addressed, team members begin to become confused about what exactly is happening, who or what is causing the conflict, and what their role in the conflict is. Communication often begins to break down in this stage. Once this happens, the team members involved in the conflict usually

---

112 These stages are based on Donald Palmer, *Managing Conflict Creatively: A Guide for Missionaries and Christian Workers* (Pasadena: William Carey Library, 1990), 61–64.

feel threatened and begin to pull apart from each other. If the conflict is not addressed at this stage, the team members involved often begin to nurse grudges and put together a list of all the negative things the other person, or people, involved have done towards them. This is usually a preparation for some kind of confrontation. If it is managed poorly, then the injustices that have been collected by the various parties can be brought out in a way that damages relationships. If managed well, though, this can still be an opportunity for clarifying and resolving differences. This stage cannot continue for very long, as it is very emotionally draining. Sooner or later everyone looks for ways to make adjustments to end the confrontation.

When a conflict cannot be resolved in a multicultural team, there are several possible outcomes. In some cases the issue causing conflict is initially covered over, but the fundamental problem remains and often resurfaces. In other cases the team stagnates or "gets stuck." In some teams, unresolved conflict leads to the team dissolving and to ongoing confusion and trauma to team members that they carry for years afterwards. Team members who had been part of teams that disbanded because of unresolved conflict pointed to unforgiveness and burnout in team members as the main causes. In other cases of unresolved conflict, the team stays together but trust between team members becomes eroded. One team member gave a particularly poignant description of the consequences of unresolved team conflict:

> Conflict explodes and then it is left. The big thing is that the local people see it—that we are not of one accord, that we don't think the same way. That's really sad, that's an agony. We all feel very hurt. . . . Some of us feel a deep ache, like a hole in the heart in a way, because we know it's not right.

CONFLICT AND CULTURE

While different cultural values in a team are a seedbed for conflict, team members often do not become aware of these different values until they experience conflict. Conflict can therefore play an important role in helping the team negotiate a set of shared team values. Team members may think they can discuss cultural differences and show respect to each other in the process, but then discover that they are experiencing negative emotional reactions and find themselves in conflict with their teammates. This happens because they see their deeply held values being contravened. It is not until we have experienced the emotions associated with conflict that we begin to realize how deeply and passionately we hold our values. Powerful emotions can be aroused by unexpectedly minor issues when our values are threatened. An East Asian family, for example, found themselves in conflict with an EDG leader when the amount of food given to their children was regulated by the leader. Each party found that they had a different culturally shaped value concerning food, and the clash of values led to strong emotional reactions. It is the strength of the emotion and the unpredictability of it that makes conflict so difficult to manage.

Once conflict has arisen, it can be made more complex and intense by team members from different cultures perceiving it to be caused by different things. Trying to resolve a conflict is also made more difficult in a multicultural team, because people from different cultures approach the negotiation process of conflict management in different ways. What is helpful in one culture may be a hindrance in others. For example, EDG cultures usually need to hear a spoken apology incorporating the words "I'm sorry" when they perceive that someone else has acted inappropriately. Some East Asian cultures, in contrast, use mainly nonverbal means of resolving conflict and restoring the relationship, such as inviting the other person(s) to a meal together or giving a gift. Conflict can also escalate when team members are unaware of the different possible cultural styles of conflict management. They can easily misinterpret their teammates' style of interaction as being rude, aggressive, deceptive, or lacking in commitment.[113]

The causes of conflict are, more often than not, embedded in deeply held assumptions that continue to simmer under the surface and give rise to more conflicts even after the initial conflict has been resolved. An example of this is the power dynamics between different ethnic groups in countries and organizations. If a team member who is from a minority culture group in their own country is involved in a conflict with a majority-culture team

---

113 Mitchell Hammer, "The Intercultural Conflict Style Inventory: A Conceptual Framework and Measure of Intercultural Conflict Resolution Approaches," *International Journal of Intercultural Relations* 29 (2005): 675–95.

member (e.g., a Hispanic team member in conflict with an EDG American in a predominantly EDG American organization), although the acute conflict may appear to be resolved, it is very difficult to be sure that the process of resolution has not been influenced by majority-culture biases. For this reason, for teams to understand and effectively manage conflicts, the deeper meanings behind the conflict for all participants need to be explored. Ethnocentric assumptions and feelings that "our way is the right way" can keep us from being open to considering other ways of thinking and doing and should, as much as possible, be brought out into the open. Any type of rigidity magnifies conflict. Rigidly held aspirations relating to security, identity, respect, strongly felt principles, and either/or options tend to magnify conflict and make it difficult to resolve.[114]

UNDERSTANDING HOW TEAM MEMBERS APPROACH CONFLICT

Before we look at ways of approaching conflict resolution, it is important to realize that not all conflicts can be resolved and there is not always a solution for every issue. Even when there is a solution, it is not always clear whether resolution has been achieved. For these reasons, even if the leader has outstanding conflict resolution skills, they do not always guarantee a solution. In some cases intervention by outside leaders or others is necessary. This can involve structural reorganization, reassignment, or the exit of one or more members. These strategies are more likely to be necessary when the team has split up into various subgroups, when negative attitudes cannot be adjusted, when emotions are too volatile, or when team members have lost too much face.

EDG approaches to conflict management tend to separate people from issues and often focus on efficiency at the expense of relationships. Values such as fairness, individual choice, and empowerment are stressed. In contrast, people from collectivist cultures do not usually separate the issue from the person they are having the conflict with. Japanese managers, for example,

---

114 Dean Pruitt and Sung Hee Kim, *Social Conflict: Escalation, Stalemate, and Settlement* (Boston: McGraw-Hill, 2004), 19.

have been found to take criticism and objections to their ideas as personal attacks, while EDG managers usually do not.[115] People from collectivist cultures stress values such as honor and group harmony and are more likely to see situations holistically. They will look for solutions that involve combining various options. EDG approaches tend to treat problems as either/or situations in which one option must be selected and the other rejected. EDG team members often see Asian and Latin American conflict styles as weak or passive. People from these and other collectivistic cultures, though, do not see their approaches to conflict resolution as negative but as the best ways to preserve face and relationships and to achieve each party's goals.[116]

Members of multicultural teams will use different styles of dealing with conflict. Each team member's style of managing conflict is influenced partly by culture and partly by their unique individual background. A widely used model for categorizing approaches to conflict describes five personal responses to conflict: avoiding (also known as withdrawing), accommodating (also known as yielding or obliging), competing (also known as dominating), compromising, and collaborating (also known as integrating).[117] These are shown in the diagram (fig. 15) below, which plots each style according to the degree of assertiveness (attempting to satisfy one's own concerns) and cooperativeness (attempting to satisfy the other party's concerns) that each style represents.

---

115 Gudykunst, *Bridging Differences*, 278.

116 Stella Ting-Toomey, "The Matrix of Face: An Updated Face-negotiation Theory," in *Theorizing about Intercultural Communication*, ed. William Gudykunst (Thousand Oaks, CA: SAGE, 2005), 80.

117 This model is described by Kenneth Thomas, "Conflict and Conflict Management," in *Handbook of Industrial and Organizational Psychology*, ed. Marvin Dunette (Chicago: Rand-McNally, 1976), 889–935. The alternative descriptive terms are from Afzalur Rahim, "A Measure of Styles of Handling Interpersonal Conflict," *Academy of Management Journal* 26 (1983): 368–76.

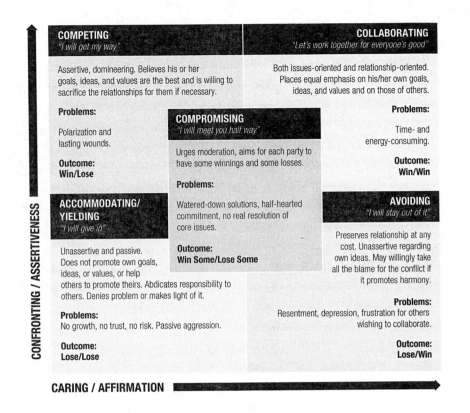

Figure 15: Conflict management styles
(adapted from Thomas, "Conflict," 889–935)

There are positive and negative aspects to each of these styles. Collaboration is usually seen as the best style by writers from EDG cultures, and it ideally produces a solution that addresses both parties' needs, but it can take a lot of time and effort to achieve. Collaboration is also described as "carefronting," a term that expresses directly approaching the other person in a caring way and working towards a win-win solution.[118] The other four styles are usually seen as having more drawbacks than collaboration. Competition may resolve the conflict quickly but harm relationships. Accommodation may preserve relationships but in the long run can lead to the person harboring resentment. Avoidance averts danger in the short term but fails to deal with either parties' real needs or fears. Compromise only

118 David Augsburger, *Caring Enough to Confront* (Glendale, CA: Regal Books, 1973).

partially achieves the needs of each party, but is the best approach in some circumstances and may be necessary when time is critical.

Each conflict resolution style is appropriate in particular situations. In the book of Genesis, Abram seems to have used an accommodating approach when it became clear that he and Lot could not stay in the same place. While, as the uncle and more senior of the two, he could have chosen the land he wanted, he offered Lot the first choice. Perhaps this was partly to avoid messy negotiations and a possible loss of family honor, but most of all it seemed to be the way Abram communicated the priority he put on their relationship (Gen 13:1–12).

Avoiding conflict is negative and damaging to relationships when it involves pretending to be tolerant and that there is nothing wrong but meanwhile feeling hurt and avoiding the relationship. But there is a positive type of avoiding conflict. It can be appropriate when the issue is relatively insignificant or temporary, or when a decision will not affect the long-term vision or goals of the team. When a teammate's ways of doing things offend you, there are many situations in which the best course of action is to overlook what they are doing. There are times when applying the biblical proverb "A person's wisdom yields patience; it is to one's glory to overlook an offense" (Prov 19:11 NIV) is the best approach to conflict. It also seems to be what Paul anticipated was needed in Christian community when he wrote, "Be completely humble and gentle; be patient, bearing with one another in love" (Eph 4:2 NIV). Overlooking an offense is a typically Confucian approach to conflict and likely to be used frequently by Chinese and Korean team members. Tolerance, forbearance, and overlooking others' faults are considered necessary for life in community. This approach involves a largely nonverbal action of mercy on the part of just one party in the conflict.[119]

Using a competitive style in conflict in order to get what you want can be an expression of selfishness, but it may not always be. When you are sure that a teammate is acting in a way that contravenes the heart of the gospel, it is important to keep holding on to what is right and true. Paul's dispute with Peter, recorded in Galatians 2:11–21, in which he says, "I opposed him to his face" (2:11 NIV), concerned salvation by grace alone and required him to

---

119 David Augsburger, *Conflict Mediation across Cultures: Pathways and Patterns* (Louisville: Westminster / John Knox, 1992), 264–66.

engage in a competing style of conflict resolution. These kinds of conflicts are relatively rare, but when such theologically based conflicts do arise in teams, they can result in the team separating into two or more parts. The issues of whether or not women can lead and teach men and whether or not all the gifts of the Spirit are in operation today are the two theologically based conflicts that we have seen divide teams.

A wonderful example of collaborative conflict resolution is found in Acts 6:1–7. Hellenistic Jews were complaining that their widows were missing out on food provisions distributed by the church while the Hebraic Jewish widows were receiving this help. As soon as they became aware of the conflict, the apostles established guidelines for resolving the conflict by telling them to appoint seven men to oversee food distribution and by specifying their qualities. The believers were happy with this decision and were entrusted with choosing the seven men. All of the men they chose have Hellenistic names, and yet everyone seems to have been happy with the collaborative outcome. It was a genuine win-win situation.

Later in Acts, in chapter 15, there is an example of compromise that opened the way for the church to keep growing. A sharp dispute arose between Paul and Barnabas and a group of Jews who insisted that Gentiles be circumcised to become Christians. Everyone was included in the process of discussing this issue, and each group was allowed to express its views. James, the leader of the Jerusalem church, after hearing all the different points of view, discerned that God was leading the group to not require Gentiles to be circumcised, because it was an issue that was at the heart of the gospel. On secondary issues, however, they compromised by requesting that Gentile believers avoid some practices that would have caused offense to Jewish Christians.

Even though these five styles were described with EDG individualists in mind, they also help us to understand some of the ways team members from other cultural backgrounds approach conflict. It is important to realize, though, that these five styles do not encompass all the possible ways people, and especially people from collectivistic cultures (which represent most of the world's societies), deal with conflict.

To find out how to resolve conflict in a multicultural team, we need to look beyond the literature that assumes an EDG monocultural context and the assumption that collaboration is always the best approach. The Bible supports other ways of dealing with conflict that are different from the five approaches. It is vital that team leaders and members appreciate these other ways of handling conflict and realize that, in some situations and with team members of some cultural backgrounds, they will be the best ways of resolving conflict and reconciling people.

Culturally learned approaches to handling conflict vary along two dimensions, which are described by Mitchell Hammer, who studied multicultural astronaut and ground-crew teams in NASA.[120] He found that people from different cultures vary according to how directly they communicate in conflict and how emotionally expressive they are in conflicts. Cultures that use direct communication focus attention on the specific words people use in discussing issues and emphasize precise, explicit language. They prefer face-to-face methods of resolving conflict and want people to speak their mind. People from cultures that use indirect communication look primarily at the context of communication, including nonverbal behavior rather than the words being spoken, to find out what people mean, and they often prefer to use mediators to help resolve conflict. Along the second dimension, emotionally expressive cultures value overt displays of emotion during conflict and want to hear how the other person is feeling as well as what they are thinking about an issue. To be authentic and sincere in an emotionally expressive culture, you have to show your emotions. Emotionally restrained cultures, in contrast, focus on maintaining emotional control and hiding strong feelings. For them, staying calm communicates sincerity.

These variations led Hammer to describe four main styles of communicating in conflict that are shown in figure 16: (1) an "engagement" style that is verbally direct and emotionally expressive—typical of African Americans; (2) a "discussion" style that is verbally direct and emotionally restrained—typical of EDG cultures, European-background North Americans, Canadians, Australians, and New Zealanders; (3) a "dynamic" style that is emotionally expressive but verbally indirect—typical of Arabs; and (4) an "accommodation" style that is verbally indirect and emotionally restrained—typical of East and Southeast Asia (including China, Japan, Thailand, Indonesia, and Malaysia) and Latin America.

---

120 Hammer, "Intercultural Conflict Style Inventory."

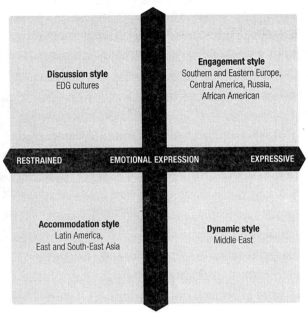

Figure 16: Intercultural conflict styles
(Hammer, "Intercultural Conflict Style Inventory," 691)

This model of intercultural variation highlights the fact that there is no single, universal way that people resolve conflict. It is important for team leaders to help their teams realize that there is no ideal level of emotional expression or directness that team members should show during conflict. The model also challenges the idea that everybody should always use the collaboration approach to resolving conflict. For people from some cultures—particularly collectivist, high-context cultures—the kind of direct verbal communication that is central to the collaborating or carefronting approach can easily cause people to lose face. This is powerfully expressed in the Chinese proverb "Do not remove a fly from your neighbor's face with a hatchet."[121] A person's face is their public self-image or social honor. It is about being liked and accepted by others. While an EDG person's face depends largely on their feeling successful, self-sufficient, and in control of themselves, face for people from collectivist cultures depends on others seeing them positively and wanting to include them in their group. Collectivists hope not so much to be self-sufficiently successful (and so be viewed positively by others) but to be seen as likeable and cooperative and good to have in a group. Since face for them depends so much on the quality of their relationships, their focus is on not losing the face they have.[122]

In order to avoid causing a loss of face to themselves or those they are in conflict with, people from collectivistic cultures often handle conflict in ways that are more indirect than approaches used in EDG cultures. These ways include using a mediator, adopting a "one-down position" (explained below), giving gifts, telling a story, and other indirect means of communication. Each of these is a communication strategy that protects both parties' need to continue to be included in the group and to be seen positively by others.

A mediator is a third person who acts as a go-between for the two conflicting parties. Using a mediator avoids face-to-face confrontation and so minimizes the possibility of either of the parties in the conflict losing face or feeling dishonored. A key purpose of using a mediator is to avoid offense and, in this way, preserve the relationship between the two parties and the harmony in the team. One of the benefits of using a mediator is that they can interpret the messages of each party to the other and act as a buffer by filtering out unhelpful, negative, or potentially offensive words, tone of voice, or body language. The mediator needs to be someone who is respected and trusted by both parties and seen as neutral and fair. They also need to be able to exert some influence over both parties and be someone both will take seriously. For multicultural teams, organizational leaders such as field and regional leaders or team coaches make ideal mediators.

Mediators are frequently referred to in the Bible, and their role is portrayed positively. God addressed the ultimate conflict—the enmity between humanity and God as a result of human rebellion—by sending Jesus Christ

---

121 Augsburger, *Caring Enough to Confront*, 84.

122 Christopher Flanders, *About Face: Rethinking Face for 21st Century Mission* (Eugene, OR: Pickwick, 2011), 93.

as a mediator. "For there is one God and one mediator between God and mankind, the man Christ Jesus, who gave himself as a ransom for all people" (1 Tim 2:5,6 NIV). When Absalom had fled from his father, King David, after killing another of David's sons, Joab acted as a mediator to enable David to bring Absalom back to Jerusalem (2 Sam 14). Barnabas acted as a mediator between the Christians in Jerusalem and Saul, who they believed could not have become a Christian, by bringing Saul to the apostles and explaining to them what had happened to him (Acts 9:26–28). Paul himself acted as a mediator between Philemon and his runaway slave Onesimus, pleading, "So if you consider me a partner, welcome him as you would welcome me" (Phlm 17 NIV).

Duane Elmer coined the term "the one-down position" as a conflict resolution approach in which one person makes themselves vulnerable by taking a position of need and asking for the other person's help. This approach can be used when there is no suitable mediator available or when there is not time to find one. It often involves asking the other party to preserve your honor and in the process to preserve theirs too.[123] Taking the one-down position communicates that, above all else, you value the relationship with the other person and trust them to be able to help you. In the Bible, Abigail used this approach when pleading with David, who was on his way to kill all the men of Nabal's household (1 Sam 25). The prodigal son, in Jesus' parable, also lowered himself before his father when he sought to return to his father's home (Luke 15:21).

Gift giving can be a way of signaling to another person that you want to be reconciled with them. In one team we interviewed, a Korean couple and an English couple had been in conflict with each other for some time. One morning the English couple found a gift at their doorstep that had been placed there by the Korean couple. For the Koreans the gift was an indirect and nonverbal way of expressing that they were sorry for their part in the conflict and wanted to be reconciled with the English couple. Jacob used gifts to communicate to Esau that he wanted to be reconciled with him (Gen 32:13–20; 33:8–11). In the theological concept of propitiation, Jesus is himself a gift to appease God's wrath so that relationship can be restored with mankind.

---

123 Elmer, *Cross-cultural Conflict*, 80–98.

Related to gift giving are other nonverbal ways of expressing that you care about your teammates and want the best for them, even though you have different ideas of how to go about the team's ministry. In the first few months of leading a multicultural team, a Spanish team member and Evelyn had a series of sharp disagreements. They so intensely and openly disagreed that Richard thought the team would collapse before it even reached the norming stage and began to do useful work. Then our whole family became very sick so that we could not even get out of bed for several weeks. Every day the Spanish team member brought over a meal to our house, carefully laid out with everything we would need. The act of bringing a meal communicated more powerfully than any words could that she cared about us. From that point, it didn't matter to us that there were disagreements about the way we should approach our task of training local leaders. We knew that we could work through these disagreements, because underneath them our relationship was built on mutual appreciation and care. We could discuss our different views openly and passionately, confident that our differences would not damage the foundational trust and care we had for each other.

Storytelling is another powerful approach to resolving conflict that uses indirect communication to preserve face and honor. When the prophet Nathan confronted David about his adultery with Bathsheba and murder of her husband, he told a story (2 Sam 12:1–9). In his many conflict-filled interactions with Jewish religious leaders, Jesus often told stories. When, for example, the Pharisees and teachers of the law were muttering about Jesus spending time with "sinners," Jesus told the parables of the lost sheep, lost coin, and lost son (Luke 15). This approach avoided direct offense but also clearly communicated his message. Storytelling is still used in many societies when there are conflicts. Keith Basso explains how the American Indian Apache tell stories to indirectly let someone know they have done something to offend the group. A teenage Apache girl who contravened traditional norms in a ceremonial event by attending it in hair curlers came to a party two weeks later; at the party, her grandmother told everyone a story about a forgetful Apache policeman who became too much like a white man. Even though the story had been told to everyone, the teenager knew it was about her.[124]

Storytelling can also be used by teams that are in conflict. First, parties in conflict can use stories to communicate indirectly what they cannot communicate directly. Team members can also tell stories of their own lives to help their teammates understand them, including their needs and fears, which are often caught up in the conflict. Storytelling can help to defuse the tension and help members build a deeper understanding of each other.

Each member of a multicultural team will have one or more preferred conflict resolution styles. The broad outlines of these styles are culturally learned but also shaped according to each person's unique individual personality. It is important that team leaders recognize each of these approaches as a valid attempt to resolve conflict and that they help team members to see this too. Team members will need to adjust their conflict management styles in order to communicate in a way that is understood and is least likely to cause harm to relationships. Although it feels uncomfortable for team members to make these adjustments, it is necessary for effective communication.

Team members from individualistic, low-context cultures should be encouraged to use less direct approaches than they are used to when approaching high-context teammates. They should try to help their collectivist teammates to maintain face by not embarrassing them in public, by paying attention to nonverbal behavior, by being more tentative in their use of language, and by using more qualifier words such as "maybe" and "possibly." Team members from high-context, collectivistic cultures should consider adapting their approach and being more direct in communicating than they would with someone from their own cultural background. This approach will include using more "I" statements than they would normally use, directly stating opinions and feelings, and providing more verbal feedback to individualists than they usually would provide. Team members will need to be sensitive to how emotionally expressive other teammates are during conflict and try to adjust their own expression of emotion accordingly so that they are seen to be taking the conflict seriously.

---

124 Keith Basso, "Stalking with Stories: Names, Places, and Moral Narratives among the Western Apache," in *Text, Play, and Story: The Construction and Reconstruction of Self and Society*, ed. Stuart Plattner and Edward Bruner (Washington, DC: American Ethnological Society, 1984), 40–41.

Every team member will be stretched as they begin to engage in conflicts in ways that are outside of their comfort zone. When conflict escalates or seems irresolvable, team members need to be willing to use unfamiliar conflict management methods, such as mediators and gift giving for EDG team members, as a part of the process for relationship restoration. It is also important that emotions are acknowledged and appropriately dealt with. There should also be permission for team members who are struggling with their emotions to temporarily withdraw so that they can work out their emotions with God and truly forgive any perceived offenses. Surface forgiveness that does not adequately deal with feelings will only lead to ongoing, festering conflict. Leaders must be alert for this occurring on the team and insist that team members do what is necessary to manage their feelings and then deal with the issue that has provoked the feelings.

THE ROLE OF THE TEAM LEADER IN MANAGING CONFLICT

The first thing a team leader can do to prepare teams to manage conflict well is to enable each team member to understand their own preferred style of conflict resolution and those of their teammates. It is helpful for each team member both to be aware of each of the five styles of conflict resolution described in figure 15 and to work out which style or styles they use most of the time. One way of doing this is to complete one of the conflict style inventories available online.[125] Team members can also use figure 16 to discuss their culture's preferred approaches to conflict and the implications for managing conflict on the team. Another way of helping the team discuss different approaches to conflict management is for the team to engage in a storytelling exercise together in which each team member shares a story about a conflict and how it was addressed in their home culture. From these initial discussions, the team can prepare a draft set of guidelines that state

---

125 A good example of a free conflict management style inventory (based on the five styles) is the widely used Thomas-Kilmann Conflict Mode Instrument. Another very similar tool that helps people assess their use of the five styles is the Rahim Organizational Conflict Inventory.

how they would like to approach conflict management when conflicts arise on the team. The more specific these guidelines are in terms of concrete steps that team members can take, the more useful they will be and the easier they will be to review after conflict has occurred. Working through a case study of a specific conflict that another team has experienced may help to make the issues and potential problems more specific and concrete.

Communication is the cornerstone of conflict resolution. The team leader must model communicating clearly and help team members to communicate with each other openly and honestly. The purpose of communication is restoring relationships. It doesn't matter what conflict resolution style members use as long as it involves communication. Members from high-context cultures will usually use and expect more nonverbal communication than members from low-context cultures, and it is important for team members to learn the "silent language" of their teammates. But it is also vital for communication to include a verbal component, especially for members from low-context cultures who place a lot of value on words. God communicates with humanity both verbally (through the prophets, angels, and the Bible) and nonverbally (through creation, the tabernacle, temple, and sacrificial system; through miracles, his provision for us, and his personal presence). Jesus epitomizes God's communicating with us through both his person and his words—all he is, does, and says. He expects us to follow his lead by doing our best to communicate in ways that our teammates are most likely to understand, using both verbal and nonverbal means.

Once team members have an understanding of their different preferred styles of conflict resolution, the leader can help the team to work towards adjusting their ways of communicating, so that their teammates can hear what they are saying clearly, and decreasing interference from jarring extremes of emotional expression and verbal directness. Team members we interviewed stressed the importance of team leaders and members adjusting their manner of communication, behavior, and expectations when confronting problems.

One of the most important things a leader can do to help a team prepare for conflict is to establish a positive team climate. Creating an atmosphere in which team members feel safe to be themselves and say what they think enables everyone to share freely and to work through misunderstandings and feelings. The team leader needs to create a climate in which members feel emotionally secure and free to disagree with each other. Team members are much more likely to be willing to share things that trouble them when they feel that others on the team, including the team leader, encourage diversity and will not force them to adopt any one culture's preferred way of doing things.

Another key aspect of a positive climate is flexibility. Being flexible means suspending judgment and being open to ambiguity and complexity. A stubborn adherence to our own culturally learned ways of thinking and behaving will only worsen conflict. Team leaders can most help team members to be flexible in their ways of seeing things by modeling flexibility through suspending judgment and patiently taking time with the team to consider different aspects of the issues they are discussing.

Once the team is aware of each member's preferred style of conflict resolution and team members have begun to adjust their own styles so that their communication is better understood by their teammates, the leader should help the team establish some commonly agreed-on guidelines about how to approach conflict. These guidelines will at least partially be based on the values that the team has agreed on, and they should be expressed in written form in a section of the team covenant that focuses on how the team intends to handle conflict. The process of having to agree on what is written down helps the team to articulate clearly and specifically what they think is important. One leader in our study found that making these agreed-on guidelines very clear helped the team to avoid problems related to saving face, because everybody had owned the decisions about how to approach conflict. Guidelines need to be discussed and agreed on by the team, but could include statements like the following:

> We commit to communicating openly, honestly, simply, and clearly with each other about our thoughts and feelings, using 'I' statements where possible rather than 'you' statements, and using concrete rather than abstract language as much as possible (Josh 22).

> We agree to actively listen to our teammates to understand what they are thinking and feeling, needing, and afraid of.

We will give every team member frequent opportunities to tell us what they are doing, thinking, and feeling (Jas 1:19).

We will do all we can to trust, respect, and think the best of each other (Phil 4:8,9). This means that we will also avoid divisive comments and gossip, we will speak in ways that build the other person up, and we will check with teammates directly if we have heard rumors about them (Eph 4:29).

When we realize we may have conflict with a teammate, we will

- Ask the Lord to reveal any wrong attitude, grudge, or behavior in ourselves and deal with it (Matt 7:1–5);
- Ask the Lord to help us forgive the other person in our heart (Luke 17:3,4; Col 3:13);
- Approach them to talk about the issue and not allow the relationship to deteriorate (Matt 18:15);
- Affirm the other person and listen to them carefully (Jas 1:19);
- Identify areas of agreement and disagreement, and explore options for resolving the conflict (Eph 4:15);
- Commit ourselves to do everything we can to be reconciled with them, including being willing to adopt their culture's preferred conflict management style. (Add here the specific cultural approaches of team members to conflict that have been identified in team discussions—e.g., saying "sorry" to North Americans, having a meal with Koreans.)

If we are unable to resolve the conflict by communicating with our teammates, we will ask for the help of a mediator (cf. Acts 9:26–28). We agree to do this as soon as possible (e.g., within two days of talking with our teammates) so that relationships do not have time to deteriorate further.

As a team we agree that restoring relationships is a major priority in our team. When conflict occurs, its resolution has priority over scheduled team activities. This means that if teammates are in conflict, their meeting together to resolve the issue is more important than their attending a regular team meeting or doing some other team activity.

These guidelines are oriented around constructively dealing with conflicts based on a commitment to preserve relationships, be reconciled when there is a conflict, and communicate clearly and openly. This is the emphasis of the New Testament concerning conflict in relationships. Once the team has a clear set of guidelines, the team leader must keep everyone accountable to them as they work through conflicts.

Team leaders should do their best to anticipate conflicts and deal with issues before they escalate. They should try to recognize early signs that a conflict may be brewing, such as when team members start to complain more frequently or to oppose their leadership. The team leader ought to be especially alert to potential conflict when someone in the team is having serious problems in life and ministry, a major change is pending, or there is a longstanding problem that has not been dealt with. When a team member seems not to be contributing to the team or its task, other team members can become annoyed. In this situation the team leader ought to address this problem early by going and talking with the team member involved to explore issues they may be struggling with and try to help address them. Interviewees in our study said that it is important to "try to resolve problems right away" and that the leader needs to "nip things in the bud." One interviewee said,

If you think there's something wrong, there probably is, and you probably don't know what it is, especially if you're in an environment that is unusual or you've got someone who may not know that they're offending. You probably would say, "Oh, that's because of the culture. I wouldn't talk to them about it. I don't know how to." Well, you've got to find a way.

Addressing conflict early means that when two or more team members seem to be in conflict, the team leader should encourage the team members to talk with each other. They may also need to meet with the members who are in conflict and help to clarify and resolve issues or misunderstandings. Team leaders need to be sensitive and tactful when doing this. Doing this can take a lot of time, but it is a key investment in the health of the team. Leaders also need to be sensitive to the setting in which they raise issues with team members. They should do everything they can to make sure that the team members feel comfortable, relaxed, and safe.

The nonverbal messages communicated by the place and time in which the leader talks to team members about sensitive issues have the potential to either make the person feel accepted and put them at ease or make them feel very uncomfortable. Team members from East and Southeast Asia may especially appreciate being invited to a meal as the setting for talking about something difficult. A meal communicates care, concern for them as a person, respect, and a desire to get to know them better, and it is an opportunity to talk with them about how are they are doing, their family, and many other things. After the meal is a good time to gently raise the issue related to the conflict.

The team leader's own behavior in conflict acts as a vital model that can help the team handle conflict. Being approachable and welcoming towards team members is a vital part of this example and a powerful encouragement for team members to be open to one another. Interviewees in our study stressed the value of the team leader's approachability in enabling team members to raise concerns and talk through problems. One team member contrasted approachable and unapproachable leaders:

> I know that in many cases when there's been conflict or problems, if the team leader is approachable, that makes a big difference, and team members feel they can get the problems sorted out because they know their team leader doesn't mind being approached. Other team leaders I've seen . . . Their busy lives kind of almost speak, "Don't bother me with anything else."

Other key aspects of the leader's modeling include forgiving team members, asking them for forgiveness, dying to self, and limiting their expression of frustration. One interviewee admired her team leader because he was ready to ask forgiveness when he hurt others. If the team leader is both approachable and forgiving, team members will feel safe to raise issues with the leader and to confess to inappropriate behavior. One interviewee felt that "unless you have a heart of forgiveness, you'll have conflict all the time." Leaders also need to die to themselves by letting go of prejudices, ideas, and values that stop them from working effectively together with the team. This may require the leader giving up something precious from their cultural heritage, such as a North American leader learning to tolerate team members arriving late for meetings. Finally, the leader must work on managing their expression of emotions, especially frustration and anger, so that uncontrolled emotional expression does not hurt team members, close doors to further communication, and damage relationships.

The storming phase of team life is characterized by more frequent and intense conflict than at other times. The team leader must be prepared for the transition from the forming phase, when members are typically optimistic and on their best behavior. Storming usually occurs within the first year of a team's life. During storming, team members often experience dissatisfaction as their hopes and dreams for team life are threatened by the realities, and they experience tension concerning how much to give themselves to the team and to merge their individual identity with the team's identity. There are healthy and unhealthy types of storming. The team leader's goal in this phase is to help the team work through conflicts healthily in such a way that relationships remain good and norms for team life are established. Team leaders can help their teams through storming by enabling members to recognize that storming is a normal part of team development, by expecting and welcoming team members to express their expectations about team life and work, by scheduling frequent team meetings with times to discuss ideas, by making open and continuous communication a priority, and by organizing "clearing the air" sessions for team members in conflict.

Team leaders may need to find a mediator when a conflict cannot be resolved or when they are deeply embroiled in the conflict themselves. When two or more team members are locked in conflict and unable to resolve it, it is important for the team leader to offer to act as a mediator in order to enable those in conflict to interact with each other. If the team leader cannot resolve the issue, or is personally involved, the team leader may need to arrange for a person from outside the team to act as a mediator. A mediator, acting as an outside person to the conflict, can bring a helpful perspective to the issues, as those involved do not always see the issues clearly.

In addition to building a healthy team community, it can be helpful for the team to negotiate a team covenant together. The process of agreeing on the covenant can be as important as or more important than the document itself. In the first few months of a multicultural team, this document has to be flexible, as it is not possible for team members to predict all the possibilities of scenarios that will cause conflict in the team and how they will react. The covenant should be prepared during team formation and used in debriefing after each conflict is resolved.

As part of the process of preparing the covenant, teams should discuss each member's expectations of the team and of leadership and assumptions about how the team will function. Questions for helping the team to do this are provided in appendix 2. The team also needs to work through how it plans to work together to solve problems and make decisions. The team's agreed-on process for managing conflict that has come out of discussions relating to different cultural approaches to conflict resolution should also be included. In the early stages of team life, the team covenant should also be reviewed after each incident of team conflict to see if it needs to be modified. The process of preparing and refining the covenant is an opportunity for the team to further develop its capacity to work through conflict and make decisions together.

CHAPTER 8

CHARACTER QUALITIES TO NURTURE

In our work of training mission teams we searched for resources to help struggling team leaders. We found a lot of helpful tools aimed at monocultural and especially North American teams but very little that was designed to address the complexity of multicultural teams. The few resources that were available were mostly based on opinion rather than research.

To address this need, we set out to discover what supervisors, leaders, and members of multicultural teams considered the essential characteristics and competencies of multicultural team leaders. We wanted to create a profile of a good multicultural team leader that could be used to help select and train leaders of multicultural teams, and we wanted this profile to reflect the actual experience of team leaders and members working in multicultural teams and to embody their opinions.[126]

We began by reviewing the literature on teams and multicultural organizations. We then conducted focus groups with fifty team members from multicultural organizations, asking them what they saw as the characteristics and competencies of good multicultural team leaders.[127] This list of characteristics and competencies from the focus groups was compared with a leadership profile that had been developed from surveying more than one hundred leaders in one international mission agency[128] and with

---

126 Evelyn Hibbert, "Identifying Essential Characteristics and Competencies of Good Multicultural Team Leaders: A Pilot Study" (EdD diss., University of New England, 2010).

127 Members of three large and highly multicultural organizations in Australia took part in these groups.

128 Leaders in WEC International, an international and interdenominational mission

characteristics and competencies in the team leadership literature. This comparison and analysis led to a composite list of over fifty characteristics and competencies of good multicultural team leaders. We then interviewed fifty-one supervisors, leaders, and team members—all of whom had previously worked or were currently working in a multicultural team—to further refine this list. Most of our interviewees were from Christian missionary agencies,[129] but we also included some people from secular organizations that had multicultural teams. Interviewees came from eighteen different cultural backgrounds and had worked with an average of five different cultures represented on their teams. Collectively the interviewees had worked with people from seventy-five different cultures.

Interviewees were asked to rank the importance of each of the items on the list and, for the five characteristics they considered most important, explain what they understood by that characteristic and give concrete examples of that characteristic from their own experience. They were also asked to add any extra characteristics of team leaders that were missing from the list. After analyzing their responses we were able to develop a refined list of characteristics and competencies of a good multicultural team leader. We have adapted this list into a Multicultural Team Leader Inventory that can be used by team leaders and members to assess how the leader is doing. This is found in appendix 3.

The characteristics and competencies of good multicultural team leaders are described in this chapter, using the words of the team leaders and members we interviewed as much as possible in this and the next chapter. This chapter focuses on the character qualities of the multicultural team leader—the things the leader needs to be. Chapter 9 describes the competencies of good multicultural team leaders—the things they need to be able to do.

---

agency, which then had about 1,700 members from over fifty countries working in over seventy countries.

129 Interviewees came from a number of international mission agencies including SIM, World Team, OM, CMS, and WEC International.

CHARACTER IS ULTIMATELY MORE IMPORTANT THAN COMPETENCE

Character qualities figured more prominently than competencies in both interviewees' responses and the literature. Competencies are still important, but character is ultimately foundational. Competence can be learned on the job, as necessary, while character usually takes much longer to develop. A key implication for organizations is that character rather than competence is the first area to look for in selecting people for team leadership.

Character is developed through life experience, not in classrooms. Character takes time to develop and requires exposure to good role models. Character development requires a willingness to change deeply held attitudes and approaches to life, an openness to the Holy Spirit to give us insight into other cultures, and a disciplined openness to receive feedback from others regarding how well we relate and respond to them. When we are in situations of high stress, even if we have learned to respond well to others under normal conditions, we often revert to less mature attitudes and ways of behaving. As multicultural teams are often stressful, this means that we usually respond less well to others than we do in a monocultural situation.[130] In a multicultural team, then, we need to learn to how to manage ourselves when under stress, as well as how to ask for forgiveness when we behave in ways that cause problems for others.

Competencies, in contrast to character qualities, are skills. This means that it is possible to train people in them even when they are complex and difficult. With the right character qualities, multicultural team leaders will want to work at and be willing to persevere in developing these skills and will be more able to seek forgiveness when they make mistakes or offend team members.

One of the leader's most important tasks is to develop a positive "emotional bank balance" in the team. An emotional bank account is "a metaphor that describes the amount of trust that's been built up in a relationship.

---

130 Mitchell Hammer, "Solving Problems and Resolving Conflict Using the Intercultural Conflict Style Model and Inventory," in *Contemporary Leadership and Intercultural Competence: Exploring the Cross-cultural Dynamics within Organizations*, ed. Michael Moodian (Los Angeles: SAGE, 2009), 221.

It's the feeling of safeness you have with another human being."[131] We make deposits into an emotional bank account with someone else through expressing qualities like compassion, kindness, humility, gentleness, and patience (Col 3:12). In a team, the emotional bank balance refers to the degree of trust that each team member has in each other and especially in the leader. When the emotional bank balance in a team is positive and high, it means that there has been strong investment in the relationships. When things go wrong or team members are hurt, it is easier for them to forgive because they have built a level of trust in and care for one another. This kind of relationship building requires good communication skills, but more than that it requires the character qualities that enable the leader to engage with others, genuinely care about them, seek their best, and build trust.

WHAT ARE THE CHARACTER QUALITIES OF A GOOD MULTICULTURAL TEAM LEADER?

Leading a multicultural team is a demanding task, and not everyone is convinced that it is worth the effort. Not only is it demanding, but multicultural teams take longer to build and face more conflict than monocultural teams. In the face of these challenges, leaders of multicultural teams have to be convinced that it is worth the effort of attempting to build a multicultural team and be convinced enough to persevere when the going gets tough. For this reason, the first character quality in the Multicultural Team Leader Inventory is a measure of the team leader's conviction that multicultural teams are worth working for.

The next two character qualities listed in the Inventory—a broad knowledge of other cultures, and specific knowledge of the cultures represented on the team—have been discussed in chapters 2 and 3. A fourth quality in the Inventory—a commitment to work through conflict to reach resolution—is described in chapter 7. The remaining character qualities are described here.

---

131   Covey, *7 Habits*, 188.

A positive attitude towards other cultures

People are very sensitive to negative attitudes towards them and are quick to recognize if team leaders have a problem with their culture or other cultures. To have a positive attitude does not mean to naively assume everything is good about a particular culture, but it does mean having an authentic, positive orientation towards it, which will be demonstrated through continually wanting to learn more about that culture and being respectful about frustrations. Several of our interviewees felt that how team leaders talked about other cultures was an indicator of how those leaders would respond to their cultures.

When leaders have a positive attitude towards other cultures, they intentionally look for positives in situations where cultural differences are causing problems. One supervisor gave the example of a more consultative team member who consistently failed to meet organizational deadlines. The team leader recognized the positive aspects of this team member's consultative approach, and this made it easier for the leader to find ways to work around the problem.

Having a positive attitude does not mean pretending that leaders think everything they see or experience is good. One team leader explained:

> It doesn't mean you have to love everything about the other culture or about the other person. I think from experience that sometimes people think that naively you've got to like everything or everyone, but I don't think that's real or normal or even possible, but I do think that you can positively orient yourself towards another people's culture, and it has to be authentic. If team members think that the leader just loves everything about a certain people group and everything they do is great, that's unrealistic and people won't follow it. I think the leader has to be authentic, and having a positive attitude doesn't exclude respectfully and appropriately being real about their frustrations.

Team leaders do have to be careful, though, about how they talk about other cultures, especially when they make jokes. Even a small thing, such as making a comment about an accent, can express what is perceived as a negative attitude and make it very difficult for the team to function. One supervisor commented,

> Team members sense how you tell stories about other cultures when you've made a visit as leader. It may be that you tell a joke or something about another culture that is not even represented on the team, but people pick up, "Aha, that's how he or she thinks about cultures, so I will never know how he thinks about my culture."

When a team is working cross-culturally, leaders may go out of their way to be positive about the host culture but neglect to be positive about cultures in the team. One way to overcome this is to be committed to keep learning about and finding aspects to appreciate in the other cultures on the team.

Humble

Humility was described by interviewees mainly in terms of things the humble leader does not do. Humble leaders do not tower over members or alienate them, do not think they know everything, do not demand that others follow them, and are not "puffed up, condescending, and arrogant."[132] Humble leaders are not threatened by people on the team having different views. They are not scared by people on the team wanting to try things that are different to policy.

On the positive side, because they do not assume they know everything, humble leaders are continually learning and trying to understand others. They consult with other people, listen to what others say, and ask team members what they think would be best to do in different situations. One team member described a humble team leader as

> a person [who] has nothing to defend or nothing to hide or nothing to prove, will be willing to listen, take things on board and make mistakes and still continue and ask for forgiveness. . . . It's not putting themselves forward but giv-

---

132 Individual interviewees are not identified in order to preserve their anonymity.

ing room to many different ways of living and going about
things and drawing things out.

Part of being humble, according to team members, was that their leaders
made themselves vulnerable. Humble leaders are careful to hear concerns
and make sure they understand what team members are saying, even when
they feel attacked. This means that humble leaders do not feel threatened
by team members' reactions. Humble leaders are relaxed when being challenged and are able to "receive team members into their heart" without
worrying about themselves. A humble team leader does not put his or her
own interests first but is, according to one team member, "ready to be hurt
and asks for our ideas about things, or opinions, and wants to listen, . . .
[does] not defend himself quickly, but [is] patient enough to wait and ask
and find out what we mean."

Humble leaders are able to work with the "grassroots" and are not always
hanging around with more powerful people. Being comfortable working with
"grassroots" people means that leaders do not consider themselves superior.
Several interviewees were quick to point out that being humble as a leader
does not mean, though, that they are unable to confront. A leader can be
both courageous and humble. Humble leaders still must have the courage
to confront team members when necessary.

Patient

In multicultural teams the complexity of relating to different cultures and
languages means that it takes longer to communicate, ensure understanding, make decisions, and achieve outcomes. This requires the leader to be
patient. One leader emphasized that when working with people from different cultures,

> [p]eople will go slower than you. People will take time to
> try and understand the direction that you might want to
> go in, and in some cases the direction you may want to go
> in is at odds with their cultural heritage. Therefore things
> or achievements that you want to attain would take two
> or three times as long than if it was in your own culture.

Another leader gave more detail about what being patient involves when working with people from very different cultures:

> Patience is actually really a given in the context of a multicultural team purely because . . . there's a lot of different cultures that are very, very quiet by nature and don't like to speak out when they don't understand something, so sometimes you've got to be really patient and explain things as well. And if they don't understand or have a language barrier, or they don't quite fully understand the tone that you're delivering it or the words you're using, you've really got to show a lot of patience to make sure they understand.

A supervisor explained that patience is necessary because sometimes the resolution of issues can take years:

> One of the big issues went on for a number of years. So it's not even a week thing or a month thing. It can be a long process. God is taking people on a journey. It is a process for them. You can't rush it. People aren't ready to do certain things. You have to wait.

Ready to listen and approachable

Many team members and leaders emphasized the importance of multicultural team leaders being ready to listen. Being ready to listen means drawing others out, going to the team members, being curious, asking questions to better understand and to check that what was heard was what was truly meant, as well as actually wanting to hear the answers. It means patiently waiting to be sure the team members have finished saying what they wanted to say. It includes listening to feelings and understanding the emotional state of team members.

Listening involves a real openness in the leader to the possibility of different ways of doing things. It means having an open heart so as to hear where team members are coming from and what they feel about things. Listening involves not just letting others speak but actively drawing them out, in culturally sensitive ways, and making sure that you are clearly hearing what the other person is trying to communicate. It means making team members feel comfortable and relaxed, not only through words but also nonverbally, so that team members feel "at home." It means having a manner that invites questions and expresses availability. One team member put it this way:

> In a multicultural setting people share, and the ideas that are expressed from different cultures always come across in different ways. I think I've noticed that in a good multicultural leader they're able to listen very carefully to ideas from other cultures and make people from other cultures feel at home and welcome to share.

Being ready to listen is not only about listening to the words people say. Listening involves a genuine desire to understand the person, their background, their feelings, their current emotional state, their culture, and who they are. It involves taking time beyond the immediate conversation. It is about communicating respect and value. Interviewees expected that their leaders would demonstrate curiosity and ask them lots of questions about themselves. One young team member expected her team leader to appreciate where she was at as an individual, in terms of her stage of life, the problems she was having, and how that might affect her work on the team. A supervisor talked about the importance of spending time with each team member "to ask them their story" and learn about "their family, their backgrounds, and who they are" and then to continue to build on this relationship. A team member reinforced this by referring to the positive example of her leader: "I felt respected by my leader because she took time to listen to my experiences, to listen to my background experiences, experiences in the past as well as in the present, and this listening felt like it was endless, and by this I felt valued and I really appreciated that."

Even when team leaders have more experience than team members, team leaders need to put aside their own preferences and listen to the suggestions and contributions of team members. A team leader described an incident when she needed to go to team members and ask them to help her understand what was going on. Although this did not immediately resolve the issue, she said, "Several times they said how much they appreciated just being heard and someone just trying to understand things from their point of view rather than trying to achieve results."

Being ready to listen means that the leader is approachable, and this relates to the leader's manner. An approachable leader does not seem too busy and freely gives time to team members. Team members need to feel that it is "easy to ask the leader anything." One supervisor explained that being approachable involves "how we bear ourselves" and having "a friendly face."

One supervisor described a crisis that resulted in major pain and division but was then turned around in a very short time through the gentle, quiet listening of new leaders. Because of their approachability, the struggling team member at the heart of the crisis "felt able to unload onto them and share her heart with them, which led to good resolution." The leader's approachability is essential for resolving conflict and sorting out problems on the team. It provides security to team members in that team members know they can get their problems sorted out.

Always learning

A good multicultural team leader is always learning by talking with people and by reading. Good multicultural team leaders demonstrate this continual learning by asking questions and by letting others know that questions are welcome. They are also willing to try new things and new ways of doing things. Several team members stated that people are more ready to listen to leaders who are learners than leaders who think they know everything.

Three supervisors stressed the importance of the leader's continuing to read. One commented that good multicultural team leaders are always learning in multiple disciplines. They read broadly and their breadth of learning is reflected in their conversations. A team member observed that the leaders he has seen who have been most sensitive to other cultures are those who read about other cultures and are always taking note of them. Another supervisor also thought that it is necessary to keep reading new books, reflecting on them, and applying the insights gained. She saw this as a way of helping to keep her mind open.

Being a continual learner is coupled with a sense of having so much more to learn, which is the opposite of arrogance or the assumption that the leader knows best. Two supervisors ruefully acknowledged that more recent experience and study had helped them to see the mistakes they had made in the past in relating to people from other cultures. One leader said that he had so much more to learn, even after decades on the job and years of study. The more leaders had experienced, the less they felt they knew.

Ready to try new ways of doing things

Successful leaders in multicultural teams are open-minded and open to new experiences. They have an attitude of openness to and appreciation of others' values and practices and a willingness to experiment with different ways of doing things. They create a culture of openness and exploration and encourage creativity. They are curious, nonjudgmental, willing to take risks, flexible, and good at thinking in new ways.

An open-minded leader gives the impression to team members that their opinion will be accepted, and this makes team members feel comfortable. A team member elaborated:

> If I think this particular thing should be done in this way and somebody comes from a different culture who can do it differently, I have to be ready to listen to the person and to accept it and listen to the reasons, because maybe what the person is saying is true; maybe it's a better way of doing it.

Being willing to try new things requires a safe team context in which to explore new ideas and being open to making mistakes. Mistakes are inevitable, but they can be learned from. One leader stressed that making mistakes is inevitable in trying new things but also an essential part of growing as a person. In order to try new things, team leaders need to be willing to take the risk that the team will make mistakes.

When new ideas or ways of doing things are suppressed, team members may not want to continue working together. It is important for team members "to feel safe, to be able to say, 'Look, I've got this new idea' and not feel like this can get shot straight out of the [water] from the word go. We appreciate that." One team member talked about the negative feeling she had as a result of her team leader's unwillingness to try new things or to listen to anything new. She submitted to his leadership but wanted to leave and no longer felt safe to say what she thought.

Respectful of others regardless of background

Good leaders respect team members regardless of their cultural background or role on the team. Interviewees said that this requires patience, open-mindedness, and flexibility in the leader. It also means that leaders must invest time in listening to team members' stories and learning to understand them, intentionally valuing them as individuals, and acknowledging their skills and professional qualifications. The leader must also be willing to learn from team members.

The leader who respects others regardless of their cultural background adjusts his or her approach according to the values and expectations inherent in those backgrounds. The leader demonstrates respect by being willing to adopt different ways of doing things. Although it is not sustainable for the leader to meet everyone's expectations all the time, it is still important that in interacting with individuals on the team, the leader demonstrates a willingness to be sensitive to their cultural background. The challenge for the multicultural team leader is being able to fairly balance the adjustments for each team member without compromising the relationships and functioning of the team as a whole. The good multicultural team leader enables his or her team not only to embrace difference but also to work with it.

One leader recommended making an "investment of respect" into team members. This means taking the time to get to understand team members better and being willing to adjust one's approach in order to suit their background better. It also means being willing to allow different team members do the same things in different ways. Respect means honoring team members, being tolerant of them and patient in interacting with them.

Team members felt that good leaders avoided stereotyping people according to their cultural background and recognized that individuals differed within cultural groups. One team member gave an example from her team life where the team needed to work with a Muslim. People on the team became very paranoid based on their stereotypes of Muslims. When they finally realized what they were doing, they talked about their fears and were able to recognize and overcome them. Another example comes from a supervisor who related his experience of interacting with Koreans from two different generations and how his assumptions about Koreans based on one generation did not apply to the other. He was very frustrated until he worked out that the stereotype he had created in his mind was not appropriate. He pointed out that the way to overcome this tendency to stereotype is to be continually learning about other cultures. Another leader commented that stereotyping emerges from expectations based on previous experiences and that the only way to overcome this is to treat everyone individually. One supervisor expressed it in the following way:

> One of the things we tried to do was not only to recognize the different cultures but even within cultures try not to put all members together, as if to say, "So now I understand all Australians, now I understand all Dutch." Each brings their own environmental baggage, experiences, personality styles, as well as cultural generalities.

Another aspect of respect is fairness. Team leaders need to be fair in how they relate to team members. Team members are sensitive to any variance in how leaders express that they care for or respect different team members. A perception of fair treatment is dependent on feeling that leaders can be trusted, that they are unbiased in judgments, and that they treat all people with the dignity and respect appropriate for full group members. When people are treated fairly, this communicates that they are important, included in the group, and equally valued.

Inclusive

The good multicultural team leader is able to help every team member fully participate in the team and its decision-making processes. The barriers to team members' full participation include language, shyness, quietness, introversion, and cultural orientations, which preclude active participation in group discussion. Good team leaders include each team member in the decision-making process, making a decision based on what everyone has said.

Interviewees reported several reasons for team members being excluded from full participation in the team: lack of proficiency in the team's language, culture shock, errors they had made, strong reactions they had displayed, and being quiet in team meetings. One person said that those who waited to be asked their opinion were often excluded. It was only when the leader specifically asked the quiet people to contribute that they gained valuable insights that helped their decision making. Referring to quieter or less vocal team members, one supervisor reinforced the need to continually "bring them in" and make them "feel part of it" by encouraging those who are more timid to talk. One team leader needed to help his team adjust their language use and way of communicating to help nonnative speakers of the team's language feel included. Another leader described how her own experience of working overseas helped her to understand why new team members feel alienated and led her to be more tolerant and to ensure that her team was not "exclusionary."

Including everyone on the team in decision making requires the leader to consult with team members about decisions affecting their work and then make a decision or help the team make a decision based on what everyone has said. This means that it feels like the whole team made the decision together. One team leader was reported to have made a conscious effort to avoid putting "his own interests first" by listening to team members' ideas and opinions. In contrast, another interviewee reported that their team leader made decisions on his own without asking team members and simply announced them to his team. This eventually led to the team disbanding.

Self-aware

To be self-aware means that multicultural team leaders are honest with themselves about themselves. Leaders who are self-aware understand their limitations and failings. A supervisor described how her own self-awareness affected her as a leader:

> The more I can be in touch with myself—who I am, my own limitations, the utter desperation that I can't do it differently than I am—it helps me to be compassionate or even to want to accommodate or respect somebody else who says I can't do it differently. So that self-awareness of who I am gives me authority in leading.

One leader described self-awareness as being authentic, which means being yourself and not trying to be like others. He also felt that it is important for him to model authenticity to team members. One interviewee described self-awareness as "understanding how you're being received by others." This understanding is developed through getting feedback from others. The most accurate assessment of team leaders comes from the people who see their leadership most clearly—the team members.

Self-aware leaders accept their own uniqueness and how God has made them. It is particularly important for multicultural team leaders to have a strong conception of their own identity, because they will often feel that their personal boundaries are threatened by the demands that culturally diverse teammates put on them.[133] Leaders who are confident of their own identity in Christ do not feel the need to hide their weaknesses from others. They can be transparent about their motives and behavior because they are not afraid of team members seeing them for who they really are.

Self-awareness is developed through being personally stretched and receiving feedback from others. Prior experience of difficulties develops empathy and enables leaders to understand how they are being perceived by others. A supervisor described how experience helped her grow in self-awareness:

> I know more than theory and how much it might hurt or how much effort it takes to really connect and really under-stand, so it's more than something we can study. As we hurt each other in different cultures, it is good to have had an experience of being out of my own depths, being stretched, opening a file in my brain to even have a sense for things that are not in my worldview. I have grown through it, and that has widened who I am.

The demands on multicultural leaders can be so great that they threaten the leader's own sense of being. Interviewees expected their multicultural team leaders to be open and vulnerable yet not feel threatened, even when criticized. To be vulnerable and to open up to others, especially when others are upset or wanting to criticize, requires a high degree of self-confidence and self-awareness. This can be particularly challenging in cross-cultural

---

133 Susan Schneider and Jean-Louis Barsoux, *Managing across Cultures* (Harlow, UK: Prentice Hall, 2002), 208.

interactions where boundaries defining appropriate behavior are unclear. These kinds of demands on the leader require emotional stability.

An emotionally stable leader also regulates how they express their emotions. Leaders need to be self-controlled when interacting with others. One team member stressed the importance of leaders' being able to control their physical reactions when they feel strong emotions. For example, if leaders are angry, they should be able to control their facial expression so as not to show it.

HOW DO YOU DEVELOP THESE QUALITIES?

Our foundational character development occurs during childhood and adolescence through observing and imitating prominent adults in our lives. It also occurs through reflecting on difficult experiences. There is some normal progression in character over the life span, such as from the hotheadedness of adolescence to the (usually!) more measured maturity of older adults. Character development as an adult requires intentionality and hard work.

In our experience, intentional character development requires a definite commitment to changing a specific attitude or way of behaving. An example of this kind of commitment is when we intentionally decide to forgive someone who has hurt us, and commit ourselves to becoming a forgiving person in the future. Recognizing that the change is impossible without the help of the Holy Spirit, we start putting into practice the new behavior because of the change that God is bringing about inside us. But putting the new behavior into practice just once is inadequate, because character change is about developing a habit of attitude and behavior. In the case of forgiveness, it involves a constant discipline of deciding to forgive, seeking God's help, and refusing to be unforgiving even when you would really prefer to take revenge.

Role models are a key to character development. More mature Christians who demonstrate the qualities that we want to develop become a benchmark by which we examine our own attitudes and behavior. The Apostle Paul wrote to Christians on many occasions telling them to follow his example and to follow the example of people like him. For example, he said to the church at Philippi, "Join together in following my example, brothers and sisters, and just as you have us as a model, keep your eyes on those who live as we do" (Phil 3:17 NIV). The best role models are living people whom we know personally, though it is also possible to find role models in historical figures.

Another way of developing the character qualities needed for leading a multicultural team is to find a mentor who will give you feedback about your attitudes and behavior. It is best to have a mentor who sees how you live rather than one who only hears your own reports about the issues you are dealing with. Some leaders ask their team to give them feedback on how they are doing. While this may be helpful in certain situations, it is important to be aware that this may disturb some team members' confidence in the leader and create unhelpful dynamics in the team.

MAINTAINING YOUR SPIRITUAL, EMOTIONAL, PSYCHOLOGICAL, AND PHYSICAL WELL-BEING

Many leaders are painfully aware of their imperfection, as one team leader reminded us when he said, "Looking at the criteria in here, do I personify all those? I wish! If I personified even half of these, it would be nice, wouldn't it?" Although leaders are imperfect people, God, who is perfect, makes his strength available and is able to make his strength perfect in our weakness and enable us, through Christ, to do everything he has called us to do (2 Cor 4:7; 12:9; Phil 4:13). Nevertheless, appointing people to be multicultural team leaders who do not already display the above personal qualities, at least in rudimentary form, is a recipe for disaster, not just for the leader but also for the team.

Once leaders are appointed they need to develop a sense of dependence on God in order to find strength to persevere, focus in the chaos, and healing for the hurt they will experience. Sometimes leaders receive unsolicited feedback that can be very hurtful. Being able to work through this builds character. When the knife of criticism has gone in deep, we find it helpful to imagine an open wound in our heart and to offer it up to Jesus for him to pour his healing blood over it. The ability to deal with accusations and emotional hurt is crucial to the multicultural team leader's survival. As one writer has put it, "You can only exercise leadership to the extent that you can bear pain."[134] Organizational leaders should therefore be careful not to add to the team leader's hurt in the way they interact with them. Instead they should listen for this kind of hurt and ask God for words and actions of encouragement and affirmation to give to the leader.

It is important that as leaders we do not take on burdens that are not ours to carry. In the end, God's people are his, even when they are team members. His requirements on them are the same as those on us. Whatever cultural background team members are from, they have to learn to love and forgive. The leader does not have to fix everything, and sometimes a team will not work and will need to disband. It is not failure, but just the way things are. Teams have to be free to dissolve as well as to continue. As leaders we need to cultivate the ability to let go of the need to control and make things happen, and to let God do his work both in us and in other team members. Multicultural ministry teams are working for God's purposes. We have to let God work out his purpose in his way, and not try and do what only God can do.

It is important to identify reasonable boundaries that balance family and ministry priorities with what you are able to cope with. In any ministry situation, the demands on leaders are usually far greater than they can endure on their own. Defining boundaries and working out practical ways of ensuring you can keep to them is very important for your physical, mental, and spiritual well-being in the long term. Mentors or other people from outside the team who can offer an objective viewpoint are good people to help you work out reasonable boundaries.

We are all human beings, made in the image of God. Multicultural team leaders need to have a clear sense of their own identity, accept themselves as God has made them, and not try to be something they are not. It can be tempting to try to be superhuman, but then subsequently burn yourself out. Give yourself permission to be human. Set reasonable boundaries (preferably with some help from an objective person from outside the situation). Do what you can, and leave the rest to God. Meanwhile, make sure you keep up adequate rest, relaxation, exercise, sleep, food, and time with your family and friends. If you are rested and healthy and your family relationships are good, you will have more strength and sensible perspectives when faced with the demands and storms of multicultural team life and work.

---

134 Gary Corwin, "Leadership as Pain-bearing," *Evangelical Missions Quarterly* 34 (1998): 16.

CHAPTER 9

SKILLS TO WORK ON

Some of the skills that multicultural team leaders need have already been discussed in other chapters. Chapter 4 elaborates on the skill of communicating and enabling the team to communicate well. Chapter 5 describes the skill of communicating and clarifying common vision. Chapter 6 focuses on the skill of helping the team understand and balance the personalities and roles on the team, and chapter 7 talks about managing intercultural conflict on the team. In this chapter we present the remaining skills that the team members, leaders, and supervisors we interviewed considered essential for good multicultural team leaders.

VALUE AND SHOW RESPECT FOR EACH TEAM MEMBER

Good team leaders value and show respect for each team member. They demonstrate this by affirming each person's contributions. They communicate how much they value their contributions to each team member personally, to the rest of the team, and to those outside the team. It is helpful for the leader to specifically identify the contributions of each team member, as this makes their value clear and specific rather than general and easy to question.

Part of showing respect for each team member's uniqueness is done by responding to them according to their specific needs, rather than approaching everyone in exactly the same way. A supervisor found that in some cases he had to encourage some team members who felt negatively about aspects of their own culture that "that's who they had to be" and that the team "needed to be positive to each other in order to also be authentic to ourselves."

Respect and value should be shown by the leader even when he or she does not yet understand team members well. One team member expressed it in the following way:

> I see that in our team leader that he might not really under-
> stand what's going on in our Korean friend, but in the way
> he relates to him, he continues to draw him in. It shows a
> respect, and of course how the respect is exerted or expressed
> again is culturally different and needs to be learned.

Respect and value are communicated through listening to and delight-ing in the person and their culture. It is not sufficient just to know about a different culture, as this does not necessarily result in appreciation for it. Appreciation will be evident in action. Team leaders can foster the celebration of cultural difference by incorporating the cultural celebrations of everyone on the team into team life and enjoying them together. It includes affirming the contributions of every team member and emphasizing the differences that allow them to work well together. It also means laughing about differ-ences. One team member put it this way:

> Delight in that person. Delight in being with that person. It's
> close to celebrating differences, but it isn't celebrating just
> the differences. It's celebrating the person and who they are.
> ... I think when team members feel that even when they're
> going through rough times, if they know that someone is
> delighting in who they are, they'll hang in there and stick
> with the roughness.

One way for team leaders to show respect for and value team members is to welcome them into their homes and into the team's ministry. A couple said of their husband-and-wife leaders:

> Straight away we felt welcome to their house. They wel-
> comed us into their house personally. They welcomed us

to the ministry and said, "You're an essential part of this ministry now, you belong to us, you belong to the ministry, we welcome you." They just accepted us all the way through.

ADJUST YOUR APPROACH IN THE LIGHT OF TEAM MEMBERS' CULTURES

Team leaders need to adjust their approach to communicating with team members from different cultures. These adjustments include varying the degree of directness they use in communication with different team members. One leader gave an illustration of how he learned to adjust his communication style to a more indirect one with a Singaporean worker after he had terribly offended her:

> We learned with time how to ask her to do things. You had to ask in a very indirect way. You can't say, "Will you empty the trash?" If you wanted her to empty the trash you'd say, "You know, the trash is awfully full. Do you have any thoughts about how we can handle that?" And so she'd say, "Well I'll do it."

The adjustments in communication style that a leader makes need to be culture specific. Inviting Korean team members to a meal before addressing an issue towards the end of their time together is one kind of specific adjustment that will not be helpful for members from many other cultures. A leader explained:

> I learned that with the Koreans, to deal with difficult issues oftentimes, it's really good to do it around a meal and do it very indirectly. But then when I would talk to a Scottish team member—she was a very, very direct person—she did not appreciate a beat-around-the-bush, eventually-get-there kind of thing. If you've got something to say, just say it. And so in both cases you really had to adjust in terms of how you approached it.

Team leaders also need to make adjustments in their communication in team meetings. The adjustments include specifically drawing out members from cultures that tend not to speak in group discussions, and learning how to be more expressive in discussions with more expressive cultures. A team leader working with Americans, for example, found she needed to adjust her style so that she could "jump in" in team discussions.

Skilled leaders are diplomatic with more than just words. They need to be able to control their own emotions and recognize and respond to team members' emotion appropriately. Appropriate nonverbal communication, especially facial expression, is essential for effective communication. Skilled leaders also need to adjust the way they interpret the behavior of team members. They must come to realize, for example, that critical comments from direct-culture members are often simply a comment on an issue rather than an attack on them personally, and that loud argumentation from members from emotionally expressive cultures does not necessarily mean they are deeply upset or that the team is about to fall apart. A team leader explained how he learned to understand comments from another of his team members:

> We had a Swedish lady on our team who seemed to us, from our background, always critical and always cutting in her remarks. Finally somebody told us about the Swedish character, which is very direct, very forthright. And I suppose it's just like the lightbulb turned on for us. That was a real moment of transition for us—working with her, understanding her, understanding that her directness was not criticalness, it was just a comment.

EMPOWER TEAM MEMBERS

Empowering team members means identifying their potential and enabling them to achieve it. Empowering is helping people to feel confident and capable to do a specific task through directing, delegating, and encouraging them. In the words of one team leader, it means developing people through "mentoring and helping them, challenging them, and being graceful to push them forward." It involves identifying people's gifts and providing them with opportunities to do what they are really good at. One team leader described his role as "being there to help people find their ministry" and develop it in the best possible way "according to their gifting and circumstances." Another leader explained that he empowered team members by spending time listening to them, talking with them through issues, encouraging them, and giving them ideas, tools, and resources. His focus was on helping them feel fruitful and fulfilled in their work.

Specific activities involved in empowering team members include mentoring them, helping them identify their gifts, and providing them with opportunities to use them by helping them find aspects of the team's ministry that their abilities are particularly suited for. Empowering continues by developing them in that context through listening, asking questions, encouraging, and providing tools and resources.

Empowering others always involves giving them areas of responsibility. Team leaders therefore need to "let go" and to allow team members to take on areas of the team's task that they become responsible for and lead the team in. Team members need to be given the freedom to make mistakes. Once responsibility is given, team leaders must not undermine their team members' efforts to fulfill that responsibility. This works best when the team leader allocates responsibilities according to competency and gifting, as this allows team members to do well. It builds trust and a feeling of being fulfilled, and creates a sense of security because everyone knows their role in the team and feels happy in it. When leaders have expertise in specific areas such as cross-cultural discipling or negotiating with local leaders, they can empower others in these areas by passing on to others the things they know until they can do them without the team leader.

A team member described how his new team leader asked his team members what areas of responsibility they would enjoy and tried to find the best job for each person. This meant people could "run with what they do well." Giving responsibility presupposes and builds trust and gives everyone a sense of satisfaction in feeling that they can contribute.

ADDRESS PROBLEMS

The competency most often placed at the top of the list of necessary skills by our interviewees was the ability to address problems. Good leaders identify and address problems on the team by dealing with them appropriately. If problems are not confronted, the team suffers. It takes emotional energy and commitment to do it, but it is essential. The fact that the team is multicultural increases the likelihood of clashes, which means that it is vital that team leaders have the courage to address problems.

To address problems always involves talking about the problem with one or more team members. It necessitates communicating about the problem. Doing this well provides opportunity for people to learn and grow. Where problems are avoided, they do not go away but instead have a tendency to grow bigger and to fester. The only way to prevent this is to bring it out into the open by talking about it.

All respondents agreed that confronting people is difficult, but that the leader needs to do it or else the team and its work suffer. One interviewee emphasized that this requires emotional energy and an intentional commitment to invest energy into this process in order to open up the issue and deal with the problem. Another insisted that even though different cultures have different ways of confronting people, the leader must still find a way to address problems by talking with those who are involved. Another team member went as far as saying that if the leader is afraid of confronting, they cannot do their job, because there are so many clashes in a multicultural team context.

In order to address problems, the leader first needs to be able to correctly identify the source of the problem. This could be a cultural difference, a personality clash, or a matter of a team member hurting others by their behavior. Multicultural team leaders often have to address behavior or attitude problems in team members and people the team interacts with. Several interviewees gave examples of how they or their team leader confronted people. One leader had to tell a driver that his behavior was offensive to others. Another leader had to talk with a local Christian who was always complaining about how the team members did not understand him.

Another problem area that multicultural team leaders have to deal with is poor performance related to work tasks. One interviewee gave the example of a teammate who insisted on preaching even though her language ability was clearly not good enough and the local people felt she should not preach. Although explaining this to the team member might hurt her, this team member felt that it was vital that the team leader talk to her. A supervisor talked about a team leader who assigned a couple to a ministry task that they really wanted to do but that did not suit them because the leader was afraid of talking with them about their unsuitability for this task. This had major consequences for the organization's recruitment in that area. A team leader gave a helpful example of how she addressed a problem of poor performance with a team member:

> I was given a team member who was a nonperformer, so I took her through a process of, you know, what's the vision of the team and stuff like that, and she had to give her feedback, and it was the first time anyone had said, "My issue is that we've agreed to this vision and you're not working towards it . . . and we're just not getting anywhere. What's going on?"

> The team member broke down and cried, realizing for the first time that she had been letting the team down. She began to commit herself to the vision and work of the team and eventually became the leader of that team.

Another kind of problem that team leaders need to address is the emotional upset of team members, even when they have no idea what has caused it. A team member expressed appreciation for her team leader recognizing when she was emotional or upset. She particularly appreciated that her leader initiated the conversation by asking her about it, rather than her having to bring it up.

Team members praised leaders who were consistently willing and courageous enough to deal with problems. A supervisor emphasized how crucial it is to confront issues early before they begin to cause major damage:

> If there's an elephant in the room, you've got to deal with it. It's also that thing about nipping things in the bud. If you think there is something wrong, there probably is, and you probably don't know what it is, especially if you're in an environment that is unusual or you've got someone who doesn't know that they're offending.

One team member explained that misunderstandings in his team were particularly hard to resolve, as one person wanted to avoid the conflict by not saying anything. But he emphasized the importance of having someone who addressed the conflict: "As a group we had someone who just stood up and said, 'No, let's tackle this conflict again.' And I think that really helped as a group." This team member stressed the importance of having a person who was committed to seeing the conflict resolved despite others wanting to avoid or ignore it. He commented that sometimes issues came up in the team and they were quick to push them aside, but it was better when they were brought up and dealt with. When they had not been dealt with, they tended to keep on growing bigger and bigger. A supervisor commented, "If there's something that's ongoing and the team leader isn't really willing to confront the situation, it just kind of festers and festers and festers until it blows up."

Effectively addressing problems requires the team leader to communicate clearly. One team member reported that her leader attempted to resolve problems but in a confusing, indirect manner by posting written notices on a notice board. Team members could not understand from these notices who was causing the problem or even what the issue was. When the team leader talked with team members face-to-face, she acted as if everything was okay. Another team leader went a step further by punishing an offending team member without explicitly telling them what their offense was. This team member stressed the importance of the leader talking with the team member causing the problems in order to find a solution. In another team, the leader never talked with the person causing the problem, but only with other team members, causing a lot of hurt.

FORGIVE MISTAKES

Good multicultural team leaders demonstrate their trust in team members and that they value them by giving them responsibility and allowing them to make mistakes. Unless new workers are given the freedom to try new things and to make mistakes, they cannot learn. Mistakes are an integral part of the learning process. The team leader therefore must readily forgive mistakes. Without this forgiveness the team is in danger of collapse.

One team member went as far as to say that "if there's no forgiveness of mistakes, there cannot be any team." His team had disbanded with damaging consequences to the members, and he attributed that to things that were not forgiven. A team leader commented that mistakes are inevitable on a multicultural team when the team language is the second or third language of some team members: "People are not going to understand clearly what the task may be or what the direction is, and they may think they understand and they go and do a job which may not necessarily be correct, and so unless you have a heart of forgiveness, you'll have conflict all the time." Another team member gave a personal example of how helpful it was to him and to his team when his team leader forgave a mistake he had made:

> I was tired and I needed a break and I just decided I needed to get away from the city, and I wanted to go hiking on Sunday, but it was Easter Sunday, and without telling anybody I left and I went hiking on this very, very important day in Christian minds, and when I got back, everyone was disappointed with me. The leader was almost angry with me. But it was a mistake, it was confessed, and it was forgotten, and we moved on.

NETWORK WELL WITH THE ORGANIZATION AND OTHERS OUTSIDE THE TEAM

Effective leaders act as a bridge between the team and the rest of the world by building relationships between the team and outside groups.[135] Being able to network well with the organization and others outside the team is a key skill interviewees felt that good multicultural team leaders have. Every team is affected by the social networks in which it is embedded, and especially by the organization the team belongs to. Good leaders communicate with the wider organization to seek the resources the team needs and to influence the organization for the benefit of the team. They communicate the team's vision to other groups and ensure that the organization endorses the team's vision.

---

135 Philip Harris and Kevin Harris, "Managing Effectively through Teams," *Team Performance Management* 2, no. 3 (1996): 23–36.

By managing the external environment of the team, the team leader protects the team from unnecessary outside pressures, protects team members from unhelpful criticism, ensures that communication is occurring with other ministry teams working in the same area, informs the organization of the needs of the team, and tries to make sure resources—such as training, professional development, or material resources—are made available to team members. Good team leaders also take the initiative to raise issues relevant to the team with organizational leadership, such as the need to reduce administrative processes that are hindering the team, or the need to decrease external demands on team members, such as managing many short-term ministry teams, so that the team can focus on its task.

Being able to network well also means that leaders understand and can relate to the organization the team is part of, and because of this they can help team members to adjust to and function effectively within the organizational system. Members of multicultural teams sometimes find it very difficult to understand and function effectively in the wider organization's culture. Team leaders play a special role in interpreting the organizational culture to team members. This is often a challenging task.

It is also important that team leaders are able to network with others outside the team and outside the organization. This enables the leader to be aware of the kinds of issues team members are facing as they interact with people in the community and how these have an impact on the way the team approaches its task. A team leader explained that it is important to be aware of "who your team members network with in the community, because it has an impact on what kind of programs you need to provide." Networking outside the team also enables the leader to have a better idea of the resources that team members need to fulfill their tasks. Finally, networking includes promoting the work of the team in the wider community and to other groups.

HOW CAN YOU DEVELOP THESE COMPETENCIES?

Competencies are skills—things that people can do. Because skills are about doing, they can only be learned by doing. Too often people try to teach skills by talking about them. But being able to talk about changing a washer on a dripping tap does not mean you are actually able to change a washer. Choosing and being able to use the right tools, taking the tap apart, dealing with the gushing water when you forget to turn off the main water tap, working out the right size of washer and how to insert it, and putting the tap back together again so that it does not leak, all require physical action. Skills are learned by practicing them and receiving feedback, either from observers or, in the case of the dripping tap, from other factors such as whether the water is dripping or whether you can get the tap back onto its base.

Because skills are things that people do, they can be observed and measured in terms of whether the components of the skill have been performed competently or not. Observers, especially more experienced ones, are able to give specific feedback on what needs to be done in order to increase competence. We develop competence by practicing a skill, receiving feedback on it, and implementing the feedback. We further develop competence when our performance of the skill is assessed by ourselves and others and when we continue to practice the skill in the light of feedback from those assessments until it is mastered. For very complex skills, such as playing musical instruments, competence is developed through receiving feedback from master performers who intuitively assess multiple aspects of performance at the same time.[136] Regardless of whether you are aspiring to change a tap, become a concert pianist, or become more approachable, skills are learned by doing them, not talking about them.

In training to be medical practitioners, students are taught to "see one, do one, teach one." To learn how to insert an intravenous cannula, for example, a trainee doctor will progress from watching an experienced doctor put a cannula in, then attempt to put one in themselves, and then, when they have mastered that, teach another trainee doctor how to do it. This is a good approach to all skills development. It is the same approach that is embodied in what Paul told Timothy to do: "You have heard me teach things that have been confirmed by many reliable witnesses. Now teach these truths to other trustworthy people who will be able to pass them on to others" (2 Tim 2:2). He was telling Timothy to pass on the things he had heard Paul say to other people, who would in turn be able to pass them on to others.

---

136 Schön, *The Reflective Practitioner.*

The model of "see one, do one, teach one" implies that in order to learn to do a skill well, you first need to see someone else do it well. Team coaches, mentors, leaders you admire, and trainers at seminars can provide models for you to emulate. Ask these people to show you how they do it. Accompany and observe them when they work with others. Ask your organization to give you opportunities to see what you need to do. Unless you can observe what you need to do, it will be difficult for you to reproduce it. Jesus first modeled for his disciples what he wanted them to do, and then he sent them out. Very often team leaders are left to their own devices without this crucial step of demonstration being provided, and they remain unclear about exactly what they need to be able to do.

Once you have seen what you need to do, you need opportunity to practice doing it. While practice occurs in the context of the team you are leading, it is good to first be able to practice the skill in a more neutral situation, such as in a seminar or with the team coach in your own living room. Another way is to practice in a simulated ministry setting or in a situation where you will not be doing ministry in the future. It is also good if the practice is supervised by someone who is more experienced and can give supportive and immediate feedback. Again, this is how Jesus trained his disciples before he sent them out into the world.

Practice involves learning to control the way you think and act. It includes talking to yourself in constructive ways about how and why you are doing what you are doing, and learning to control how you express the emotions you experience as you work on a skill. At times it may involve preparing and practicing specific scripts of how to respond to certain scenarios that can occur in a team. A team member, for example, might consistently show impatience when the team has to work on guidelines for things like crisis management or when reviewing goal progress. Other team members respond to their teammate's impatience with cutting remarks, and these meetings descend into chaos. As the team leader, you have contributed to the chaos by showing a lot of frustration through your words, behavior, and nonverbal expressions. Preparing a script to help respond more appropriately in this situation involves putting together an ordered set of better responses and practicing using those responses in a neutral environment such as with a coach or mentor or in a seminar. Simulations and role plays can re-create the stressful experiences that some multicultural team situations involve so that you can experience what the stress feels like and practice learning to control your physical, emotional, verbal, and thinking responses.

Some skills, such as listening, are relatively straightforward to develop, but they too can be honed by having others observe how we do them and give us feedback. We might think it is easy to assess ourselves about whether we are talking instead of listening, but as we are not always very aware of what we are doing, we can have a distorted perception of our actions. For this reason it is good to have more objective measures. In the case of listening, someone else can observe our interaction with others and measure the precise amount of time we talk or listen. Another important way to measure listening is how much we actually hear of what we are listening to. We can do this by summarizing to the speaker what they have said and getting the speaker to give feedback to us about how well we have captured the main points of what they said. Observers can also give feedback to listeners about their nonverbal communication, such as whether they seemed to be actively listening or looked bored or impatient. Listening exercises can also be filmed so that leaders can observe themselves.

Having a role model can be very important for more complex skills. Some of these complex skills are closely related to character qualities. The character quality of being ready to listen and approachable, for example, involves skills that help people to feel welcome. Our concept of what approachability looks like is built on what people we judge as approachable do. To develop skills in this area, we try to emulate what they do. If we observe that they always have an open office door, then we are also likely to adopt this practice. If we notice that they always look up from whatever they are doing and smile at whoever has indicated they would like their attention, then we try to do the same. The more specifically you can identify what the role model does, the more you will be able to evaluate your own behavior and modify it to become more like them.

Another way of developing competency is to train others. In doing this we further train ourselves. We do not have to become master practitioners before we can start helping others to develop the skills we want to acquire. As we try to teach others to do things, we have to very specifically think about what doing the skill involves and how we can help others to produce it. Being forced to think about these specifics helps us to reflect on what we ourselves are doing.

Training others also helps us recognize some of our own mistakes more clearly and become better able to address them. We might be training someone in the skills related to being approachable, for example. We explain to a trainee that they need to have an open door policy so that people feel welcome. Then we notice that although the trainee welcomes people at the door, they stand in the doorway so that people feel they cannot proceed into the room. We notice that potential visitors feel happy that their presence is acknowledged but are unsure about how welcome they really are. From this we learn that in order to be approachable, we need to stand to the side of our door so that the way into our room or home is open and visitors do not receive mixed messages about whether or not they are welcome into our personal space.

Most Christian teaching in the West, and wherever the West has exported its educational approach, is word based. This is consistent with the low-context communication common to Western cultures, but it unfortunately means that learning how to do things is often neglected. Multicultural team leaders need to learn how to do the various competencies that are essential for effective team function. These competencies are best learned by observing competent practitioners, practicing the skills, receiving feedback on performance, putting that feedback into practice, and reflecting on personal practice. Training others in these competencies will also help us to hone our own skills.

CHAPTER 10

HOW ORGANIZATIONS CAN SUPPORT TEAM LEADERS

Teams do not just happen. They require a lot of hard work and significant outside support to enable them to become effective. Intercultural ministry training specialist Kenneth Harder sums up the importance of providing support for missionary teams:

> Missionary teams, of course, do not develop automatically. Like plants, they must be cultivated during their formation and subsequent stages. . . . Teams require periodic, planned care and regularly scheduled times for coaching and team growth activities.[137]

Multicultural teams require more support than monocultural teams and often take longer to become effective because of the increased complexity of their conflicts and difficulty in building multicultural team community. This chapter gives suggestions to organizations about how best to train and support leaders and their teams through each of the stages of team life, and how they can select the right leaders for their teams. The recommendations in this chapter have been compiled from what team members told us they felt they needed in terms of support and the factors they felt most hindered

---

137 Kenneth Harder, "Introduction to Part 3: Team Development," in *Missionary Care: Counting the Cost for World Evangelization*, ed. Kelly O'Donnell (Pasadena: William Carey Library, 1992), 163.

and helped team effectiveness, as well as key insights from the literature on how organizations can help teams.

Every team is unique because of the unique set of people and relationships in it, but every team also reflects to some extent the organization it is part of. In a sense each team is a microcosm of its parent organization. Teams will either be helped and supported by their organizational culture and leadership, or adversely affected by that culture and leadership if these work against the things the team is trying to accomplish. Organizations that want healthy, effective teams need to examine their organizational culture and shape it to support rather than hinder healthy team development.

MODEL IN THE ORGANIZATION WHAT YOU WANT TO SEE IN TEAMS

Organizations need to model the things they want to see in teams. Firstly, since teamwork requires shared decision making, the parent organization should model and support this type of decision making to help teams thrive. Team leaders and members we interviewed had found that their organization helped them make participative decisions by modeling this at higher levels of leadership. If collaborative decision making is important in the microculture of the team, it should also be evident in the macroculture of the organization and in interteam interactions.

Organizations should also model to team leaders how they want them to lead. Team leaders must be able to help their teams to grasp clear, compelling vision and values and continually communicate those to the team. They must also ensure that team members understand their roles clearly, and they must be able to deal with problems rather than avoiding them. An organization that wants to support its team leaders in carrying out each of these vital functions must model them. Organizational leaders, then, need to communicate and act according to a clear and compelling vision and values, clarify the roles of each member of the organization, and deal with problems. Team members from one of the organizations in our research, for example, felt that the organization's failure to confront performance problems and strive for excellence in ministry were key weaknesses hindering their teams' effectiveness.

For multicultural teams to flourish in an organization, the organizational leadership needs to model multicultural community. Concentrating power in the hands of members of just one culture is often a source of problems.[138] The majority of leaders in many mission organizations that were started in the West, for example, continue to be from EDG cultures, although there is an encouraging increase in the number of leaders from other cultures.

Organizational culture tends to mirror the culture of its founders and leaders.[139] Because of this, organizations founded and mostly led by people from EDG cultures tend to operate according to the norms of those cultures. Such organizations would do well to examine the cultural diversity of their leadership with respect to the cultural diversity of the organization's membership and, if necessary, proactively recruit more people from other cultural regions—South America, Asia, and Africa—into leadership. If multicultural teams are to prosper, organizations need to work towards cultural diversity at all levels and to explicitly state the importance of cultural diversity in mission and strategy documents.[140]

There can be a tendency for international missionary organizations to assume that they are doing well in promoting diversity just because they recruit and accept people from multiple cultures into the organization. However, by not intentionally addressing the challenge of diversity, the cultural blind spots of the organization are not perceived and remain blind spots. The organization will continue to default to the practices of the dominant cultural group as "the way we do things."

Organizations that are serious about promoting cultural diversity should foster a culture of mentoring emerging leaders from a variety of cultural backgrounds. Research into the pathways people from ethnic minorities take to become top leaders in North American organizations has revealed the key role that mentors play. Mentors invest in minority members, protect them, open up opportunities, and act as their advocates. These mentors also

---

138 Roembke, *Building Credible Multicultural Teams*, 96.

139 Schein, *Organizational Culture and Leadership*, 22.

140 Taylor Cox, *Creating the Multicultural Organization: A Strategy for Capturing the Power of Diversity* (San Francisco: Jossey-Bass, 2001), 253–54.

interpret organizational practice to minority members and provide access to information pathways.[141] This kind of mentoring requires more than simply making information available to prospective leaders. It means that the mentor provides active personal help in guiding their mentee in how to put organizational vision and values into practice.

The organization also has a key role to play in promoting and modeling the character qualities that leaders of multicultural teams need. The most powerful way for the organization to be an instrument in the formation of these qualities in its team leaders is for higher level supervisors, regional leaders, and international leaders to model these qualities in mentoring relationships with emerging team leaders. Character qualities are caught rather than taught.

Our study of leaders and members of multicultural teams confirmed something that is already widely known in the missions community: that missionaries are ordinary people doing an extraordinary task. Because they are ordinary people, they have hurts, character weaknesses, and areas of sin they are still dealing with. They bring to their teams unresolved issues from their past, and this "great and varied . . . cultural and psychological baggage that missionaries carry with them to the field" usually comes to the surface under the intensified stress of cross-cultural living and teamwork.[142] Team members we interviewed said that insecurity, low self-esteem, and a sense of rejection were important problems that some of their teammates had carried with them into their teams and that had hindered their working together. Marjory Foyle, a psychiatrist who focuses on missionary care, points out that many heartaches and personal failures, as well as frustrations for fellow teammates, could be avoided by carefully selecting missionaries and dealing with potential problems before the missionary arrives on the field.[143]

When an organization has a culture that reinforces excellence and continuous improvement, its teams are more likely to be effective.[144] As leaders

---

141 David Thomas, "The Truth about Mentoring Minorities: Race Matters," *Harvard Business Review* 79 (2001): 98–107.

142 Roembke, *Building Credible Multicultural Teams*, 167.

143 Foyle, *Honourably Wounded*, 84.

144 Richard Hackman, "Work Teams in Organizations: An Orienting Framework," in *Groups That Work (and Those That Don't): Creating Conditions for Effective Teamwork*, ed. Richard Hackman (San Francisco: Jossey-Bass, 1990), 9–11.

are the key influencers of organizational culture formation and evolution, they are the ones who must take responsibility for shaping a climate of working towards excellence. A first step towards this is to articulate a vision for excellence and communicate that vision through words and action. Secondly, leaders should model personal development in understanding and skills through engaging in disciplined study. Thirdly, they should periodically evaluate their own and their organization's practice.

SUPPORT TEAMS IN THE FORMING PROCESS

Organizations can help teams become effective by selecting appropriate team members and helping teams in the formation process. Interviewees expressed a strong felt need for help and support from organizational leaders in the process of team formation. Team members particularly felt that many of the problems they had faced as teams could have been avoided if they had a more appropriate mix of people on the team, and if they had known what issues they needed to discuss and resolve early in team life. This emphasis on the importance of team formation accords with Richard Hackman's extensive research into teams, which shows that one of the most powerful and constructive interventions a leader can make is to help the team get off to a good start.[145]

There is no guarantee that the "chemistry" between people will always work. Appointing a team coach to help each team can help to build interpersonal and intercultural understanding that can offset many of the problems. Team coaches can also help the team to work through issues that have consistently been a problem with similar teams, such as theological incompatibilities in church planting teams. However, there should be a time limit set on the formation process and, if there are overwhelming problems, the team should be given permission to disband without it being viewed as a failure. The disbanded team's members are then less likely to give up on the idea of working in a team and more likely to learn resilience from the experience and be willing to try working in a team with a different mix of people. In this situation a facilitator from outside the team can be very help-

---

145 Hackman, "More Effective Work Groups," 503.

ful in working through the process of disbanding and redeployment of the team's members to new teams, as the team leader will often be too invested in the team to view it objectively.

Four areas that should be considered when selecting team members are (1) their character qualities; (2) their personalities in the light of the personalities of the other team members; (3) their competencies—that is, their gifts, skills, and strengths in relation to the team's task and the gifts, skills, and strengths of the other team members; and (4) the chemistry of the relationships—that is, the degree to which team members feel like they get on with the other members of the team and want to work with them.

The team members we interviewed had the following four recommendations for their organizations' leaders (international, regional, and field leaders) to consider:

1.   Appoint the team leader before the team forms. This avoids the problem of the team having to work through this issue alone when they have no principles or procedures for selecting a leader. This recommendation is supported by Lester Hirst, who studied urban church planting teams and points out, "A leadership vacuum tends to foster competition for informal leadership of the team."[146]

2.   Take an active role in helping potential team members work out whether they would work well together. The most effective team interviewed had help from the field leadership in selecting members. Lianne Roembke suggests that this process should take into account the existing team members' choice of who they would like to work with if they know the potential members.[147] We found that the best situations were ones in which

---

146 Lester Hirst, "Urban Church Planting Missionary Teams: A Study of Member Characteristics and Experiences Related to Teamwork" (PhD diss., Trinity Evangelical Divinity School, 1994), 155.

147 Roembke, *Building Credible Multicultural Teams*, 177.

the field leadership, the existing team, and the potential team members all had a say in and consulted together about whether or not the potential members joined a particular team.

3. Provide a list of things that need to be discussed and resolved early in the team's life. Things to be discussed include the purpose or vision of the team, goals or faith targets for the first few months, how conflict will be resolved, the leadership style, and how decisions will be made.

4. Provide guidelines on how teams should form. These guidelines could incorporate the recommendations above, a statement about the vision and values of the organization that should be reflected in its teams, the overall purpose of the team, and any other specific recommendations the organization has found to be helpful.

These four types of support to teams in formation help to achieve a better balance between authority outside the team and authority inside the team. Keeping this balance is difficult, but leadership outside the team must exercise authority in terms of the overall team direction and the "outer limit constraints" on team behavior—what they must always or never do.[148] In too many cases, teams are left to flounder without enough direction or support from outside leadership. Without a set of guidelines from the organization about the overall purpose of the team, ways of measuring progress, and the boundaries of the team in terms of their areas of responsibility and authority, many teams flounder because there is too much ambiguity. The organization must provide these guidelines.

It is important for organizational leadership to urge members of forming teams to find accommodation close enough to one another so that members can easily meet together and visit each other outside the formal team meetings. Spending time together apart from the ministry of the team was

---

148 Hackman, "More Effective Work Groups," 496.

considered by many team members we interviewed to be very important to team effectiveness. This was much easier when members lived sufficiently close to one another. The cultural differences between members, and especially between those from individualist and those from collectivist cultures, mean that living close together is even more important, as the relationship aspects of team building are especially important when there is cultural diversity.

PROVIDE TRAINING FOR TEAM MEMBERS

Another way that organizations can support team leaders is by providing training for team members. Team members we interviewed keenly felt their teams needed training in skills for teamwork. They especially wanted training in (1) how to resolve conflict, (2) how to understand and appreciate the personalities and cultures of team members, (3) how to communicate clearly, and (4) how to recognize one another's gifts. Training focused on these areas should ideally be provided very early in a team's life so that good foundations are in place for appreciating and understanding one another and resolving conflict.

Providing training to teams in intercultural competence—the ability to respond and relate effectively to teammates from a wide variety of cultures—is especially important, as cultural differences have such a deep impact on the way people communicate and make decisions, and hinder team effectiveness if they are not understood and appreciated by team members. People who have low levels of intercultural competence find it difficult to form a team identity with culturally different team members, and a lack of cross-cultural empathy and understanding can cause team dysfunction. The implication of this for multicultural teams is that recruiting guidelines for multicultural team membership should include assessment of intercultural competence, or team members should be intentionally and specifically trained in this.

Just as team leaders need to keep developing in Christian character qualities, so do team members. They cannot be relegated only to the selection process and prefield orientation and training. On the field, missionaries need to continue to develop towards Christlikeness. Organizations, at the whole agency, field, and team levels, need to support this development by fostering true community, characterized by mutual submission and walking in the light, and by shaping a climate in which teams can hear God speaking to them through activities such as corporate prayer and devotional input from the Bible (Gal 6:1; Eph 5:21; Col 3:15,16; 1 John 1:5–7).

Organizational leadership should do all they can to keep team personnel, and especially team leaders, as stable as possible, as changes in personnel— both addition of new members and departure of existing members—effectively mean that the team enters the forming stage again and experiences a new wave of culture shock.[149] Team members find changes of team leadership especially jarring and difficult to adapt to.[150]

Organizations need to do everything possible to keep missionaries on the field and to keep teams functioning. Effectiveness is strongly related to both tenure on the field and to the time teams have been operating. Developing an organizational culture that fosters spirituality, training in relational and ministry skills, member care, and opportunities for periodic self-assessment will help people stay on fields and in teams.[151]

HOW A TEAM COACH CAN HELP

Team members we interviewed strongly felt they needed ongoing support in the form of coaching and mentoring. The most frequently mentioned areas for input from the coach were (1) conflict resolution and mediation; (2) helping teams work out principles of how to operate, and especially how to set up lines of accountability; and (3) advice in how to go about the task of church planting.

The team coach should be involved from the first moment of the team's life. There are two important things for the coach to do: (1) establish the overall task of the team and (2) select and provide training for team leaders.

---

149 Roembke, *Building Credible Multicultural Teams*, 176–77.

150 Hirst, "Missionary Teams," 155

151 William Taylor, "Challenging the Mission Stakeholders: Conclusions and Implications; Further Research," in *Too Valuable to Lose: Exploring the Causes and Cures of Missionary Attrition*, ed. William Taylor (Pasadena: William Carey Library, 1997), 359.

Establish as clearly as possible what will be the overall task of the team

Lead—or help the team leader lead—the team through several team-building sessions, preferably over several days. Pay particular attention to first meetings and actions. These tend to set a tone, and first impressions are especially important.

Help the team to draw up a team covenant in their first month of operation. This should include:

- A clear vision statement
- Team values
- Major goals, including a few immediate performance-oriented tasks and goals
- Some mutually agreed on strategies
- How the team will resolve conflict

Once the team has formed, the team coach should continue to visit the team regularly, stay alert for signs of storming, and meet with the team leader, preferably every week or two. From now on the team coach's focus should be on supporting the team leader. In the weekly meetings the team coach should listen to the team leader explain how things are going, answer the leader's questions, stimulate further learning, give words of encouragement, and pray with the leader. Team leadership is hard work, and team leaders very much appreciate this kind of support.

Once team storming commences, the team coach should keep visiting frequently. In this stage the team coach's role is to support the team leader, be aware of relationships in the team, facilitate intercultural understanding and the processes of conflict management, and help the team reflect on and learn from team conflict.

When the worst of the storming has passed and the coach is confident that the team can manage its own conflict, the coach can reduce the frequency of visits to perhaps once every two to three months. As the team moves into the performing stage, it is time to start training the leader and other team members to be coaches for new teams. If the team accepts new members, the coach should again increase the frequency of visits as the team has to re-form, and they may have been lulled by recent performing success to forget how difficult the forming and storming process can be.

It can be very difficult for individualists to give up their independence. It can also be very difficult for them to cope with the higher group orientation and social expectations of collectivist team members. Many will default to a working group approach if they are not specifically encouraged to develop a true team approach to working together. Katzenbach and Smith emphasize the difficulties individualists have in giving themselves fully to teams: "Because of deep-seated values of individualism and a natural reluctance to trust one's fate to the performance of others, the team choice demands a leap of faith."[152] In the light of the challenge that becoming a real team is, team coaches will need to encourage team members from individualistic cultures to take the risk of giving up control of individual work and results and becoming part of the "we" that is a team. Team members from collectivistic cultures may, in contrast, need help to understand the behavior of individualists that may, especially early on in a team's life, come across to them as aloof and disengaged.

Team coaches should continually read about teams and their development and collect resources that will help teams grow. They should teach others what they learn and build libraries of articles, books, and resources that they can loan or give to teams. In this way, they provide a valuable resource for the organization, not just about how the organization's teams are doing but about best practice for teams.

The role of a team coach is intensive at the beginning of the life of the team, but if coaches do their work well through team formation and storming, there will be fewer problems in the future and the coach will be able to concentrate on other teams. Team coaches help team members evaluate, reflect, synthesize, and change according to the different cultural dynamics in any team. Coaches must understand the different ways that different cultures resolve conflict and preserve face. They also help teams to critically reflect on their practice and can help the whole organization learn from the experience of its teams. In this way the whole organization and its coaches develop a body of experience that they can then pass on to new teams.

---

152 Katzenbach and Smith, *The Wisdom of Teams*, 92.

Select and provide training for team leaders

A vital step that comes before the training of team leaders is selecting appropriate trainees. This is particularly important in Christian ministry contexts where resources—human, financial, and other material resources—are often in short supply. Selecting the right people and making sure they are equipped for the job can prevent emotional and spiritual trauma to both leaders and their teams. As working in multicultural teams requires personal maturity, and character development is a long-term task, it is critical to carefully select for character qualities. Interpersonal skills can be honed through training and experience, but it is important that team leaders are selected on the basis of already having good interpersonal skills. It is also important that multicultural team leaders already have some intercultural experience. Potential team leaders who have not had intercultural experience should ideally be placed in a cross-cultural ministry internship in their home country or another context before joining the team. This will help to screen out potential leaders for inflexibility and avoid the trauma to the team if they cannot cope with the demands of intercultural relationships. Where possible, it is preferable to choose leaders who have previously been members of multicultural teams.

Not everyone can lead a multicultural team. Even someone who has successfully led a monocultural team may find leading a multicultural team too much of a challenge if they do not have a basic level of intercultural competence. Unfortunately, people who do not have knowledge of or training in working with people from other cultures are still sometimes appointed to lead multicultural teams. Diana Simkhovych states, "One of the principal causes of failure or subperformance in international projects . . . is the challenge of culture—failure to recognize the pervasive influence of culture on all activities and to select and train personnel accordingly."[153]

Multicultural team leaders need to be familiar with other cultures and should be specifically selected and/or trained for intercultural competence. Simply having knowledge about other cultures is not sufficient, as intercultural interactions affect both behavior and emotions, and multicultural

---

153 Diana Simkhovych, "The Relationship between Intercultural Effectiveness and Perceived Project Team Performance in the Context of International Development," *International Journal of Intercultural Relations* 33 (2009): 383.

team leaders must have the competence and self-discipline to control and adapt their own reactions.

Intercultural competence is not developed in a classroom. It is developed in real life with real people. It is risky and demanding. Trainees will make mistakes and feel uncomfortable and at times humiliated, but through this process they have the potential to develop the skills and character qualities necessary for effective intercultural interaction. Where cultural training programs are restricted to lectures or information transfer, they have a tendency to cause trainees to stereotype people from other cultures. Intercultural training programs should focus on developing trainees to be curious and motivated to explore, experiment, and persevere in new situations.[154]

There is no substitute for experiencing other cultures firsthand and over an extended period as a key part of training for intercultural competence. One interviewee explained that understanding other cultures "can't be learned in any other way but actually experiencing it and feeling those kind of things—your soul and your body, your nose and everywhere." One of the reasons why cultural difference needs to be experienced is the emotion that this experience evokes. Although we can intellectually know about emotions, experiencing them can powerfully affect us, and it can be difficult to learn how to react appropriately when we feel so strongly about something. Emotions can also be unpredictable, and how a leader reacts emotionally when faced with challenging situations critically affects relationships on the team. It is hard to develop self-control, especially control of facial and other nonverbal expression, if you are unaware of what needs to be controlled until it is too late. Learning about other cultures needs to be intentional and ongoing. It has to extend beyond superficial differences such as food and greetings to include developing openness to the huge diversity of human experience, as well as an understanding of potential issues that can arise between culturally different team members.

On the other hand, simply exposing trainee team leaders to other cultures will not necessarily lead to their developing intercultural competence. It is possible to live close to people from other cultures for many years and

---

154 Julia Brandl and Anne-Katrin Neyer, "Applying Cognitive Adjustment Theory to Cross-cultural Training for Global Virtual Teams," *Human Resource Management* 48 (2009): 341–53.

never really engage with their experience or worldview. This lack of deep engagement is evident in many cases of interethnic tension in the world today and is particularly the case for majority-culture members who have little interest in or understanding of the minority people groups who live among them. Development of intercultural understanding requires experience in relating closely with people from different cultural backgrounds. This experience creates discomfort sufficient to make people adjust their meaning frameworks and change their behavior in appropriate ways. In order to grow in appreciation for other cultures and intercultural skills, team leaders must be intentional in learning about other cultures. They need to study and ask questions, observe people who have good levels of intercultural competence, receive feedback on performance, and reflect on experiences. The best way to do this is by living in another culture and having an experienced mentor.[155]

Mentoring team leaders is the key way that organizations can help them to develop in the character qualities they need. Research has demonstrated the impact of being able to observe good role models.[156] Mentors should be experienced multicultural team leaders who regularly interact with the leader. They suggest to the leader things they should do to grow in their leadership, help the leader reflect on how they are doing, and give feedback and encouragement in the light of their own experience. In an ideal situation they are close enough to the team leader that the leader is able to see the mentor interact with people from other cultures. The mentor then also acts as a role model for the developing leader.

The character and skills needed to effectively lead multicultural teams are not developed in a classroom, nor can they be gained through lectures. They require both experience in relating to and leading people from other cultures and guided reflection on that experience. They take years to develop, not hours or weeks. This means that organizations that are committed to developing effective multicultural teams must be willing to make a long-term investment in developing their leaders by providing mentors.

---

155 Joyce Osland and Allan Bird, "Beyond Sophisticated Stereotyping: Cultural Sensemaking in Context / Executive Commentaries," *Academy of Management Executive* 14 (2000): 65–79.

156 Evan Offstein and Ronald Dufresne, "Building Strong Ethics and Promoting Positive Character Development: The Influence of HRM at the United States Military Academy at West Point," *Human Resource Management* 46 (2007): 95–114.

Team leaders need training in specific areas. The team leaders we interviewed particularly felt the need for further training in setting and clarifying expectations, helping team members clarify their roles, and confronting problems. Due to the complexity of multicultural interaction, and because each team will be unique according to the specific mix of personalities and cultures represented on it, this training is best done on the job so that it can be adapted to meet the specific needs of each leader.

A good approach to providing training is to offer a selection of periodic seminars that are easily accessible to leaders where they can consult with and learn from other leaders' experiences and combine these with ongoing support from a team coach. Seminars provide exposure to key issues in leading multicultural teams and an opportunity to participate in a learning community with other team leaders who are dealing with similar issues. They also provide opportunities for organizational leaders to reenvision team leaders about multicultural teams and to discuss organizational issues that affect teams. In these seminars leaders can practice skills in safe environments by examining case studies, developing good responses, practicing these responses in role plays, and receiving feedback from other leaders and trainers. Role plays are helpful because issues that arise in multicultural teams are often very emotive, and role playing allows the leader to experience emotion, analyze and understand it, as well as prepare and practice appropriate verbal and nonverbal responses.

A team coach can help team leaders work through the specific problems they are facing, provide relevant resources, give specific training in skills where needed, and work with the whole team when necessary. Just-in-time training from coaches, coupled with seminars, balances the more predictable needs of multicultural teams with the less predictable issues that will arise. For example, a seminar offered prior to the forming of a team can alert the leader to the issues and challenges that are likely to arise in the early life of the team. This can be followed up with specific advice and help given by a team coach in the context of the team. As the team moves into the storming phase, for example, a seminar on managing conflict could be followed up with specific feedback and advice from a team coach that is targeted to the specific conflicts the team experiences. Team coaches are then able to help the leaders apply the principles they have learned in seminars to the specifics of the team. Adults learn best when specific help is provided just when they feel the need for it.[157] This means that when issues arise on teams, specific help that addresses each issue not only helps to address the issue but also provides a lesson that will be readily remembered in the future when similar issues arise.

The Multicultural Team Leader Inventory provided in appendix 3 can be used to highlight areas that a multicultural team leader needs to be aware of and to work on. Team leaders can use it as a self-assessment tool, but they will get a better picture of what they most need to work on by asking their team members to complete it as well. It can be used for selecting team leaders and assessing how they are doing. When it is used as part of the process of selecting a team leader, it is best to ask people who have worked with the potential leader to fill it in, and ideally this will include members of teams the leader has previously participated in and previous supervisors.

---

157 Evelyn Hibbert, "Designing Training for Adults," in *Integral Ministry Training: Design and Evaluation*, ed. Rob Brynjolfson and Jonathan Lewis (Pasadena: William Carey Library, 2006), 57.

APPENDIX 1

LEADERSHIP DISCUSSION QUESTIONS[158]

STATUS AND INFLUENCE

Who are the most influential people in your community?

How many different ranks of status are recognized?

How does a person mark the transition from one rank of status to the next?

Is there any struggle for status?

Can a person lose one's status? Can a person rise in status? How?

What kinds of class distinctions are there?

Can rank be inherited? Through what lineage?

How does one become a wise man?

Are old people considered wise? Do old people have authority?

Who do people go to for advice?

---

158 Taken from Jacob A. Loewen, "Missionaries and Anthropologists Cooperate in Research," in *Readings in Missionary Anthropology II*, 2nd ed., ed. William A. Smalley (Pasadena: William Carey Library, 1978), 860–76.

LEADERSHIP

How do people become leaders?

Is there any kind of election or choosing for leadership?

Do you need to have power in order to become a person of worth?

Can women become leaders? In what areas?

Does the wife of a leader have any more authority than an ordinary woman?

What is the division of labor between leaders and followers?

What is done with the bodies of leaders?

How are leaders developed?

DECISION MAKING

How does the family make decisions? Who takes the lead? Is there discussion? How does the family settle quarrels? Describe some quarrels you have seen or have been told about.

What is the community decision-making unit? What is the process?

How much can each member participate in the gathering? On what basis is this determined?

Is there any ranking in the right to speak?

GATHERINGS AND MEETINGS

Why do people gather?

Who gathers them?

What do they do when they gather?

Who initiates meetings?

Who leads them once they are gathered?

How is the gathered group led?

How much can each member participate in the gathering? On what basis is this determined?

CHURCH

How is the church organized?

How much power do church leaders have over other Christians?

What is the relationship between church leaders and political or social leaders?

How much power do church leaders have in the wider community?

How are Christian leaders chosen and organized?

APPENDIX 2

IDENTIFYING YOUR ASSUMPTIONS AND EXPECTATIONS[159]

An expectation is something we're planning on, looking forward to, or regard as likely to happen. An assumption is something taken for granted. Expectations are stabilizing and motivating factors when they are communicated and understood by the appropriate parties. They are dangerous and potentially deadly when they are assumed. Unrealistic expectations and assumptions not based on fact are a major source of missionary stress and contribute to a host of problems and misunderstandings.

The following is an exercise designed to help you identify your expectations and which among them are potentially dangerous assumptions. If you are not already in a team, think about the next team you expect to be part of, discuss your expectations in pairs, and then reflect on your discussion as a whole group.

Try to identify your expectations for as many of the areas below as you can. Write a brief statement about what you look forward to and think is likely to happen. Circle those that may be assumptions because you have not yet discussed them as a team. Discuss your circled items with your team. What are your expectations in the following areas?

---

159 We think these questions came from a Frontiers Training Manual, but we are having difficulty tracing the original source. Please let us know if you know where they came from.

YOUR PERSONAL LIFE

What are you expecting in terms of your living situation (house and neighborhood)? How will you find it?

What will the demands of daily living be?

How will you relax, and what will you do for recreation? How much of this will you do with other members of the team?

What do you think the biggest sources of stress will be?

LANGUAGE AND CULTURE LEARNING

How many languages will you have to learn?

How fluent will you need to be in the language(s)?

How will you go about learning?

How much structure or guidance will be available and how adequate will it be?

How much time will you have available on a daily or weekly basis for language learning?

How long will it take to reach your ultimate goal in learning the language?

How difficult will it be for you personally?

How will your teammates do, and how will this affect you?

Do you have any fears about things that you may find difficult to cope with in the culture?

How do you expect others to help you with this?

THE WAY THE TEAM WILL FUNCTION

How will your team make decisions, and on what kinds of issues?

How often will you meet as a whole team? For what purposes?

How will your team leader lead (leadership style)? How much authority will he or she have?

What will your team leader do for you?

What will your team leader expect of you?

What will your teammates expect of you?

What level of friendships will you develop on your team, and how much time you will spend together?

What degree and nature of interpersonal tensions and conflict do you expect you will experience?

What is your ability to deal with and resolve interpersonal problems?

How will your team resolve conflicts?

What role will you play on the team?

How will you support and encourage one another?

What do you expect your working environment to be? How do you prefer it to be organized?

How will your team handle finances? Will you have a pooling fund?

How will you keep yourselves accountable to one another?

How much holiday and free time will you have? How often will you go back to your home country?

What role will wives play on the team?

CHURCH PLANTING ISSUES

When will converts be baptized and by whom?

Will home groups be open to nonbelievers?

How will spiritual gifts, including tongues and prophecy, be used in church meetings?

What will be the position on women in leadership?

What will be the position on the use of money by team members?

What type of church government (Episcopalian, Presbyterian, Congregational, or other) will you nurture?

What model of church will you be aiming for?

YOUR PERSONAL MINISTRY

What do you expect will be your role and primary responsibility?

What will your supporters and home church expect of you?

What will the field and your supporters provide?

What do you expect the field leader, international or home country leaders, and/or team coach will provide for your team?

How will you negotiate this with them?

What will be your major personal and team accomplishments by the end of the first three months?

REFLECT AND DISCUSS

1. In which areas are the expectations of all team members similar?

2. In which areas do your expectations differ?

3. What will you do about the areas in which you have differing expectations?

Put any values or ways of operating on which you all agree as a result of this discussion into a draft memo of understanding (team covenant).

MULTICULTURAL TEAM LEADER INVENTORY

This inventory has been developed from the profile of the good multicultural team leader. The profile outlines the things a leader of a multicultural team leader needs to know, be, and do (personally and in terms of building the team community); it was derived from the questionnaire responses and interviews of fifty-one multicultural team members, leaders, and supervisors representing eighteen cultures who were working in teams with people from seventy-five cultures.

Instructions for using this inventory:

1. Complete the inventory yourself.

2. Ask each member to complete the inventory anonymously and return it to you. For each item of the inventory, add up all the numbers assigned by the team members, then divide the total by the number of team members. This will give you the average of your team's assessment for each item.

3. Compare the team's average with your own assessment of yourself. In particular, look for any areas where there are major discrepancies between yourself and what your team thinks.

4. Ask your supervisor or team coach to complete the inventory as their assessment of you.

5. Use the results to reflect on which areas you especially need to work on developing. Prepare a plan to intentionally develop these areas. If you are not sure how to improve in particular areas, discuss options with your supervisor or team coach.

MULTICULTURAL TEAM LEADER INVENTORY

Circle the number that best indicates how well you think your leader is doing.	Needs Work	Okay			Excellent
The team leader has:					
A deeply held conviction of the value of multicultural teams	1	2	3	4	5
With respect to other cultures, the team leader has:					
A broad knowledge of other cultures	1	2	3	4	5
Specific knowledge of the cultures represented on the team	1	2	3	4	5
A positive attitude towards different cultures	1	2	3	4	5
With respect to personal qualities, the team leader is:					
Humble	1	2	3	4	5
Patient	1	2	3	4	5
Ready to listen and approachable	1	2	3	4	5
Always learning	1	2	3	4	5
Ready to try new ways of doing things	1	2	3	4	5
Respectful of others regardless of background	1	2	3	4	5
Inclusive	1	2	3	4	5

MULTICULTURAL TEAM LEADER INVENTORY

Circle the number that best indicates how well you think your leader is doing.	Needs Work		Okay		Excellent
Committed to work through conflict to reach resolution	1	2	3	4	5
Self-aware	1	2	3	4	5
With respect to skills, the team leader:					
Clarifies and communicates common vision	1	2	3	4	5
Communicates and helps the team to communicate well	1	2	3	4	5
Values and shows respect for each team member	1	2	3	4	5
Adjusts his or her approach in the light of team members' cultures	1	2	3	4	5
Helps the team understand and balance the personalities and roles on the team	1	2	3	4	5
Empowers team members	1	2	3	4	5
Addresses problems	1	2	3	4	5
Forgives mistakes	1	2	3	4	5
Manages intercultural conflict on the team	1	2	3	4	5
Networks with the organization and others outside the team	1	2	3	4	5

This profile may be freely copied and used for ministry or nonprofit purposes as long as Evelyn and Richard's authorship of the Multicultural Team Leader Inventory is acknowledged.

BIBLIOGRAPHY

Abdalla, Ikhlas, and Moudi Al-Homoud. "Exploring the Implicit Leadership Theory in the Arabian Gulf States." *Applied Psychology: An International Review* 50 (2001): 506–31.

Augsburger, David. *Caring Enough to Confront*. Glendale, CA: Regal Books, 1973.

———. *Conflict Mediation across Cultures: Pathways and Patterns*. Louisville: Westminster / John Knox, 1992.

Barth, Fredrik, ed. *Ethnic Groups and Boundaries: The Social Organization of Culture Difference*. Long Grove, IL: Waveland, 1969.

Basso, Keith. "Stalking with Stories: Names, Places, and Moral Narratives among the Western Apache." In *Text, Play, and Story: The Construction and Reconstruction of Self and Society*, edited by Stuart Plattner and Edward Bruner, 37–70. Washington, DC: American Ethnological Society, 1984).

Bates, Gerald. "Missions and Cross-cultural Conflict." *Missiology: An International Review* 5 (1980): 93–98.

Belbin, Meredith. *Management Teams: Why They Succeed or Fail*. Oxford: Butterworth-Heinemann, 2010.

———. *Team Roles at Work*. Oxford: Butterworth-Heinemann, 2010.

Bennett, Janet. "Transformative Training: Designing Programs for Culture Learning." In *Contemporary Leadership and Intercultural Competence: Exploring the Cross-cultural Dynamics within Organizations*, edited by Michael Moodian, 95–110. Los Angeles: SAGE, 2009.

Bhabha, Homi. "The Third Space: Interview with Homi Bhabha." In *Identity: Community, Culture, Difference*, edited by Jonathan Rutherford, 207–31. London: Routledge, 1990.

Bond, Charles, Adnan Omar, Adnar Mahmoud, and Richard Bonser. "Lie Detection across Cultures." *Journal of Nonverbal Behavior* 14, no. 3 (1990): 189–204.

Brandl, Julia, and Anne-Katrin Neyer. "Applying Cognitive Adjustment Theory to Cross-cultural Training for Global Virtual Teams." *Human Resource Management* 48 (2009): 341–53.

Cacioppe, Ron. "An Integrated Model and Approach for the Design of Effective Leadership Development Programs." *Leadership and Organization Development Journal* 19 (1998): 44–53.

Campion, Michael, Ellen Papper, and Catherine Higgs. "Relations between Work Team Characteristics and Effectiveness: Implications for Designing Effective Work Groups." *Personnel Psychology* 46 (1993): 823–50.

Canen, Alberto, and Ana Canen. "Multicultural Leadership: The Costs of Its Absence in Organizational Conflict Management." *International Journal of Conflict Management* 19 (2008): 4–19.

Chan, Frank. "Biblical Materials for a Theology of Cultural Diversity: A Proposal." In *Understanding Diversity: Theological Views on Diversity*, 140–41. Dubuque, IA: Kendall Hunt, 2005.

Chen, Stephen, Ronald Geluykens, and Chong Ju Choi. "The Importance of Language in Global Teams: A Linguistic Perspective." *Management International Review* 46 (2006): 679–96.

Cortes, Carlos, and Louise Wilkinson. "Developing and Implementing a Multicultural Vision." In *Contemporary Leadership and Intercultural Competence: Exploring the Cross-cultural Dynamics within Organizations*, edited by Michael Moodian, 17–31. Los Angeles: SAGE, 2009.

Corwin, Gary. "Leadership as Pain-bearing." *Evangelical Missions Quarterly* 34 (1998): 16–17.

Covey, Stephen. *The 7 Habits of Highly Effective People*. New York: Free Press, 1989.

Cox, Taylor. *Creating the Multicultural Organization: A Strategy for Capturing the Power of Diversity*. San Francisco: Jossey-Bass, 2001.

Dierck, Lorraine. "Teams That Work: Leadership, Power, and Decision-making in Multicultural Teams in Thailand." DMiss diss., Biola University, 2007.

Dodd, Carley. *Dynamics of Intercultural Communication*. 5th ed. Boston: Abilene Christian University, 1998.

Dorfman, Peter, Paul Hanges, and Felix Brodbeck. "Leadership and Cultural Variation: The Identification of Culturally Endorsed Leadership Profiles." In *Culture, Leadership, and Organizations: The GLOBE Study of 62 Societies*, edited by Robert House, Paul Hanges, Mansour Javidan, Peter Dorfman, and Vipin Gupta, 669–719. Thousand Oaks, CA: SAGE, 2004.

Douglas, Mary. *Purity and Danger*. London: Routledge, 1966.

Earley, Christopher, and Elaine Mosakowski. "Creating Hybrid Team Cultures: An Empirical Test of Transnational Team Functioning." *Academy of Management Journal* 43 (2000): 26–49.

Elmer, Duane. *Cross-cultural Conflict: Building Relationships for Effective Ministry*. Downers Grove, IL: InterVarsity Press, 1993.

———. *Cross-cultural Connections: Stepping Out and Fitting In around the World*. Downers Grove, IL: InterVarsity Press, 2002.

———. *Cross-cultural Servanthood: Serving the World in Christlike Humility*. Downers Grove, IL: IVP Books, 2006.

Farhadian, Charles. "Comparing Conversions among the Dani of Irian Jaya." In *The Anthropology of Religious Conversion*, edited by Andrew Buckser and Stephen Glazier, 55–68. Oxford: Rowman & Littlefield, 2003.

Flanders, Christopher. *About Face: Rethinking Face for 21st Century Mission*. Eugene, OR: Pickwick, 2011.

Foyle, Marjory. *Honourably Wounded: Stress among Christian Workers*. London: Monarch Books, 2001.

Gibson, Cristina, and Mary Zellmer-Bruhn. "Metaphors and Meaning: An Intercultural Analysis of the Concept of Teamwork." *Administrative Science Quarterly* 46, no. 2 (2001): 274–303.

Goetz, David, and Marshall Shelley. "Standing in the Crossfire: Interview with Bill Hybels." *Leadership: A Practical Journal for Church Leaders* (Winter 1993): 14–25.

Greenlee, David. *One Cross, One Way, Many Journeys: Thinking Again about Conversion*. Tyrone, GA: Authentic, 2007.

Gudykunst, William. "Applying Anxiety/Uncertainty Management (AUM) Theory to Intercultural Adjustment Training." *International Journal of Intercultural Relations* 22, no. 2 (1998): 227–50.

———. *Bridging Differences: Effective Intergroup Communication*. London: SAGE, 2004.

Hackman, Richard. "Creating More Effective Work Groups in Organizations." In *Groups That Work (and Those That Don't): Creating Conditions for Effective Teamwork*, edited by Richard Hackman, 479–504. San Francisco: Jossey-Bass, 1989.

———. "Work Teams in Organizations: An Orienting Framework." In *Groups That Work (and Those That Don't): Creating Conditions for Effective Teamwork*, edited by Richard Hackman, 9–11. San Francisco: Jossey-Bass, 1990.

Hall, Edward. *Beyond Culture*. New York: Anchor, 1976.

Halverson, Claire. "Group Process and Meetings." In *Effective Multicultural Teams: Theory and Practice*, edited by Claire Halverson and Aqeel Tirmizi, 111–33. Dordrecht, The Netherlands: Springer, 2008.

Hammer, Mitchell. "The Intercultural Conflict Style Inventory: A Conceptual Framework and Measure of Intercultural Conflict Resolution Approaches." *International Journal of Intercultural Relations* 29 (2005): 675–95.

———. "Solving Problems and Resolving Conflict Using the Intercultural Conflict Style Model and Inventory." In *Contemporary Leadership and Intercultural Competence: Exploring the Cross-cultural Dynamics within Organizations*, edited by Michael Moodian, 219–32. Los Angeles: SAGE, 2009.

Harder, Kenneth. "Introduction to Part 3: Team Development." In *Missionary Care: Counting the Cost for World Evangelization*, edited by Kelly O'Donnell, 163–65. Pasadena: William Carey Library, 1992.

Harris, Philip, and Kevin Harris. "Managing Effectively through Teams." *Team Performance Management* 2, no. 3 (1996): 23–36.

Hibbert, Evelyn. "Designing Training for Adults." In *Integral Ministry Training: Design and Evaluation*, edited by Rob Brynjolfson and Jonathan Lewis, 51–64. Pasadena: William Carey Library, 2006.

———. "Identifying Essential Characteristics and Competencies of Good Multicultural Team Leaders: A Pilot Study." EdD diss., University of New England, 2010.

Hibbert, Richard. "Enhancing WEC Church Planting Teams: A Study of the Factors Influencing Their Effectiveness." DMin diss., Columbia International University, 2002.

Hibbert, Richard, and Evelyn Hibbert. "Contextualizing Sin for Cross-cultural Evangelism." Unpublished manuscript, 2012.

Hiebert, Paul. *Anthropological Reflections on Missiological Issues*. Grand Rapids: Baker Books, 1994.

———. *The Gospel in Human Contexts: Anthropological Explorations for Contemporary Missions*. Grand Rapids: Baker Academic, 2009.

———. *Transforming Worldviews: An Anthropological Understanding of How People Change*. Grand Rapids: Baker Academic, 2008.

———. "Western Images of Others and Otherness." In *This Side of Heaven: Race, Ethnicity, and Christian Faith*, edited by Robert Priest and Alvaro Nieves, 97–110. Oxford: Oxford University Press, 2007.

Hirst, Lester. "Urban Church Planting Missionary Teams: A Study of Member Characteristics and Experiences Related to Teamwork." PhD diss., Trinity Evangelical Divinity School, 1994.

Hofstede, Geert. Foreword to *Leadership in a Diverse and Multicultural Environment: Developing Awareness, Knowledge, and Skills*, edited by Mary L. Connerley and Paul Pedersen, ix. Thousand Oaks, CA: SAGE, 2005.

Hofstede, Geert, Gert Jan Hofstede, and Michael Minkov. *Cultures and Organizations: Software of the Mind*. New York: McGraw-Hill, 2010.

House, Robert, Paul Hanges, Mansour Javidan, Peter Dorfman, and Vipin Gupta. *Culture, Leadership, and Organizations: The Globe Study of 62 Societies*. Thousand Oaks, CA: SAGE, 2004.

Hughes, Dewi. *Ethnic Identity from the Margins: A Christian Perspective*. Pasadena: William Carey Library, 2011.

Jarvenpaa, Sirkka L., and Dorothy E. Leidner. "Communication and Trust in Global Virtual Teams." *Journal of Computer-mediated Communication* 3, no. 4 (1998): 0.

Jehn, Karen A., Gregory Northcraft, and Margaret Neale. "Why Differences Make a Difference: A Field Study of Diversity, Conflict, and Performance in Workgroups." *Administrative Science Quarterly* 44, no. 4 (1999): 741–63.

Johnson, David, and Jeff VanVonderen. *The Subtle Power of Spiritual Abuse: Recognizing and Escaping Spiritual Manipulation and False Spiritual Authority within the Church.* Minneapolis: Bethany House, 1991.

Jones, Gordon, and Rosemary Jones. *Teamwork: How to Build Relationships.* Bletchley, UK: Scripture Union, 2003.

Katzenbach, Jon. *Teams at the Top: Unleashing the Potential of Both Teams and Individual Leaders.* Boston: Harvard Business School Press, 1998.

Katzenbach, Jon, and Douglas Smith. *The Wisdom of Teams: Creating the High-performance Organization.* New York: HarperCollins, 1999.

Keirsey, David. *Please Understand Me II: Temperament, Character, Intelligence.* Del Mar, CA: Prometheus Nemesis, 1998.

Kim, Dongsoo. "The Healing of Han in Korean Pentecostalism," *Journal of Pentecostal Theology* 15 (1999): 125–26.

Kroeger, Otto, Janet Thuesen, and Hile Rutledge. *Type Talk at Work: How the 16 Personality Types Determine Your Success at Work.* New York: Dell, 2002.

Kummerow, Jean, Nancy Barger, and Linda Kirby. *Work Types.* New York: Warner Books, 1997.

Lanier, Sarah. *Foreign to Familiar: A Guide to Understanding Hot- and Cold-climate Cultures.* Hagerstown, MD: McDougal, 2000.

Larson, Carl, and Frank LaFasto. *Teamwork: What Must Go Right / What Can Go Wrong.* Thousand Oaks, CA: SAGE, 2001.

Loewen, Jacob A. *Culture and Human Values: Christian Intervention in Anthropological Perspective.* Pasadena: William Carey Library, 1975.

Loewen, William. "Participation and Decision-making in a Changing Workforce." In *Cultural Diversity and Employee Ownership*, edited by Margaret Showers, Cathy Ivancic, William Loewen, Anthony Mathews, and Pamela Stout, 59–74. Oakland: National Center for Employee Ownership, 2002.

Matsumoto, David. *Culture and Psychology: People around the World.* London: Wadsworth, 2000.

Maznevski, Martha, and Mark Peterson. "Societal Values, Social Interpretation, and Multinational Teams." In *Cross-cultural Work Groups*, edited by Cherlyn Granrose and Stuart Oskamp, 61–89. London: SAGE, 1997.

Mellahi, Kamel. "The Teaching of Leadership on UK MBA Programmes: A Critical Analysis from an International Perspective." *Journal of Management Development* 19 (2000): 297–308.

Mezirow, Jack. "How Critical Reflection Triggers Transformative Learning." In *Fostering Critical Reflection in Adulthood*, edited by Jack Mezirow, 1–20. San Francisco: Jossey-Bass, 1991.

Myers, Isabel. *Gifts Differing: Understanding Personality Type*. Mountain View, CA: Davies-Black, 1995.

Myers, Isabel, Mary H. McCaulley, Naomi L. Quenk, and Allen L. Hammer. *MBTI Manual*, 3rd ed. Mountain View, CA: Consulting Psychologists Press, 1998.

Nkomo, Stella. "The Emperor Has No Clothes: Rewriting 'Race in Organizations.'" *Academy of Management Review* 17 (1992): 487–513.

Nykodym, Nick, Sonny Ariss, Jack Simonetti, and Jean Plotner. "Empowerment for the Year 2000 and Beyond." *Empowerment in Organizations* 3, no. 4 (1995): 36–42.

O'Dea, Thomas. "Five Dilemmas in the Institutionalization of Religion." *Journal for the Scientific Study of Religion* 1 (1961): 30–39.

Offstein, Evan, and Ronald Dufresne. "Building Strong Ethics and Promoting Positive Character Development: The Influence of HRM at the United States Military Academy at West Point." *Human Resource Management* 46 (2007): 95–114.

Osland, Joyce, and Allan Bird. "Beyond Sophisticated Stereotyping: Cultural Sensemaking in Context / Executive Commentaries." *Academy of Management Executive* 14 (2000): 65–79.

Palmer, Donald. *Managing Conflict Creatively: A Guide for Missionaries and Christian Workers*. Pasadena: William Carey Library, 1990.

Pasa, Selda, Hayat Kabasakal, and Muzaffer Bodur. "Society, Organisations, and Leadership in Turkey." *Applied Psychology: An International Review* 50 (2001): 559–89.

Peck, Scott. *The Different Drum*. London: Arrow Books, 1987.

Priest, Kersten, and Robert Priest. "Divergent Worship Practices." In *This Side of Heaven: Race, Ethnicity, and Christian Faith*, edited by Robert Priest and Alvaro Nieves, 275–91. Oxford: Oxford University Press, 2007.

Pruitt, Dean, and Sung Hee Kim. *Social Conflict: Escalation, Stalemate, and Settlement*. Boston: McGraw-Hill, 2004.

Rahim, Afzalur. "A Measure of Styles of Handling Interpersonal Conflict." *Academy of Management Journal* 26 (1983): 368–76.

Roembke, Lianne. *Building Credible Multicultural Teams*. Pasadena: William Carey Library, 2000.

Rosenberg, Noah, Jonathan Pritchard, James Weber, Howard Cann, Kenneth Kidd, Lev Zhivotovsky, and Marcus Feldman. "Genetic Structure of Human Populations." *Science* 298 (2002): 2381–85.

Said, Edward. *Orientalism*. London: Penguin, 1995.

Schein, Edgar. *Organizational Culture and Leadership*. 4th ed. San Francisco: Jossey-Bass, 2010.

Schneider, Susan, and Jean-Louis Barsoux. *Managing across Cultures*. Harlow, UK: Prentice-Hall, 2002.

Schön, Donald. *The Reflective Practitioner: How Professionals Think in Action*. Aldershot, England: Arena, 1995.

Senge, Peter. *The Fifth Discipline: The Art and Practice of the Learning Organization*. New York: Doubleday, 1990.

Shapiro, Debra, Blair Sheppard, and Lisa Cheraskin. "Business on a Handshake." *Negotiation Journal* 8, no. 4 (1992): 365–77.

Simkhovych, Diana. "The Relationship between Intercultural Effectiveness and Perceived Project Team Performance in the Context of International Development." *International Journal of Intercultural Relations* 33 (2009): 383–90.

Sinclair, Amanda. *Leadership for the Disillusioned: Moving Beyond Myths and Heroes to Leading That Liberates*. Crows Nest, Australia: Allen & Unwin, 2007.

Solansky, Stephanie. "Leadership Style and Team Processes in Self-managed Teams." *Journal of Leadership and Organizational Studies* 14 (2008): 332–41.

Span, John. "God Saves . . . Go in Peace: Wholeness Affirmed or Promotion Piece?" *St. Francis Magazine* 6 (2010): 218–36.

Taylor, William. "Challenging the Mission Stakeholders: Conclusions and Implications; Further Research." In *Too Valuable to Lose: Exploring the Causes and Cures of Missionary Attrition*, edited by William Taylor, 341–60. Pasadena: William Carey Library, 1997.

Thomas, David. "The Truth about Mentoring Minorities: Race Matters." *Harvard Business Review* 79 (2001): 98–107.

Thomas, Kenneth. "Conflict and Conflict Management." In *Handbook of Industrial and Organizational Psychology*, edited by Marvin Dunette, 889–935. Chicago: Rand-McNally, 1976.

Tillett, Gregory, and Brendan French. *Resolving Conflict*. Melbourne: Oxford University Press, 2010.

Ting-Toomey, Stella. "The Matrix of Face: An Updated Face-negotiation Theory." In *Theorizing about Intercultural Communication*, edited by William Gudykunst, 71–92. Thousand Oaks, CA: SAGE, 2005.

Triandis, Harry. *Individualism and Collectivism: New Directions in Social Psychology*. Boulder, CO: Westview, 1995.

Tuckman, Bruce. "Developmental Sequence in Small Groups." *Psychological Bulletin* 63 (1965): 384–99.

Turkle, Sherry. *Alone Together: Why We Expect More from Technology and Less from Each Other*. New York: Basic Books, 2011.

Turner, Victor, and Edith Turner. *Image and Pilgrimage in Christian Culture: Anthropological Perspectives*. New York: Columbia University Press, 1996.

Ungerleider, John. "Conflict." In *Effective Multicultural Teams: Theory and Practice*, edited by Claire Halverson and Aqeel Tirmizi, 211–38. Dordrecht, The Netherlands: Springer, 2008.

Van Gennep, Arnold. *The Rites of Passage*. London: Routledge & Kegan Paul, 1960.

Volf, Miroslav. *Exclusion and Embrace: A Theological Exploration of Identity, Otherness, and Reconciliation*. Nashville: Abingdon, 1996.

Walls, Andrew. *The Missionary Movement in Christian History: Studies in the Transmission of Faith*. Maryknoll, NY: Orbis, 1996.

Wu, Jenai, and David Laws. "Trust and Other-anxiety in Negotiations: Dynamics across Boundaries of Self and Culture." *Negotiation Journal* 19, no. 4 (2003): 329–67.

Yip, Jeffrey. "Leading through Paradox." In *Leading across Differences: Cases and Perspectives*, edited by Kelly Hannum, Belinda McFeeters, and Lize Booysen, 171–79. San Francisco: Pfeiffer, 2010.